POSTCOLONIAL CULTURES

Postcolonial Cultures

SIMON FEATHERSTONE

EDINBURGH UNIVERSITY PRESS

© Simon Featherstone, 2005

Edinburgh University Press Ltd
22 George Square, Edinburgh

Typeset in Ehrhardt
by Hewer Text Ltd, Edinburgh, and
printed and bound in Great Britain by
The Cromwell Press, Trowbridge, Wilts

A CIP record for this book is available from the British Library

ISBN 0 7486 1742 6 (hardback)
ISBN 0 7486 1743 4 (paperback)

Contents

Acknowledgements

I am grateful to the following for their help: Jean Breese; Eddie Lenihan; Anthony Tibbles; Catherine Silverstone; Rachel Dwyer; Jackie Jones; Tony Bilton; and Ann Vinnicombe.

CHAPTER ONE

The Nervous Conditions
of Postcolonial Studies

Few areas of study are at once so lively and so beset by doubts and
dilemmas as postcolonial studies. The term 'postcolonial' prefixes
courses in literature, cinema, critical theory and cultural studies,
and its concerns form part of a wider range of interests in the
humanities and social sciences – postmodernism, globalism, diaspora studies, area studies. Anthologies, monographs, journals and,
increasingly, explanatory guides – the surest evidence of academic
popularity – proliferate. And yet that expansion has also engen-
dered a nervous condition of self-definition, content and method.
Few other disciplines, for example, so regularly worry about their
own defining term. As Terry Eagleton once suggested, one of the
rules of the handbook for postcolonial theorists is '[b]egin your
essay by calling into question the whole notion of postcolonialism'
(Eagleton 1998: 24). At their worst, these expressions of disciplinary self-doubt can appear something of a self-indulgence; in other
ways, though, they are products of a necessary caution and self-
questioning in an area that tests sensitivities to a bewildering range
of materials and ideas, and calls to account engagements that are
ethical as well as intellectual, political as well as academic, personal
as well as professional.

These difficult engagements are the principal concerns of this
book. It aims to present a range of the critical practices and
materials for study that are available to the discipline, and to
discuss the political, ethical and methodological debates that they
provoke. The case studies that form the bulk of these discussions
are deliberately eclectic, reflecting the richness of postcolonial
cultures, and the possibilities and problems of studying diverse
cultural practices. The theoretical material that is deployed in
the discussions draws upon the work of the established, well-

anthologised theorists of the field, as well as introducing less familiar ideas from outside this core, again testing the limits and potential of an emergent discipline. Current debates on such areas as national identity, cultural hybridities, race, diaspora and gender will be described and developed by reference to some frequently studied literary texts, films and theoretical materials, and to other less familiar features of postcolonial cultures such as popular music, dance, sport and oral performance. Throughout, the emphasis is upon the detailed practice of studying postcolonial cultures and upon confronting the challenges that such inter-disciplinarity and its living politics inevitably create.

This first chapter introduces three main debates. The first of these, following Eagleton's handbook, focuses upon the term 'postcolonial' itself, and the ways in which it both describes the field and flags difficulties in such description. The second concerns the content of postcolonial studies courses and academic approaches to that material – what can be studied and how. It touches upon current dominant trends of theoretical practice and their relationship to older and emergent versions, and upon the principled and pragmatic decisions that course-designers take in setting materials for academic study. The problems and compromises that these involve open up debates about value, representation and representativeness, and also pose questions about critical language, the politics of publication and recording practices, and the material effects of publishers' and producers' marketing and distribution policies. The third area of debate is perhaps the most difficult of all, and concerns the purpose and the audience of the discipline. In his recent history of the subject, Robert Young has argued that 'the assumption guiding postcolonial critique is that it is possible to make effective political interventions within and beyond its own disciplinary field by developing significant connections between the different forms of intellectual engagement and activism in the world today' (Young 2001: 11). What these fields might be, how they can be connected, who can be involved in that connection, and what might imperil the process are important questions.

Three case studies allow a more detailed examination of these issues. The first considers a polemical challenge to the very concept of postcolonial studies posed by the historian Arif Dirlik. Dirlik's pungent critique of the discipline as an academic practice complicit with the very forces that it is notionally 'interrogating' is a provocation to an analysis of the relationship between the academy and the postcolonial. The next case study explores two different responses to Dirlik's arguments. The first links ethnography's strategic responses to its implication in the history and ideology of colonialism with current arguments in postcolonial studies. Of particular interest is its attention to the cultural and literal conversations between student and studied, privileged observer and observed. Its examination of its own implication in the various systems of power that define such dialogues and its strategies to reconfigure those dialogues through such knowledge provide a valuable resource for postcolonial practice more generally. This sense of a field recovering a past and re-articulating a method is differently inflected in the second academic revision of postcolonial practice. Robert Young's *Postcolonialism: An Historical Introduction*, referred to earlier, is one of the first sustained attempts to bring together current academic practice and a much longer history of activist thought and agitation in the periods of anti-colonial struggle and postcolonial nation-building before and after the Second World War. Young's sense of the potential for a reintegration of what have become largely divergent histories – those of practice and theory, crudely put – both offers a new perspective upon the 'linguistic turn' of postcolonial studies, and suggests new emphases for the curriculum. These are the concerns of the final case study, which deals with the life and work of the twentieth-century Trinidadian activist and cultural theorist C. L. R. James, a figure who bridges the two worlds of Young's history. James's idiosyncratic version of postcolonial studies, formed before the subject was even named, offers another resource for thinking through the challenges of the postcolonial, and redefining a contemporary field of study.

Describing the Postcolonial

The title of Kwame Anthony Appiah's essay 'Is the Post- in Postmodernism the Post- in Postcolonial?' poses a question that is both one of verbal nicety and one of the nature of the subject at hand (Appiah 1991). In 'postmodernism', 'poststructuralism' and the other intellectual movements or cultural descriptors to which 'posts' attach themselves, the prefix is there to delimit the scope and chronology of an intellectual field of study or of a set of characteristic stylistic and methodological assumptions. The 'post' in postcolonialism shares this general historical placement that signifies 'a development from' or 'replacement of' ideas on a cognate subject – here, those associated with colonialism. However, the 'post' in postcolonialism can also have a much sharper historical sense. Here, its field is defined chronologically as 'the time after colonialism', indicating the legacies of a vast political, economic and military force that, in its modern variant, extended over three hundred years. It is this second sense and its relationship to the first that have caused the most difficulty in the intellectual practices of the field. Embedded in this 'post' is a notion of colonialism coming to an end and being superseded by another set of political and cultural practices. The implicitly neat break between the colonial and the postcolonial consequently threatens to elide both the often lengthy transitional periods of change and struggle between colony and 'independence' – actually, the most intense moments of physical risk, ideological debate and cultural redefinition – and the persistence of colonialism in other economic, cultural and political forms after the formal end of its military or governmental presence.

Equally troubling are the ideological assumptions implied by a prefix that, ironically enough, privileges the very force that it appears to dismiss. Colonialism squats unqualified as history is defined around it, pre- and post. Whilst it can elide other possible historical qualifiers – what price a discipline of 'non-colonialism'? – its own verbal persistence in the very grain of a discipline that seeks to unpick its effects confirms a continuing influence. The Martiniquean theorist Frantz Fanon has a parable to illustrate the relationship of power and rhetoric in which a master tells a slave 'From now on you are free' (Fanon 1986: 220). Just as that 'gift' cannot be made because the performance of the giving perpetuates the very condition that it appears to negate, so 'postcolonialism' can be said to inscribe a predicament of continuing deference, even as it develops theories of liberation. The difficulty has led to much debate, to hyphens and parentheses demarcating the prefix, and to some theorists (Edward Said and Gayatri Spivak, for example) avoiding the term altogether. Yet it remains a useful cypher for many of the problems of defining a discipline complicated by long histories, varied geographies, diverse cultures and significant movements of population.

The constitution of postcolonialism's field of study is also difficult. To classify as 'postcolonial' those cultures which have experienced colonialism but have, to whatever extent and by whatever means, freed themselves from it, is only to raise other questions about historical boundaries and the usefulness of cross-historical and cross-cultural comparisons and parallels. To what extent, for example, is the United States of America a postcolonial nation? Its revolutionary war of independence in the 1770s defined strategies and intellectual traditions of modern anti-colonialism, even as it laid the foundations for a state that became a primary generator of the economic systems that were later to empower global neocolonial practices. The fact that it is much easier to apply the term 'postcolonial' to a state such as Haiti (which also staged a successful rebellion against a European power in the eighteenth century, but which went on to endure a very different history) might indicate that the term copes uneasily with implication in structures of domination. Should the term, therefore, be restricted to 'developing', 'emergent' or 'Third World' states (the terms and their problematic implications multiply)? In which case, the USA is only 'postcolonial' to the point at which it reconstituted itself from being an emergent revolutionary state to being a purveyor of manifest destiny. But such a restriction limits the history and agency of the field, denying the capacity for political change, as well as occluding emergent forms of postcolonial practices within dominant cultures.

Another solution to the problem of postcolonialism is to restrict its terms of reference. The 'post' in 'postcolonial' might make most sense when it is read in the more limited compass of the liberation struggles of the twentieth century and their aftermath – from the independence of India in 1947, say, to the present. This also presents difficulties, though, by artificially delimiting long and varied histories into a relatively compact synchronic moment, grouping together (and thereby disguising) disparate geographical, political and cultural conditions. What does it mean to link, however loosely, the last hundred of five hundred years of colonial activity in Ireland with the conditions of the much more recent settler states of Australia and New Zealand, or the complex ending of a complex imperialism in India with the national settlement in Ghana in 1957? And this is without raising the questions that have preoccupied the work of influential theorists like Homi Bhabha and Paul Gilroy who have sought to deconstruct 'nationhood' and the narratives of exclusion that it generates, emphasising instead mobility and difference within and between nation states. In postcolonial theory, nationhood must itself be examined as both colonial inheritance – a deeply ambivalent 'gift' of Europe – and as the unrealised, potentially reshaped, emergent cultural conscious-ness that Frantz Fanon was among the first to describe (see Fanon 1967; Bhabha 1990; Gilroy 1993). This, and Gilroy's development of concepts of non-national circuits of identity-production, linking, for example, Africa, the Caribbean and the Americas, further complicate the assumptions of political, historical and geographical demarcations that are implicit in a casual use of the concept of the postcolonial state.

The term 'postcolonialism', then, always leads to difficulties of definition and strategy. These difficulties are not only debates about the niceties of terminology, but stem from fundamental historical and political predicaments. To study postcolonialism forces some kind of definition, however arbitrary it might ulti-mately be. This book, for example, limits its discussion to areas of British colonialism – the Caribbean, Southern Africa, Australasia, India and Ireland. It also treats Great Britain itself as, in some ways, a postcolonial state, its cultures and institutions engaged in an ambivalent management of the consequences of an imperial and colonial past. The earliest case study here is from the 1930s, as anti-colonial strategies began to take a peculiarly modern shape, suggesting the unevenness of postcolonial developments both before and after national independence, and both within and beyond Britain. These are rough and ready decisions, striking a balance between coherence and diversity, and attempting to suggest the cultural and historical variety that postcolonialism implies. Nevertheless, to make such decisions necessitates an engagement with the difficulties of the term itself, its contents and methodologies.

What to Study and How

What do you study if you study postcolonialism? Two of the best readers in postcolonial studies published in the last ten years share enough interests and points of reference to make some consensus possible on an answer. Gregory Castle's *Postcolonial Discourses: A Reader* (2001) and Bill Ashcroft, Gareth Griffiths and Helen Tiffin's *The Post-Colonial Studies Reader* (1995) engage with similar core topics: questions of nationhood, cultural identity and hybridity; the effects of and responses to diaspora; a questioning of inherited, colonial-influenced historical narratives and essentialist descriptions of race. Whilst there are differences in emphasis and inflection in the treatment of these concerns, the choice of texts, and the organisation of sections, both draw upon a canon of theorists and critical methods that have become dominant in the academic field – Said, Spivak, Bhabha, Appiah. Both emphasise recent academic texts, with less attention to a longer view of postcolonial discourses. In Castle's anthology, for example, only three of its pieces were written before 1980, a chronology that, implicitly at least, locates postcolonialism in the late twentieth century and, by implication, in the academy. The earliest theorist whose work is included is Frantz Fanon, perhaps the most frequent point of pre-1980 reference for the post-1980 canon of theory. The Ashcroft does include non-academic voices, but these tend to be those of writers and poets who have ultimately made their careers in American universities, and whose work forms part of those universities' syllabi – Edward Kamau Brathwaite, Derek Walcott, Ngugi wa Thiong'o. These sources suggest what John Frow has termed the 'economies of value' of postcolonialism, that is, the hierarchies of value implicit or explicit in an intellectual practice (Frow 1997: 131ff.). In postcolonial studies these hierarchies tend to privilege the discourses of theory itself, and of literature.

The index to *Postcolonial Discourses* yields eight references to Joseph Conrad (Ashcroft has seven), six to Jean Rhys (the same in

Ashcroft), seven to Salman Rushdie (seven in Ashcroft), nine to
Chinua Achebe (fourteen in Ashcroft), twenty-three to Homi
Bhabha (sixteen in Ashcroft), and twenty-seven to Gayatri Spivak
(though only nine in Ashcroft). This is offset by a relative inattention to popular culture. Castle has essays on Irish tradition and on
'Afropop', and Ashcroft has Edward Kamau Brathwaite's 1967
piece on the relationship of jazz to Caribbean literature, but in
neither anthology is there any sustained treatment of film or sport.
Dance appears only as mediated through theatre in an essay in the
Ashcroft, and oral cultures are likewise linked to their influence on
literature, as in Brathwaite's development of the notion of 'nation
language' in Caribbean poetry, again in the Ashcroft. These are
crude measures of a discipline's interests, admittedly, but they also
reflect the emphases of the undergraduate courses that the two
anthologies were compiled to support. Any discipline works as
much through its exclusions as its inclusions, and postcolonial
studies' relative inattention to popular culture, at least in what has
become its academic mainstream, needs some consideration.

It is a neglect that is, in many ways, surprising, given postcolonialism's stated interest in reconfiguring dominant cultures,
and exploring the conditions and resistance of subalterns, to use
the term postcolonial theory has borrowed from Antonio Gramsci
to define colonised or dispossessed groups. Whilst popular forms
such as music and dance cannot be seen as unmediated 'representations' of subaltern cultures, their different manifestations do
provide contrasts and challenges to the methods and expressions
of predominantly literary/textual postcolonialism, and the latter's
own implication in the politics of the First World academy and its
relationship with the international publishing industry. Practical
concerns about the availability of set texts and access to resources
are always instructive about these economies of value. In designing
a university postcolonial studies course, novels by Salman Rushdie,
say, or Zadie Smith, or Ben Okri are both readily available and
relatively cheap, as are now-standard theoretical materials, such as
Edward Said's *Orientalism* (1978), and essays by Homi Bhabha
and Gayatri Spivak, which are widely anthologised in all the
discipline's most successful readers. Major publishers thus both
acknowledge and shape a rapidly emerging canon of postcolonial

materials. If a course-designer wishes to move beyond the conventionally 'textual', though, there are significant problems. Oral culture, for example, is much harder to 'set', even though there is a strong argument for its importance in postcolonial cultures. It is much easier to set books 'influenced by' orality than to obtain recordings of that orality itself, whether it be the work of the Irish storyteller Eddie Lenihan or Trinidad's Paul Keens-Douglas or the performances of Louise Bennett – all recorded by small, local companies, let alone orality that is not in any way commercially produced. This is not unusual, of course. Every course-designer knows about difficulties caused by the banal problem of the availability of books. However, for postcolonial studies, the issue of access is a troubling one because it touches upon the very questions of cultural and economic power, and representation and distribution that are central to the politics of the discipline itself.

The choice of case studies for the chapter on film below is a case in point. There is only limited use in writing about films that are available only through highly specialist sources or which are reproduced without subtitles, so that relatively few people will be able to see or understand them. However, to write about only postcolonial films that are readily available is to be implicated in the difficult politics of that access. These films tend to be those made with First World finance, production and distribution deals, and consequently with First World audiences in mind. This means that the films of the American-trained and resident director Mira Nair can more easily be studied as examples of postcolonial cinema in a Western academy than popular Hindi melodramas made in India for Indian audiences. Even within Nair's work, there are discrepancies of access. Her later (British- and American-funded) films such as *Mississippi Masala* and *Monsoon Wedding* are readily available on video and DVD; her early 'Indian' documentaries, such as *India Cabaret*, are not. It is a truism for many humanities subjects to say that access to texts allows, rather than reflects, representativeness. However, in postcolonial studies, it is a truism that touches upon crucial issues of representation, and upon the economic and ideological control of production and reproduction of narratives of 'other' cultures.

Language and Audience

The consideration of what constitutes representative materials for a study of postcolonialism leads inevitably to questions of audience and purpose that, in turn, take us back to the extramural political aspirations of the discipline. If, as Henry Schwarz has recently written in a survey of American postcolonial studies, the endeavour works towards 'a transformation of knowledge from static disciplinary competence to activist intervention', the means of achieving that transformation and the purpose of that intervention need some further definition (Schwarz 2000: 4). At the heart of the discipline's nervous conditions are the questions: who does it speak to, where does it speak from, and whose interests does it represent? Anxieties about the answers to these questions explain the importance to postcolonial studies of Gayatri Spivak's question in the title of her essay 'Can the Subaltern Speak?' (Spivak 1988). Spivak's answer to her own question is a qualified 'no'. A primary condition of subalternity, she argues, is, in fact, a lack of a position of speaking. For subalterns, the condition of being postcolonial is one of being relentlessly constituted in the discourses of power that control their situation and that lie beyond their agency. Spivak's piece, typically enough, is both a warning about the limitations of the intellectual endeavour of postcolonialism, and a challenge towards its transformation and the creation of the space for that speaking and self-realisation.

This influential argument for the impossibility (and undesirability) of an 'authentic' subaltern identity, that is, one unmediated by the discourses of colonial/neocolonial power, has pressed the question of postcolonialism's own capacity to represent or to speak to those with whom it is avowedly most concerned, and, more disturbingly, of its own complicity in constructing the versions of 'otherness' that police the condition of subalternity (see also Beverley 1991/2; Alcoff 1999). There has been a careful, even relentless, self-consciousness of this danger in recent postcolonial theory, an attentiveness that generates its own difficulties. It has led to the questioning, and often the effective disablement, of the generators of popular action that, in however 'untheorised' a way, produced political change in the mid-twentieth century – ideas of national identity and racial collectivity, for example. It also reinforced an institutional tendency to talk to its own, to emphasise what Neil Larsen has called 'the disparity between its generative principle – the sweeping history that the term evokes . . . and the narrow, intramural sphere in which postcolonialism is talked about and practiced [sic]' (Larsen 2000: 40–1). If subalternity cannot speak, the logic runs, there can be no subaltern voice in the discourses about its absence. And so there is no risking dealing with those subalterns who, against the odds, do think they can speak in popular forms, through dance and song, for example, on however unequal, mediated (and sometimes rebarbative) terms.

Reductive complaints about the impenetrability of the discourse of some of postcolonial studies' most influential theorists are not really the point – though language and syntax, their clarity and their obfuscation, are political issues, and it is not just Orwellian populism to celebrate a widely comprehensible style. But linguistic obscurity is only an element, albeit a highly visible one, of wider questions of the performance of postcolonial studies. The danger of constructing a populist position, of affirming 'the place of the Real *as against* the discursive', as John Frow puts it, is in the end probably no greater than the fragmentation and distance risked by theoretical discourses that are seemingly inattentive to audience and affect (1997: 164). As we will see in the discussion of Arif Dirlik's critiques of postcolonialism in the next section, there is a real difficulty in defining the politics of academic intellectuals' agency in this field. Who can seek to speak for whom, what discourses can best represent and interpret the experiences of subalternity, and who bears the cost? These questions become particularly difficult in a field that has become cagey about fixtures of identity and ethnicity, even as it recognises in its practice their continuing power and urgency.

These are some of the arguments and predicaments that constitute both the vitality and the nervous condition of doing postcolonial studies. Any student or teacher of the subject has to deal with them, not just as issues of disinterested intellectual endeavour, but as issues of performance, in the everyday practices of speaking about and responding to its world. They are part of the social, political and ethical fabric of the activity. They define the places that study, writing and debate take place in, and the relationship these activities have to other lives outside the classroom. They concern the structures of power, from global, to national, to local that, sometimes obscurely, shape writing, speaking and thinking. They define the kind of materials that are chosen for study and the way in which they are studied. The six chapters that follow attempt to give some sense of the arguments at work in specific areas of postcolonial cultures, but three case studies that conclude this chapter consider them as they relate to the academic practice of postcolonial studies, its possibilities, challenges and alternatives.

Case Study One: Postcolonial Studies and the Academy

Back in 1979, the postcolonial performer and organic intellectual Bob Marley sang of the deceptions of a vampiric 'Babylon System' as it continued to construct the physical and ideological means of perpetuating itself, '[b]uilding church and university/ Deceiving the people continually'. 'Me say them graduating thieves/And murderers. Look out now,' he warns (Marley 1979). But twenty-five years later, the university is the place to do postcolonialism, and it is on its courses that the dominant theories and discourses of the discipline have been developed. Moreover, the academic discipline has maintained ambitions of wider relevance. The task of postcolonialist academics, according to John Beverley, is to work 'against the grain of our own interests and prejudices by contesting the authority of the academy and knowledge centers at the same time that we continue to participate in them and deploy that authority as teachers, researchers, administrators, and theorists' (Beverley 1999: 31). There is something dangerously close to having your cake and eating it about this, and Bob Marley would certainly have seen the absorption of postcolonial critique by the academy as a subtle finesse on the part of Babylon system – the vampire posing as sufferer, as it were. But critiques of the political performance of postcolonial studies do not only come from the sceptical apocalypticism of Rastafari. Comparable positions are taken within the academy itself, and it is with one of these that I want to begin a consideration of postcolonialism's political position within academic Babylon – and its possible routes out.

Arif Dirlik, in a polemical essay first published in 1994, argues that the dominant concerns and strategies of contemporary post-colonialism are indicative not of engagements with an urgent present of economic and cultural oppression, suffering and resistance, but with the rather more limited circumstances of privileged diasporic academics in American universities. 'A description of a diffuse group of intellectuals and their concerns and orientations', Dirlik writes, 'was to turn by the end of [the 1980s] into a description of a global condition, in which sense it has acquired the status of a new orthodoxy both in cultural criticism and in academic programs' (Dirlik 1994: 330). It was 'not the abolition but the reconfiguration of earlier forms of domination'. The alarming conclusion of the essay is that 'postcoloniality is the condition of the intelligentsia of global capitalism', and that the particular formulations and expressions of that condition merge seamlessly with the preoccupations and interests of global capitalism (331). Far from challenging the forces of neocolonialism in the way that John Beverley affirms, Dirlik suggests that postcolonialism systematically undermines potential opposition by destabilising the traditional tools of a radical analysis of the postcolonial condition – history, causality, identity – and installing instead concepts that are much more amenable to the forces of global capitalism – the now-canonic theoretical repertoire of hybridity, diaspora and anti-essentialism. '[W]ith a global capital devoted to an ongoing scrambling and reconstitution of identities', he remarks in a later essay, 'arguments that presuppose scrambled identities come as good news' (Dirlik 1998: 176). For Dirlik, the accommodation of post-colonial theory and the defining strategies of global capitalism explain the ready welcome and financial support for the discipline in the most powerful cultural institutions of the First World.

The most disturbing effect of the 'academicisation' of post-colonialism, Dirlik argues, is the distancing of current practice and earlier histories of anti-colonialist thinking and action. 'Post-colonial or Postrevolutionary?' he asks in the title of an essay that argues that postcolonialism, in its current forms, enacts a denial of a radical political tradition. It separates theoretical concerns from the pragmatics of change that preoccupied Third World thinkers in earlier times, thereby defusing the intellectual weapons forged by those thinkers. 'The very epistemological thrust of postcolonial criticism', he writes, 'is to transcend the oppositions and identifications that informed earlier revolutionary ideologies . . . [which] have been informed by the possibility of a rational grasp of history, and the construction on that basis of subjectivities and social identities for its transformation; assumptions that are challenged by the postcolonial argument, which sees in such assumptions the promise not of liberation but of new kinds of coercion and oppression' (Dirlik 1998: 178). For Dirlik, there is in contemporary postcolonial studies a wilful rejection of the resources for a radical analysis of the postcolonial condition. To 'do postcolonialism' in this sense is to retreat from the risks of the engagements with power that defined the work of anti-colonial thinkers and activists in the first seventy years of the last century.

Dirlik's work remains a powerful call to anyone doing postcolonial studies to look to the condition and practice of that doing, to consider the relationship of the intellectual activity of an institution to the lives and conditions it seeks to understand, and to deliberate upon the means by which that understanding can best be communicated. It is part of the positive aspect of the discipline's nervous condition that it can call its practices to account, and provide an ongoing interior critique of the perils of aspirations to relevance beyond the seminar and the conference. Gayatri Spivak, one of the targets of Dirlik's polemics, has herself noted the danger of postcolonialism as a university subject responding to the academy's demands for 'an identifiable margin' (Spivak 1993: 55). For Spivak, practices of study and dissemination that appear to perform the function of introducing new voices and challenging entrenched structures of intellectual and cultural power also have the potential to participate in the very strategies of enclosure and disempowerment that they apparently seek to reverse. '[A]s teachers', Spivak warns, 'we are now involved in the construction of a new object of investigation – "the third world," "the marginal" – for institutional validation and certification . . . It is as if, in a certain way, we are becoming complicitous in the perpetuation of a "new orientalism"' (56). The danger is that the postcolonial academic and his or her students do the work of older forces of marginalisation and control whilst appearing to work towards their 'deconstruction'. Or, as another Rasta song of warning has it, '[d]on't watch the tool and the work it can do/Watch the man that behind it' (The Gladiators 1977).

One of the necessary tasks of doing postcolonial studies, then, is to analyse the context and practice of that doing. There is no need to take on the paranoia of 'Babylon System' to do this. A self-indulgent rejection of the academy from within the academy is a privileged rejection of privilege, and ignores the potential for intellectual possibility and innovation. Edward Said's idealistic vision of the university as a postcolonial ideal, 'a kind of utopian state', a place of travellers rather than potentates, in which the possibility of a 'generously integrative' endeavour can be maintained needs to be set against Dirlik's pessimism (Said et al. 2001: 157). Nevertheless, some First World universities remain ambiguously powerful institutions. Whilst they might harbour some travellers, they also police their borders with some care to repel others, limiting access physically, intellectually and economically, and generating discourses that are frequently exclusive rather than inclusive. This must give the student of postcolonialism some pause. The discipline requires him or her to negotiate methods of working that both acknowledge its own location within the First World productions of knowledge, and take seriously other less powerful sites of intellectual endeavour.

Case Study Two:
Ethnography, History and the Return of the Real

Arif Dirlik's critique of institutional practices of postcolonial studies has some parallels in the self-questioning in the disciplines of anthropology and ethnography. In the 1980s, anthropology began seriously to confront a disciplinary history and performance that were directly implicated in imperialist political structures and ideologies. The visitation, dwelling, observation and interpretation that made up the central activities of ethnographic 'field work' were enmeshed in the practices of colonialism. For pragmatic reasons, ethnologists in the early twentieth century tended to study cultures in those territories controlled by the societies from which they came: access was easier, and academic and adminis- trative contacts were already in place. Beyond this convenience, however, was a dangerous reciprocity of effect. Colonial structures were themselves buttressed by the development of a social science that worked with ideas of definably primitive and savage cultures, no matter how sophisticated the discipline might be. As Judith Okely has argued, to study a culture is to construct an implicit structure of power in which the studied becomes 'other' and the interpreter the powerful norm that it is unnecessary to study (Okely 1996). The early history of anthropology and ethnography, like that of the colonialism with which it worked, was a history of 'othering', and the two meshed in mutual support (see Clifford 1988: 55–91).

Ethnography's coming to political consciousness of this history involved a detailed questioning and reformation of the performance of the discipline, both in its physical contacts with its 'subjects', and in the products of its studies. Writing in 1988, James Clifford noted 'a pervasive postcolonial crisis of ethnographic authority': '[w]ho has the authority to speak for a group's identity or authenticity? What are the essential elements and boundaries of a culture? How do self and other clash and converse in the encounters of ethnography, travel, modern interethnic relations?' (Clifford 1988: 8). Answering these questions required a reconsideration of the power relations between student and subject (human and cultural) that both ac- knowledged the fact of that power and shaped possibilities for a new kind of ethnographic dialogue. The latter was to be a cultural encounter that produced outcomes meaningful for both parties, not just for the anthropologist. The new ethnography produced out of the sense of crisis that Clifford describes includes collaborative ethnographic projects that seek to break down the binary of 'source' and 'interpreter', and share the authorship of anthropological work with informants; a re-evaluation of the inheritance of colonial projects of collecting, display and interpretation in institutions such as the metropolitan museum; and a reappraisal of the means by which belief-systems, stories and rituals are translated and inter- preted in terms other than their own.

The recasting of anthropological and ethnographic methods has both drawn upon and, in its turn, influenced the practices of postcolonialism. The disciplines' urgent engagement with their own performances, their recognition of what Clifford Geertz has called 'the inherent moral asymmetry of the fieldwork situation', and their innovations in representing and responding to their sources are all fruitful resources for a wider postcolonial studies (Geertz 2000: 33). They are, perhaps, particularly useful in a study of postcolonial popular culture in which performance, body cultures and the relationship between scholarship and orality are significant. Also helpful, ironically enough, are the difficulties of the new ethnographic project. Its most skilful, and most consistently upbeat synthesiser and summariser, James Clifford, defines its transformation as that from the old cultural metaphor of 'roots' – implying the static positioning of a culture and of the relationship between dominant and subordinate cultures – to that of 'routes' – implying flexible and changing relationships between cultures (Clifford 1997). The task for the discipline, as he sees it, is to manage an ongoing defusing of colonial structures of power through an appreciation of the hybrid and transitive natures of cultures, whilst at the same time maintaining local integrities of making cultural meaning. Recognising that '[c]ross-cultural translation is never entirely neutral [but] enmeshed in relationships of power', Clifford nevertheless argues for the possibility of a gradual loosening of this enmeshment (182). In a global economy of routes, the possibilities for shared systems of information and interpretation proliferate. To what extent this ethnographic pluralism understates the economic imbalances and ideological compliance enforced by that same globalism is a moot point, as is a lack of specific analysis of the iniquities maintained through the funding and institutionalising of ethnographic endeavour. Baldly put, indigenous groups do not sponsor ethnographic research into First World universities, and could not afford to, even if they wanted to. Until such a route is possible, that 'moral asymmetry' to which Geertz refers persists, even if in less severe forms than before. There is a similar danger in the lauding of joint authorship of ethnographic publications between ethnographer and 'source'. Clifford himself admits '[t]he ethnographic . . . interpretations of nonuniversity authorities are seldom recognized as fully scholarly discourse', and the rewards of publication remain unequal (83). Without a disciplinary practice that establishes a 'true' relativism in its dialogue between source and interpretation, it seems inevitable that the shadows of otherness will continue to fall.

Despite these difficulties, the new ethnography's acknowledgement of the need for constructive dialogue between source and student and the scrutiny of disciplinary performance that this entails provides a useful analogue for postcolonial studies' own self-questioning. The influence of what Robert Young famously termed 'the Holy Trinity of colonial-discourse analysis' (Said, Bhabha, Spivak) and their methods defined by European post-structuralist and psychoanalytical modes of thought has been widespread, as the extent of their presence in the course readers referred to earlier suggests (Young 1995: 163). However, the very intensity of the anti-essentialising, anti-universalising deconstructive practices introduced by these thinkers, as Dirlik suggests, destabilised not only the colonial ideological legacies that were their concern, but also the very identities, narratives and analytical tools that had charged a long history of popular anti-colonial struggles. Stuart Hall, in another context, famously declared 'the end of the innocent notion of the essential black subject', but the political task for theory after the acceptance of such a declaration was to find a means of constructive dialogue with a history that had been charged by just such 'innocent' notions (Morley and Chen 1996: 443). In order to fulfil its activist aspirations, postcolonialism had to develop a strategy of analysis and action that could accommodate the deconstructive passions of theory and, at the same time, galvanise a collective consciousness that was not dependent upon the protection of First World institutions. Gayatri Spivak's celebrated get-out clause of 'strategic essentialism' – the tactical acceptance of an imaginary essential subject, such as Hall's black subject, for the purposes of political action – was at once an answer to this challenge, an intellectual sleight of hand, and an implicit acknowledgement of the limited political effectiveness of academic postcolonialism's dominant intellectual methods.

The security of the annexation of postcolonialism by the strategies associated with European poststructuralism remains startling, as a reading of its major academic journals – *Third Text*, *interventions*, *Diaspora* – and the course readers referred to earlier makes clear. More striking still is the decoupling of that theory from the intellectual and political legacy of figures who were central to the construction of 'actually-existing' postcolonies – however problematic their fates might have been. If we return to the Castle and Ashcroft anthologies, Gandhi merits one reference in each, Mao one reference in Castle, and there is no mention at all of Kwame Nkrumah, Julius Nyerere, Kenneth Kaunda, Amilcar Cabral, Ho Chi Minh, or any other of the first generation of postcolonial political leaders and theorists. The only substantial presence from this earlier period of postcolonial formation is Frantz Fanon, a revolutionary and a psychiatrist, whose work, as Henry Louis Gates argues, has been particularly amenable to mediation by various contesting versions of the contemporary postcolonial project (Gates 1991). Whilst it is too crude to present this as an effective depoliticisation and dehistoricisation of postcolonialism, there has been at least an elision of traditions of popular and intellectual activism from many contemporary versions of it. This conflict between two contrasting versions of the field was memorably defined by what is often taken to be the founding text of contemporary postcolonialism, Edward Said's *Orientalism*, first published in 1978.

One of the fascinations of *Orientalism*, as it becomes itself a historical text, is its simultaneous initiation of and resistance to a schism of theory, history and political activism. Said's scholarly examination of what he has called, after Michel Foucault, 'the affiliation of knowledge with power' heralded discourse analysis as the dominant method of understanding the intense, totalising practices of colonialism (Said 1981: ix). At the same time, though, the book was also the beginning (albeit a coded one) of Said's public commitment to the cause of Palestinian autonomy, forming the first part of a trilogy that moved on to a history of Palestinian confrontation with Zionism in *The Question of Palestine* (1980) and, in *Covering Islam* (1981), a study of contemporary media representations of the Middle East. Both of these later books (generally less well known, and certainly less often referred to on postcolonial studies courses) work in dialogue with *Orientalism* to challenge the 'pessimism of the intellect' that some have seen in the earlier work (for a helpful collection of responses to *Orientalism*, see Williams 2001). For if Said's work of the late 1970s in some ways heralded and shaped the 'linguistic turn' that was to mark the next twenty-five years of postcolonial studies, it also sought to preserve another version of intellectual work that drew upon older humanist values, defined by him as qualities of 'passionate engagement, risk, exposure, commitment to principles, vulnerability in debating, and being involved in worldly causes' (Said 1994: 81). The latter worked within and against the new political contexts within which *Orientalism* was initially read – the establishment of the New Right in Britain and America, for example, and the Islamicisation of anti-colonialism in Iran and Afghanistan. More specifically, it was published at a time when many of the postcolonial regimes associated with a previous generation of radical anti-colonial thinkers and of popular anti-colonial movements – Ghana, Tanzania, Uganda, Cuba, Jamaica – were enduring periods of crisis under combined pressures of Cold War politics, the International Monetary Fund and the political failures of national leaderships. The academic classic *Orientalism*, with its analysis of the means by which discourse constituted the practices of imperialism, was published as popular editions of the works of Nyerere, Nkrumah and Cabral were going out of print.

The humanist concerns and dissident activism that form one aspect of Said's contribution to postcolonialism have persisted in the discipline, resisting subsumption within poststructuralist models. Benita Parry, for example, criticises the 'exorbitation of discourse and a related incuriosity about the enabling socio-economic and political institutions and other forms of praxis' in a polemical essay of 1987, and it is a theme that she has pursued throughout her work (Parry 1987: 43). Her contribution to David Theo Goldberg and Ato Quayson's collection *Relocating Postcolonialism* (2002), for example, argues against '[p]ractices which privilege the signifier over the signified', promoting instead '[a] turn from a rhetoric disparaging the master narratives of revolution and liberation and a return to a politics grounded in the material, social, and existential' (Parry 2002: 73, 77). The 'real' in this case is the already-existing economic, social, and cultural plight of Third

World people. It is a theme that Parry rehearses in a recent collection of essays edited with Laura Chrisman. The editors' introduction again seeks to mark the limits of what they term a 'culturalist' approach to postcolonialism, arguing instead the 'need to foreground and extend the exploration of "materiality", so that not only socio-economic, macrological processes but also the physical materiality of human bodies . . . or the spatial materiality of domestic interiors and local environment . . . are factored into the analysis' (Chrisman and Parry 2000: vii). This attempt to reconfigure postcolonial studies from discourse to circumstance (or, rather, to discourse and circumstance) has had other expressions – two notable polemics being Aijaz Ahmad's *In Theory* (1992) and the Dirlik essay discussed earlier – but it finds perhaps its most ambitious and persuasive version in Robert Young's revisionary *Postcolonialism: An Historical Introduction*.

Young's history seeks not only to describe the last twenty-five years of the academic discipline of postcolonialism, but also to re-establish a continuity between the academic project, post-*Orientalism*, and the theory and politics of the modern period of decolonisation – roughly, from the 1930s to the late 1960s – that Said's book seemed in some ways to close. Two aspects of Young's work are particularly significant, and, in some ways, they parallel the developments in ethnography described above. The first emerges from his recognition that '[p]ostcolonial theory, despite its espousal of subaltern resistance, scarcely values subaltern resistance that does not operate according to its own secular terms' (338). This sense of the potential limitations of the methodology and assumptions of academic practice lies at the heart of his re-evaluation of earlier sources of anti-colonial resistance – religious-derived thought, for example, nationalism and pan-Africanism – both as components in a common history of anti-colonialism, and as themselves valid theoretical practices, whatever difficulties they might pose for current methods of study. The second is his social and historical contextualising of the work of recent theorists. 'Theory', he argues, 'cannot operate politically if it is conceived as operating only at a disembodied synchronic level, as if it exists in an atemporal space, without consideration of its impact in relation to specific conditions at a particular moment' (Young 2001: 11). Just

as *Orientalism* can now be read as text shaped by and active in a
moment of radical change in late Cold War anti- and neocolonialism, so other work, much of it generally intolerant of such
historicising, can nevertheless be placed within a historical-
political context of production. Young reads the ideas and methods
of Michel Foucault and Jacques Derrida, for example, as intimately
engaged with and shaped by colonial crises in Tunisia and Algeria
respectively (395–426).

   Postcolonialism, like Young's lucid popular guide to the subject,
Postcolonialism: A Very Short Introduction (2003), works to reconstitute a coherent narrative of postcolonial activity. It both fore-
grounds 'absent' histories, such as those of pan-Africanism,
Négritude and Gandhian satyagraha (or non-violent non-co-opera-
tion), as agents in the discipline, and engages with historical
materialist critiques of 'culturalist' tendencies in recent postcolonial theory by reintegrating key components of that theory within
a historical context. Young's 'long' postcolonialism – his insistence
that pre-*Orientalism* material can have theoretical as well as historical significance – is important in a number of ways. It offers the
possibility of dialogue between seemingly very different intellectual traditions, developing Said's own ideas on the necessity for
such a project explored in *Culture and Imperialism* (1993); it
restores social and political agency to the heart of the discipline;
it provokes a reconsideration of the theoretical and practical
resources of a wider field of postcolonial endeavour; and it allows
a re-imagination of the scope and practice of postcolonial studies
beyond a relatively restricted theoretical and cultural arena. Whilst
there can be no simplistic 'return of "the real" ', Young's re-
articulation of theory within a history of practice, like ethnography's re-evaluation of its methodologies, does allow a new sense of
the performance of postcolonialism within the academy, and
between the academy and other constituencies, other histories
and other practices. Such debates and re-evaluations can potentially change the shape of postcolonial studies, requiring reflection
on method and agency, thinking widely about its cultural contents,
and arguing through the historical and geographical compass of its
concerns. It might also allow a re-invigoration of the influence of
postcolonialism's older figures. The final case study will test out

some of these possibilities for expansion and diversification by considering the example and the relevance to contemporary post-colonialism of a relatively neglected theorist and writer, C. L. R. James, a writer and activist who crossed the historical divides that Young also seeks to bridge.

Case Study Three: Postcolonial Intellectuals and the Exemplary Career of C. L. R. James

C. L. R. James (1901–89) is certainly a respected figure in the field of postcolonial studies, but that respect is not reflected in his use. In the two representative readers referred to earlier, Castle contains a couple of references, Ashcroft none. James, though, is both a representative figure for a long view of postcolonialism, and a provocative questioner of the discipline's interests and methods. His life and writing span the history of high colonialism (he was born in the year of Queen Victoria's death), of the great movements of twentieth-century global power (he died in the year of the fall of the Berlin Wall) and of the politics of postcolonialism (he was present and active in the processes leading to the independence of both Ghana and his native Trinidad). He also spent fifteen years in the USA, and a formative time in Britain in the 1930s, returning to London and the 'front line' of Brixton in his last years. Biography has been downplayed in contemporary critical discourse, but there is a sense in which James's was a kind of exemplary twentieth-century anti-colonial/postcolonial life, living through and being lived through by the forces of empire and of the processes of its dissolution after the Second World War, and participating in the construction of new nations and intellectual traditions. His later fascination with autobiography, culminating in his remarkable *Beyond a Boundary* (1963), shows something of his own awareness of this representative quality, and of his search to find a narrative mode that would suggest that dialectical play between the individual life and its active historical context.

James's contribution to postcolonial theory cannot be summarised neatly – hence, perhaps, his marginal presence in textbooks and course readers. There is no single representative work, but a bewildering range of texts and genres – an early Caribbean novel, *Minty Alley* (1936); a pioneering history of the Haitian revolution, *The Black Jacobins* (1938); an extended, but incomplete, study of American culture posthumously published as *American Civilization* (1993); *Mariners, Renegades and Castaways* (1953), a Marxist reading of the work of Herman Melville; and *Beyond a Boundary* (1963), both an autobiography and a history of cricket. There are also scores of essays, some of them innovative examples of cultural studies, others locked into the minutiae of Trotskyite schisms, others again cricket reports or memoirs and opinions on the game. James's significance for contemporary postcolonialism lies, in part, in this very improvisation of method and subject, a sense of theory and practice as performances grounded in theories of historical materialism and revolutionary anti-colonialism, but at the same time open to particular moments, places and encounters. If, as Young's history suggests, postcolonialism needs to configure a long and divergent history, and, like ethnography, to encounter and respect the divergent performances and discourses of its subjects as representing potentially multiple and alternative versions of theory and practice, a figure like James offers an instructive example. Three areas are particularly relevant. First, the scope of his interests; second, his deployment of theory; and third, his sense of the performative as central to the postcolonial endeavour.

Any representative selection of James's work such as *At the Rendezvous of Victory* (1984), *Spheres of Existence* (1980), or *The C. L. R. James Reader* (1992), suggests the range of his interests. *Spheres of Existence*, for example, contains essays on Marxist theory, Ancient Greek democracy, cricket, Caribbean slavery, the calypsonian Mighty Sparrow, the novel and African-American politics. It is an eclecticism foreign to the specialisations of early twenty-first-century academic postcolonialism, but this is not only a sign of James's idiosyncratic inquisitiveness. The variety of his interests was also an imperative in a project committed to a unified understanding of the material processes of history and culture. James's work insists upon a cultural model that makes connections across divides of space, time and taste. Sport is read alongside drama and sculpture, African-American history is connected to Caribbean history, popular music is part of political discourse, and so on. This is not a free play of relativism, however. Rather, it is a performance of both the consequences of modernity, and the means of understanding and changing that modernity's most pernicious results. James's own peripatetic life enacted a process of deracination and connection, as he moved restlessly, but purposefully, along the routes of what Paul Gilroy was later to term the 'Black Atlantic'. Years before the official coming of cultural studies, James argued the necessity for a serious study of popular music, commercial films and sport alongside and in dialogue with that of history, political theory and literature. He constructed a version of culture which, as Anna Grimshaw argues in her introduction to her reconstruction of James's projected study of American civilisation, broke with ' "old bourgeois civilization" and its oppositions between art and culture, intellectuals and the people, politics and everyday life' (James 1993: 14). For James, the tasks of the cultural historian and postcolonial revolutionary were to understand the totality of his or her environment, to identify a means of describing the sources of creativity and change, and to participate in effecting that change.

James's intellectual practice can be seen an example of what Edward Said calls 'traveling theory', a set of ideas inherited and transformed by attentiveness to 'the essential untidiness, the essential unmasterable presence that constitutes a large part of historical and social situations' (Said 1983: 241). Said's celebration of the intellectual as 'exile and marginal' is peculiarly apt for James, whose political life and writing were activities conditional upon changing circumstances and locations, and were mainly developed outside of mainstream political and academic institutions. James's 'Marxism' was as much travelling method as established theory, a peripatetic set of ideas applied to and inflected by the different circumstances of colonialism and postcolonialism that he encountered in Trinidad, Lancashire, the USA, Ghana and Brixton at different moments of their and his histories. It means that his ideas are not easily summarised, sampled or 'applied'. But they offer other possibilities for framing a postcolonial studies that emphasises performance, active, changing and risky engagements with a diversity of postcolonial expression, and that re-engagement with earlier traditions of postcolonial practice that Robert Young's history encourages. Said has also spoken admiringly of qualities of 'amateurism' in intellectuals, by which he means a critical intelligence unconstrained by the imperatives of institutional scrutiny or the careful compromises of a career, but at the same time passionately engaged with the politics and ethics of their predicament (Said 1994: 57). James's work certainly presents an elegant, urgent version of these qualities in its sharp analyses of local productions of political and cultural expression framed by a sense of broader political and economic developments.

The dialectic that shaped James's cultural analyses was formed through a lifelong attention to Marxist theory (a process most fully examined in *Notes on Dialectics* (1980)). But what is startling about James is his willingness to include and absorb seemingly incompatible versions of cultural critique within this dialogue. For example, in the 1960s James was an early celebrant of the Guyanese novelist and theorist Wilson Harris. Harris's idiosyncratic work, poised between visionary narrative, existentialist philosophy and indigenous Central and South American metaphysics, is celebrated by James as an innovative and provocative counter-discourse to the narratives of nationalism and collectivism that were dominant in that period of decolonisation (James 1980: 157–72). Harris's work is one of several counter-articulations of culture and history that James engages with – and it is interesting to note, forty years later, that Harris is beginning to be used in comparable ways by contemporary theorists (see, for example, Huggan 2002). In his writings on popular culture – particularly cricket and calypso – James also argues for the capacity of the popular to deliver up its own critique of historical moments, its performers becoming knowing theorists and agents of analysis and change. His essay on Mighty Sparrow, for example, sees the calypsonian not as an example of the emergent culture of a Trinidad approaching independence, but as a critical shaper of that emergence. For James, Sparrow made the flexible popular form of calypso into a resourceful structure for analysis and intervention in the changing politics and culture of the island. This perception both celebrates the possibility of a popular 'vanguard', independent of established politics, able and willing to use its own resources to achieve a critique of its historical circumstances to transform them, and alters the relationship of the 'critic' to his or her 'subject'. Sparrow is not an object of study for James. He acknowledges the calypsonian as a fellow analyst, complete with strategic sense, political purpose and wittily appropriate vernacular discourse, with whom the commentator can maintain an equal and delighted dialogue (James 1977a: 191–201). The same kind of intellectual respect is accorded elsewhere to other practitioners of popular culture – the comedian Charlie Chaplin, for example, and cricketers such as Learie Constantine and Garfield Sobers.

James's work consistently emphasises the capacity of popular cultural forms both to achieve and express awareness of the social formations and historical processes that produced them, and through that awareness to participate in challenge and change. That expression was most forcefully achieved for James in performance, a persistent presence in his work, in his 'theory', and in his own life, and a concern that links him with the seemingly distant interests and methods of ethnography discussed in an earlier section. Performance, for James, was not limited to drama, though he wrote a play and about plays, but implicitly took on the many connotations that recent work on performativity has developed in different terms – in speech-acts, song, film and sport. The articulate body fascinated James, and his writing on these topics is informed by a sense of a meaningful theatre beyond verbal articulation. For him, the body in movement was a dynamic sculpture shaped by a dialectical tension between individual will and desire, and the forms and constraints of its social environment at a particular historical moment. Whilst the body has always been at the painful centre of colonial and imperial history, it was James who first articulated its capacity for expression and resistance, not through violence necessarily, but through the detailed aesthetics of the body's response to stimuli at a particular moment in history. This political theatre of movement occurs in various and unexpected places by no means limited to traditional definitions of 'art' or rebellion: in a batsman's stroke in cricket; in the Tramp in Charlie Chaplin's early comedies; in the details of Kwame Nkrumah's oratory (James 1977b: 114–17, 1992: 248–9). The apparent eclecticism of reference, as always, belies an intuition of connection and totality within an ongoing historical process.

Performance also defines James's own practice as a writer and

activist. His sense of theatre, in its widest sense, and his commitment to shared social knowledge and transformation, made it
impossible for him not to think carefully about the audiences of
his writing and speaking. The lists of sources for the collections of
his essays and articles made towards the end of his life and after his
death suggest a writer who more often than not improvised his
materials and outlets, using the journals and platforms that were
available, and responding to opportunity and invitation, rather
than being secure in the knowledge of publisher, reader and fee.
This instability, or, seen differently, this improvisation within a
frame of conviction and interest, is part of James's practice, rather
than an interruption to it (though, like his slightly older and ill-
fated contemporaries in Marxist theory, Antonio Gramsci and
Walter Benjamin, the dangerous openness to history stalled and
fragmented some of his projects). But James worked in the forms
available to him, always deploying an elegant, if idiosyncratic,
prose style that was itself a component of, not just a vehicle for, his
politics. The point here is less about clarity, and more about the
strategic imperatives of performance. James was committed to a
process of communication that included diverse audiences, from
African-American radicals to an emergent Black British community
to the cricket-loving Englishmen who might be thought to be the
natural readership for John Arlott's *Cricket: The Great All-Rounders*
(1969) in which one of his best political essays first appeared.

I have dwelt upon the exemplary career of C. L. R. James to
suggest the diverse narratives contained by postcolonialism, and
their potential for reconfiguring and refocusing the discipline. Just
as Gramsci and Benjamin made posthumous interventions at critical
moments of Marxist history in the 1970s and 1980s, so James
presents alternative versions of postcolonialism's field of interest,
its cultural connections, its places of performance and its political
potential. These are not necessarily coherent, summarisable theoretical statements or immediately usable conceptual tools – in fact,
James's work, in its improvisatory manner and unexpectedness of
interest, poses a different model of cultural theory and practice
from those usually associated with the field. The importance of
James is as much in his principled attention to diversity, and in his
insights into the performance of colonial/postcolonial analysis, as in

an extractable position or theoretical vocabulary. He makes it clear that to do postcolonial studies is to be interested in that diversity, involved, complicit and committed. It also requires a clear and sensitive analysis of that complicity and commitment.

Conclusion

This chapter has been concerned with grounding postcolonial studies in its fundamental debates and predicaments. These are not abstract problems, but ones that engage every practitioner and student in immediate ways, and affect every aspect of course design, reading, writing, performance and dialogue. To do post-colonial studies is to be aware of difficult complicities and challenges of method, purpose and audience. These cannot be easily resolved, but have to be recognised and argued through. The six chapters that follow offer some examples of those arguments. Some key themes will be developed and retraced: the difficult relationship between the academy as generator of knowledge and holder of its capital, and the subalternity that is postcolonialism's preoccupation; practices of performance – theoretical, dialogic, and physical – that are ethnography's primary concerns; the integration and expansion of postcolonial studies to emphasise the 'long revolution' of decolonisation and the richness of its cultural and theoretical manifestations; the wide range of subjects for study and the possibilities for dialogues within that study that C. L. R. James's work emphasises; the necessity for any student of postcolonialism to be aware of the demands for ethical thought, political engagement and worldy vulnerability that Edward Said has articulated. All of these issues have also affected the choice of subject-matter.

Three of the six chapters are devoted to the study of particular modes of cultural production and performance: film, music and body cultures, particularly dance and sport. The emphasis here is on popular cultural forms which, as suggested earlier, have tended to be underrepresented in the main anthologies and readers in the field. The serious predicaments of postcolonialism are more normally read through high cultural discourses of literature and philosophy, emphases reflected in course readers and anthologies. In other ways, though, the fluid, contested performances of popular culture allow an exploration of points of rupture in dominant cultures, through their 'aggressively indifferent attitudes toward the life of the mind and the protocols of knowledge', as Andrew Ross puts it, their trading 'on pleasures which a training in political rationality encourages us to devalue' (Ross 1989: 231). They also allow an introduction of a broader range of inter-disciplinary methodologies and complementary theoretical per-spectives. Each chapter also poses its own particular difficulties of approach. A study of body cultures, for example, requires a consideration of the stereotyping of black and 'other' physicality, even as it opens up opportunities to consider the processes of the construction of popular nationalism, and the coded challenges to colonial authority and expressions of postcolonial authority that C. L. R. James perceives in a performance such as cricket. Film poses particular challenges in its negotiation between national and ethnic representation and global structures of finance and distri-bution. Similar issues beset discussion of popular music, where local 'authenticity' is set against international consumption, and rhetorics of radicalism in language, body and posture are in uneasy complicity with the smooth marketing of such rebellion.

The three later chapters take up broader questions and more diverse examples. By focusing on issues of memory, land and rationality, they seek to address in more depth some of the key debates in postcolonialism raised in the introduction. These include the relationship of cultural expression to material dispossession, questions of representation and critical discourse, and the writing and speaking of histories in the contested spaces of colonial legacies, whether of a metropolitan museum or extramural oral traditions. The case studies in these chapters are deliberately eclectic, bringing together different kinds of cultural expressions, histories and contexts. The aim is to suggest the diversity of forms in which these questions are shaped in different historical and social contexts, and the various responses and analyses that can be studied. So, for example, the decisions taken in the construction of the slavery exhibit in the Merseyside Maritime Museum share concerns – of narrative, audience, political agency – with the decisions taken by the South African Truth and Reconciliation Commission in its – immediately dangerous and traumatic –

attempts to tell the stories of apartheid and create a meaningful political agency through that historical record. These chapters are intended to encourage students to look across cultures and their different expressive formations and functions, and to make connections as well as understand the historical and political specificities of each.

The geographical range of reference in the case studies is mainly limited to the postcolonialisms of the former British empire. Any such decision is in some way arbitrary and arguable, and that arbitrariness is itself one of the issues that are being debated. The nation states that emerged from British colonialism are themselves rough, permeable constructions, as the ruinous improvisation of borders that produced India, Pakistan and the Irish Republic go to show. Nations are defined, as recent theory has affirmed, as much by difference and hybridity as they are by ethnic or cultural coherence, but in the shorthand they allow, the discussions are confined to Ireland, the British Caribbean, India, Southern Africa and Australasia, though Britain and America are necessarily included, both as economic centres, and as sites of an internalising postcolonialism that produces their own distinct cultural forms. The decision on the historical span of the studies is, likewise, rough and ready. Some go back to late colonial periods – the discussion of Caribbean and Irish music in the 1950s, for example, and C. L. R. James's and Learie Constantine's stay in Nelson in the 1930s. But these only serve to show the messiness and overlap that postcolonial studies forces its students to confront. Its history is neither neat nor constrained, and neither is the study of it.

CHAPTER 2

Music

Musical traditions transcribe the most intimate histories of culture, where sounds, languages and bodies meet. Rhythms and harmonies, songs and dances, and shows and recordings are performances of function and pleasure that encompass, shape and express individual and communal identities, and register cultural encounters of both trauma and delight. For these reasons they provide particularly valuable materials for a study of postcolonialism and its concerns with diasporic experience, hybrid identity and contests of cultural value. However, to engage with cultural forms that are often wilfully ephemeral, that depend upon deep structures of linguistic, musical and bodily interpretation in changing cultural contexts, and that problematise questions of value and function obviously tests theoretical and interpretative resources. It also tests the academic nerve to resist celebrating what is most theoretically useful, rather than that which is most culturally significant. And the more contemporary the music, the greater is the danger.

The theoretical starting point of this chapter is the work of the sociologist Paul Gilroy. For over twenty years, Gilroy has returned to the possibilities of understanding popular music within political and cultural debates of the African diaspora, insisting on its centrality to the maintenance and furtherance of African-American, Black British and Caribbean identities and relationships. His writing has also consistently tracked and engaged with developing methodologies of reading popular music politically and sociologically, his work from 'There Ain't No Black in the Union Jack' (1987) to Between Camps (2000) providing a guide to these wider developments in the scholarship of black music. Gilroy's use of music as a central component of 'Black Atlantic' cultural formations will be explored through a study of two contrasting emigrant musics in post-Second World War London. The migration of Trinidadian calypso was one part of the major population shift of Caribbean labour to Britain, and provides a means of studying the processes of a popular music's adaptation to new social and political circumstances. It also suggests the importance of a diachronic or longer view of this material. Trinidadian calypsonians found an already-existing black music culture in Britain, one that contained both Caribbean and African performers, and their interaction provides an example of the historical circuits and emergent politics that Gilroy describes. The impact of another musical migration to London in the 1950s, that of rural Irish performers, suggests that the model of a Black Atlantic circuit is one that might be adapted to describe other musical diasporas.

Gilroy's discussions of musical value, and of the relationship between recent black music and globalised music production and marketing, provide the starting point for the other two case studies. The first concerns 'world music', a marketing term developed by First World recording companies for a variety of post-colonial musics. World music's exploitation of concepts such as hybridity and its simultaneous development of ideas of 'rooted-ness' provide a means of exploring some important concepts of postcolonial studies through the practices of popular music and its marketing. The work of the Jamaican DJ and singer Lady Saw provides another perspective on these, and upon Gilroy's pessimistic sense of the condition of Black Atlantic music at the end of the twentieth century. Lady Saw's version of postcolonial musical politics provides a more positive model of the persistence of traditional cultural practices and the adaptation of their resources to provide a challenging performance of the contradictions and confrontations of contemporary local and Black Atlantic music-making.

Black Atlantic Music

The central chapter of Gilroy's *'There Ain't No Black in the Union Jack'*, 'Diaspora, Utopia and the Critique of Capitalism', is one of the first attempts to place black musical styles at the centre of debates about diaspora, modernity and postcolonialism. Although the chapter concentrates upon Black British musics, Gilroy argues that an identity such as 'Black British' is itself a hybrid formation, a transformation of other cultural elements in response to the specific conditions of British life. 'Black Britain', he argues, 'defines itself crucially as part of a diaspora' (Gilroy 1987: 154). This diasporic shaping is part of what the American poet and cultural theorist Amiri Baraka called the 'changing same' of black music. It is a music that is at once 'rooted' in a repertoire of expressive codes, and in a process of change as those codes are adjusted in response to new circumstances (Baraka 1991: 186–209). Unconfined by national identity, it functions as a currency of cultural, intellectual, physical and commercial exchange. Whilst a music might coalesce into an identity that fixes particular moments of voice, body and politics, the wider resources of black musical culture remain in motion, and so essentially uncentred. Thus the music that was both agent and embodiment of changing Black British identity from the 1950s through to the 1980s was a shifting amalgam of American, Caribbean, African and British forms.

This model of transport and restless cultural transformation and translation becomes the centre – circumference, really – of Gilroy's influential concept of the 'Black Atlantic', developed in the book of that name published in 1993. Here he works against what he and other theorists such as Homi Bhabha and Stuart Hall, in their different ways, see as the debilitating fixity of identities founded in nationhood and race. Instead, he suggests a version of black cultural identity defined by 'the flows, exchanges, and in-between elements that call the very desire to be centred into question' (Gilroy 1993a: 190). Music is a crucial cultural practice in these exchanges. It embodies a dialectic between a specific worldly location – in its particular performances, dances, recordings – and an endless malleability and improvisation as it reshapes itself in response to particular social and historical circumstances. Music is both of the moment – an expression of voice, sound and body – and always on the move betwixt and between places, bodies and histories. The changing same of jazz, soul, reggae and other manifestations of a post-slavery black aesthetic is a current between the places of those histories – Africa, Europe, the Americas – moving in the bodies and voices of the diaspora, commodified as recordings, exported, reabsorbed, and then recast once more into other sounds and other movements.

The Black Atlantic also refines a methodology for analysing postcolonial music. Gilroy's earlier essay tended to concentrate upon lyrical analysis, identifying verbal statement as the main constituent of a song's political agency. However, as Simon Frith's work on popular song has suggested, to concentrate on the lyric as the main bearer of music's meanings is to turn performance into text, limiting the meanings of a complex interaction of non-textual elements. The real political force of popular song, Frith argues, lies in performance and its generation of tensions between text, voice and body, tensions that are in turn received and reproduced in the various social and historical contexts of the song's reception (Frith 1996: 158–82). To sing Peter Tosh's militant anthem 'Get Up, Stand Up' is not necessarily to make a radical political statement, just as, conversely, to be devoted to charting the stringencies and pitfalls of sexual relationships is not necessarily to withdraw from political concerns (see the discussion of Lady Saw below). In *The Black Atlantic*, Gilroy's emphasis is upon the complex encryption of an expressive culture inherited from responses to slavery. The Black Atlantic is constituted by cultural formations that are often masked or coded in their political expression, the political power of the performance often depending upon the very indirection of its statement. It is a formulation that broadens the interpretative possibilities for musical performance, as well as confronting post-colonial studies with familiar questions about its own interpretative methods. In an adaptation of Antonio Gramsci's concept of the organic intellectual, Gilroy re-imagines postcolonial musicians and performers as skilled operators within these cryptic musical and verbal legacies of slavery, something that C. L. R. James anticipates in his studies of cricket and calypso. Certain performers, working through the cultures of sound and body, are able to articulate and intervene in the struggles of groups in ways that were previously assigned to 'traditional' intellectuals – theorists, writers and vanguard activists. What they produce is not just 'expressive' culture, but a developing system of understanding, an interpretative culture (76).

Along with American cultural historians such as George Lipsitz,

Houston Baker and W. T. Lhamon and sociologists like Simon Frith, Paul Gilroy established song and music as central components of subaltern cultural expression, and developed a supple methodology for exploring these beyond their purely verbal expression (see Baker 1984; Lhamon 1990; Lipsitz 1990). In *The Black Atlantic*, difficult questions of value also begin to be debated. 'Diaspora, Utopianism and the Critique of Capitalism' emphasises those aspects of Black Atlantic traditions that were perceived to carry forward a message of positive development through radical politics – songs discussed include The Impressions' 'Keep on Moving', Nina Simone's 'Mississippi Goddam', and The Specials' 'Ghost Town'. But the essay had little to say about traditions of black music that articulated other concerns, or about the relationship of the music to the recording industries that are its major purveyors. In his later work, Gilroy begins to develop a sceptical political aesthetic, particularly in his dealings with the global popularity of American hip-hop and rap. At odds with the work of influential American academics such as Lipsitz and Tricia Rose, Gilroy's essays in *Small Acts* (1993) and *Between Camps* (2000) provide both a critique of black music's implication in globalised commerce, and a polemical appraisal of the etiolation of that music's political discourses. In opposition to Lipsitz's optimistic celebration of hip-hop's 'diasporic conversation' and the 'potential for contemporary commercialized leisure to carry images, ideas and icons of enormous political importance between cultures', Gilroy argues that the incorporation of hip-hop by global capitalism marks the 'final commodification of the extraordinary cultural creativity born from the slave populations of the New World' (Lipsitz 1994: 27; Gilroy 2000: 272).

The latter days of Black Atlantic music, in Gilroy's analysis, are marked by a thinning of the dense and specific cultural expressiveness of its historical forms, and their replacement by what he terms a 'culture of simulation that changes the value of blackness' (Gilroy 2000: 274). In ' "After the Love Has Gone": Biopolitics and the Decay of the Black Public Sphere', he argues the impossibility of maintaining radical political articulation when its agents are themselves trapped in 'the dismal process in which public politics became unspeakable and a body-centred bio-politics began to take hold' (Gilroy 2000: 184). The dialogic forces of the changing same of black music depend upon three elements in creative motion: an urgent memory of slave history, in sound, body and speech; a tradition of resistance through an articulation of those memories; and a continuing capacity for aesthetic reconfiguration. Such forces become calcified through an increasing complicity with global capitalism and the development of a discourse obsessed with the markers of an individualised, depoliticised present, a present that forbids, rather than continues, a dialogue with a complex past. The contraction of the black public sphere, which music once both articulated and shaped, allows the inner codes of Black Atlantic opposition to be routinised by the antipathetic forces of international capital. Instead of the dialogic, contested relationship between black music and the dominant forces of Atlantic production and performance, the successful global marketing of hip-hop leads to an empty rhetoric of marginality that effectively displaces the true strengths of subaltern history. It leads to what Gilroy calls a 'revolutionary conservatism' of gesture expressed through elaborate misogyny, the fetishism of weaponry and the reduction of a tradition of dissent to imagery of romanticised criminality expressed through corporate branding (2000: 180). Black musical performance is subdued into a scabrously articulated and ultimately solipsistic individualism, and into performative bodies that are cleansed of the marks of violent history by what he calls in another essay in the collection the 'forces of rampant iconization' (273). Such political paralysis, he suggests, echoing the arguments of Arif Dirlik about postcolonial theory itself, has been aided by the complicity of an American academy whose partiality and investment in a particular trajectory of African-American studies leads to a largely uncritical incorporation of rap into its discourses and courses. This process, Gilroy argues, prevents an analysis of 'the extent to which, in a global market for these seductive products, white consumers currently support this black culture' (181). The 'revolutionary conservatism' of performers, audiences and corporate sponsors marks the end of a Black Atlantic traffic of resistance and change.

Gilroy's work provides a productive and provocative context for a discussion of a variety of postcolonial musics, and not just of the African-American, Caribbean and Black British genres that are his immediate concern. Three of his issues are particularly relevant: the definition of music as migrant and hybrid performance rather than as an expression of stable identities, national or personal; the sense of its political agency as enacted through a complex dialogue of history, body, voice, material contexts and reception; and the need for questions of value to be argued through an exploration of music's relationship with the contexts of its production – global and local – and the contexts of its reception, whether they are dancehalls or academies. The first two case studies will develop Gilroy's ideas and arguments with reference to two contrasting versions of postcolonial music.

Case Study One: World Music

The period of Gilroy's assessments of Black Atlantic music is also that of the growth of 'world music'. This is a marketing category devised in the 1980s to widen exposure in Europe and North America of a range of music outside the circuits of Black Atlantic and Euro-American popular forms and consequently previously unincorporated by popular music producers. Its components are highly eclectic, though some styles have a stronger presence than others, particularly those that are relatively accessible to Western audiences either through their recognisable harmonic scales and rhythmic patterns or by their familiarity from earlier 'borrowings' by mainstream performers. Central and West African music is more current than North African and Middle Eastern, for example, and Latin American music is more prominent than Far Eastern styles. World music provides a parallel development to Gilroy's description of black musical processes, pressing at the relationship of local cultures to global markets, at questions of cultural performance, representation and interpretation of postcolonial performers in First World contexts, and at the political meanings of the music's hybrid forms

World music embodies a contradiction that is often given material shape in the layout of racks in record shops. There, world music is frequently set alongside folk or traditional music, and 'roots' music, such as blues. In terms of style, form and outlook, this juxtaposition makes little sense – what has Tito Puente's salsa or Fela Kuti's Afrobeat to do with English folk song, earnest 1960s protest music or Mississippi blues singers of the 1930s? However, the conjunction does make sense on other terms. Both categories appeal to notions of authenticity that, in turn, are linked to the perceived provenance of the music in pre-industrial social structures. The experience of a Western listener hearing, say, a Malian singer like Ali Farka Toure, is structurally akin to the experience of nationalist folk-collectors of the early twentieth century listening to rural 'source-singers' or the 'rediscoverers' of blues musicians in the 1960s. Central to these is a shared sense of a valued otherness and an appreciation of a culture apparently outside of or at odds with the aesthetics of mass popular music developed in the Western metropolis. At the same time, though, as well as being 'authentically other', world music is also hopelessly hybrid, a contradiction that is actually part of its strength as a commercial category. Its marketing and consumption depend upon apparently paradoxical conjunctions that both affirm a distant localness, and render that localness 'universally' comprehensible and adaptable. So, Burundi drummers can apparently be heard meaningfully at the WOMAD world-music festival, outside of the context of local rituals for which their drumming was originally intended, and Western-trained musicians like Ry Cooder can create best-selling musical 'dialogues' with Ali Farka Toure or the Indian Vishwa Mohan Bhatt. In world music, local authenticity co-exists as universal language, and locality and hybridity are simultaneously exalted and consumed.

World music's apparently contradictory values of roots and transferability, or 'routes', to use a favourite pun of its marketing, take us back to Gilroy's exposition of the historical and political contingencies of black music. For Gilroy, as for Amiri Baraka, the strength of that music was its capacity to embody a continuity of historical and cultural awareness and expression, whilst responding to new circumstances of colonial and postcolonial place, society and experience. World music actually argues for the opposite, in its affirmation of the potential for the transformability of local music outside of the specific historical and geographical circuits of its formations. In this, it takes up a utopian position where the logic of postcolonialism shades into that of postmodernism. Recalling James

Clifford's optimistic visions of '[l]ocal/global contact zones [and] sites of identity-making and transculturation', world music offers the possibility of a free, innovative play and dialogue between once remote traditions (Clifford 1997: 219). Yet despite such apparently liberating innovation, visits to world-music events and the world-music sections of the big record chains tend to raise spirits of old postcolonial controversies about representation, interpretation, agency and audience.

These begin most strikingly with body culture, or what the Irish dance scholar Catherine E. Foley has called 'body dialects', the detailed cultural expressiveness embedded in dance (Foley 1997). Dance isn't much discussed in postcolonial theory – in fact, as far as I know, it isn't discussed at all. But it should be. Dance defines a culture in performance, and is an extraordinarily sensitive transcription of its interior meanings, its transformations, and its exchanges (see Chapter 3). Performances of world music, on stage and on record, pose fundamental questions about their audiences' capacity to understand the body dialects embedded in the music. What does it mean to play a music outside of its original contexts, for example, and what does it mean to dance to a music the provenance of which the dancer is largely ignorant and the steps of which are unknown? The various guides to world music are, interestingly, of little help here, concerned as they are with listening not dancing. None gives the reader any specific guide to moving to the music, despite the fact that world music is predominantly dance music. The process of cultural dislocation implied by the effective splitting of musical practice from specific social and bodily contexts, and its reification as a predominantly aural experience, is just the most striking erasure of cultural meaning in the postcolonialism of world music.

John Hutnyk has noted of audiences at the British WOMAD world-music festival that there is 'a lack of embarrassment or irony in the face of what must be a largely incomprehensible exchange', in a 'scene where authenticity operates through incomprehension and fracture of context' (Hutnyk 1997: 109, 110). The performances are both a cultural decontextualisation and an elision of agency – a removal of what the act of music-making is for, whether it is that of social dance or religious ritual. Which is why, in truth, it is hard to know what to do with much of world music as it appears on CD or, indeed, in concert performance, and why the marketing of that music is often interested in defining a function for it. World-music CDs tend to recontextualise its material, with South and Eastern Asian and Native American and Australian musics being suggested as soundtracks for meditation, for example. Touring performances like those of the Burundi drummers, Sufi dancers and so on are transformed into striking spectacles of cultural difference, a display of otherness that recalls, quite alarmingly, the nineteenth-century predilection for living ethnic curiosities that marked the first phases of mass popular culture (see Lindfors 1999). In both cases, a functional act is transformed into a Western aesthetic act, something to be appreciated rather than something to be used in a particular context, and that act of aestheticising is one implicated in the residual power of colonialism itself. Whilst there is a danger in underestimating world musicians' own influence in the presentation and development of their work and the benefits that they gain from it, the economic contexts and cultural frames of its production nevertheless remain fixed within First World codes of reception and value.

World music's aestheticising of non-Western music and its elision of that music's contexts and utilities, what Veit Erlmann has termed the process of 'coating the sounds of the fully commodified present with the patina of use value in some other time and place', are two aspects of its engagement with postcolonial politics (Erlmann 1993: 13). A third lies in its manipulation of musical development. Gilroy's account of black music is that of a historical process that both maintains and transforms a hybrid vocabulary and gesture of subaltern resistance. This is opposed by world music's emphasis upon a recovery and preservation of neglected musical styles, and its interest in synchronic musical fusions and manufactured encounters between musicians from different cultures. Both of these strategies pose questions about world music's political relationship to postcolonialism, and, like its instinctive recourse to colonialism's repertoire of generic/racial descriptors, problematise its apparently radical, democratising ambitions for the music that it celebrates. These questions can be explored through projects associated with a leading figure in world music, the American guitarist Ry Cooder. In the academic literature on world music, Cooder tends to emerge as a principled celebrant of other musicians, often in enlightened contrast to Paul Simon, whose work of the 1980s and 1990s is frequently used as an example of exploitative cultural tourism (see, for example, Lazarus 1993; Fairley 2001: 283–6). The point may not be about principle, however. Gilroy's theory of the complex and inflected politics of subaltern music suggests that it is much more about the structures of power inherent in the performance and display of that music. It is, in other words, the old political question of postcolonial aesthetics: who is representing what to whom and why?

Wim Wenders's feature-length documentary *Buena Vista Social Club* (1999) records Ry Cooder's meetings and performances with a group of veteran Cuban musicians that included Ibrahím Ferrer and Rubén González after the success of their *World Circuit* CD, produced by Cooder. The film contains interviews with the musicians, shots of Cuban cityscapes, rehearsals in Havana and concert footage of the musicians' performances in Amsterdam and Carnegie Hall. Wenders's film, like his later documentary on American blues musicians, *The Soul of a Man* (2003), celebrates the 'rediscovery' of neglected artists and their belated success as international performers, and allows the musicians to tell their life-stories and play their music without commentary. However, the appealing directness of narrative also serves to disguise omissions of context, history and agency in its representation of the postcolonial condition of the Cuban musicians. The musicians become players of a soundtrack to the benevolent affirmation of their own fragile social survival into a post-revolutionary era, as Wenders camera lingers on the picturesque decay of Havana. The once-revolutionary modernities of the island are elided in a film that dwells upon the appealing relics of a colonial geography. Political contexts for the men's lives are notably absent, collapsed into the safety of the performance of old musical styles and the murals of Che Guevara that are now seamlessly integrated into Havana's architecture of decline. The context of that 'golden age' of music in the gangster-run American tourist economy of the pre-Castro dictatorships is not addressed. Nor is the role of world music in rendering Cuba a tourist destination once again, one advertised by reference to the

Buena Vista Social Club recordings as an authentically archaic postcolonial revolutionary state to be visited quickly before America returns. Though, as the film, in its way, makes clear, America already has.

Cooder's and Wenders's representation of the old Cuban musicians, beguiling as it is in many ways, is also characteristic of world music's approach to the postcolonial contexts of its performers. The act of historical recovery that allows the musicians to perform again, to travel and to be fêted is also an unexamined political act whereby the recovery of pre-Castro Havana is presented as the reconstitution of an apolitical aesthetic moment of Cuban jazz. It is a process that, ironically enough, reaches its culmination in the film with the Cuban musicians' apparently awed visit to New York. The history of post-1959 Cuba and the actual context of the musicians' 'rediscovery' are 'absent presences', engaged with neither by the film-makers nor, more understandably, by the musicians themselves. Without such an engagement, the narrative easily becomes that of the benign and unquestioning reassertion of American cultural influence. Whilst *Buena Vista Social Club* is in no sense an overtly anti-Castro film, its aestheticising of the contexts of the music, its uncritical narrative of 'rediscovery' and success in America and Europe, and its political silences make its position in postcolonial cultural politics an ambivalent one.

A second area of political ambivalence in world music concerns its interests in fusions and hybridity. Hybridity has become a key term in postcolonial theory, a means of destabilising the limiting essentialist intellectual inheritances of colonialism, whether it be racial identity or national identity. Gilroy's use of the concept, like Amiri Baraka's 'changing same', re-imagines music as a transformative process, responsive to shifts of site and moment, and adaptable in its tactics to meet the local demands of resistance, pleasure and identity. In the circumstances of Black Atlantic history, this hybridity was shaped by the contingencies of colonialism's own developments, particularly in its traffic of populations and commodities, and by the chance encounters of sounds, bodies and texts which that traffic delivered. But it was also energised by the subaltern agency of the musical production itself as it made meanings from those encounters and social function from its music on its own terms. World music has attempted to locate itself in such dynamic. The rationale of the Buena Vista Social Club, for example, is that of recording an encounter between Cooder and the neglected musicians that he 'rediscovered' in Cuba. That of his recordings with Ali Farka Toure is the exploration of the circuits of sound and rhythm that connect American blues and West African traditions – the Black Atlantic, indeed. In other ways, though, this rationale mistakes the nature of subaltern musical hybridity and introduces the very economic and ideological forces that Gilroy identifies as endangering the political agencies of Black Atlantic music.

In a discussion of the 'dialectics of cultural hybridity', Pnina Werbner notes the usefulness of Mikhail Bakhtin's distinction between hybridity as a deliberate artistic device and the 'unconscious, "organic" hybridity' which drives changes in the deep structures of expression (Werbner 1997: 4). It is Bakhtin's second sense that defines the changing same that Baraka and Gilroy describe. The hybrid resources of Black Atlantic music are shaped and used by its practitioners, but the formations of those resources are intimately bound to histories and movements that are uncontrolled and unplanned, but resisted through culture. Precisely how and where the great hybrid musics of colonialism and its aftermath – jazz, tango, salsa – were shaped is necessarily unknown and irrecoverable because they developed not as planned encounters, but as negotiations of unexpected collisions and particular social predicaments. As Ishmael Reed, the African-American novelist, expresses it in his satirical fictional account of the 'disease' of jazz, the music was 'jes grew' (Reed 1988). The apparent abandonment of agency in Reed's description is, in fact, witty recognition of a hybridity that necessarily improvises its processes and hides the moments of its generation and change. The Cooder–Toure hybrid, like other world-music conjunctions, is an example of Bakhtin's first category of aesthetic deliberation. It performs what Veit Erlmann, following Fredric Jameson, calls 'a kind of transversality born from the random play of unrelated differences' (Erlmann 1993: 8). The cultural meaning of such play is ultimately no different in its deep structure from any other encounter engineered by a world-music producer – that of a perhaps surprising compatibility of distant and distinct musical practices. The economic power of Western recording industries allows them to exploit that time–space compression that David Harvey has defined as a defining feature of postmodernism to bring together musicians from diverse cultures to make records (see Harvey 1990: 240ff.). The resulting encounters may produce versions of hybridity that are aesthetically pleasing, but they are quite unable to sustain the political and cultural weight and energies that Gilroy, Bakhtin and Ishmael Reed assign to the 'unintentional' histories of that process. Whilst 'jes grew' seems a distinctly untheoretical tool, it nevertheless expresses a truth about the development of subaltern musics in modernity that students of postcolonialism need to ponder.

Case Study Two:
Three Emigrant Music Cultures in England

The implications of the 'anti-theory' of 'jes grew' might be developed alongside Gilroy's concept of the Black Atlantic through three musical styles that were developed in post-war Britain. The first revisits the dangers and possibilities of academic study of recent popular cultures through a consideration of readings of the British-Asian performer Apache Indian. The others argue for the value of a longer view of postcolonial cultures in a study of some of the first musical styles of post-war emigration to Britain, those of the Caribbean and Ireland. The Trinidadian Lord Kitchener's calypsos are a relatively little-known component of Gilroy's Black Atlantic, but they are the first to articulate a sustained response to the experiences of that emigration. Exploiting calypso traditions of topical commentary, coded statement and sexual fascination, and of a rapid absorption of musical styles, Kitchener was able to explore the world of the Caribbean man in England. His engagement with an already-existing African and Caribbean culture in England and his links with an experimental post-war recording industry also allowed him to develop an innovative and playful diasporic voice that addressed West Africans as well as British-based Caribbeans, Trinidadians as well as white British audiences. The musical culture of the rural Irish musicians who were part of the large influx of

Irish labour to London and other cities in the late 1940s and 1950s is a contemporary, but differently inflected, version of postcolonial music. Whilst Irish traditional music is in no sense a static cultural form, and was affected by twentieth-century technologies as much as any other, its presence in emigrant communities was locally functional and shaped by distinct traditions and perhaps unexpected cultural dynamics.

Watching out for the Indian

The case of Apache Indian is a postcolonial morality tale about the dangers of using popular music in academic study. It concerns the brief love affair and subsequent quarrel between postcolonial cultural critics and the British-Asian DJ Steve Kapur, otherwise known as Apache Indian, born in the Punjab and raised in Birmingham. Apache Indian's debut record *No Reservations* (1993), issued by the Island record label, launched the brief career of a recording artist who seemed to represent a classic example of postcolonial hybridity of Bakhtin's second kind – one that emerged unbidden from the density of social and historical circumstance. *No Reservations* defined a style that mixed Jamaican dancehall rhythms and DJ lyric styles with Punjabi bhangra, emphasising their similar drum patterns and creating chants that mingled English, Jamaican and Punjabi. His work also crossed distinct boundaries of audience as the song/video 'Arranged Marriage' became 'the biggest Western music hit in the history of the subcontinent' (Zuberi 2001: 204). It was a success that seemed to herald a new cultural synthesis.

Apache Indian's music on his first record and its successor *Make Way for the Indian* (1994) was striking both in its integration of Punjabi dhol drum patterns within Jamaican dancehall sounds, and in its lyrical range and inventiveness. The songs addressed subjects such as arranged marriage, bilingualism and the relationship between diasporic Indians and the homeland. Such a mix proved irresistible to some postcolonial critics engaged with a theory of what Nabeel Zuberi, citing Homi Bhabha's essay 'How Newness Enters the World', calls 'the revenge of the migrant hybrid' (200). Apache Indian's music seemed the realisation of what hybridity should bring, given the social and cultural mixes of contemporary urban Britain: 'a real British Indian toaster chatting on the mic in Jamaican Patois and Punjabi', as Zuberi puts it (201). Soon after the release of *No Reservations*, the American cultural historian George Lipsitz referred to Apache Indian as a representative of a new kind of postmodern performance. He demonstrated how 'artists from aggrieved communities can use the very instruments of their displacement and dispossession to forge a new public sphere with emancipatory potential' (Lipsitz 1994: 14). For Lipsitz, Kapur's hybridity – personal and cultural – illustrated the possibility for postmodern/postcolonial popular music to bring together subaltern audiences in mutual recognition both of common rhythm and common political cause. And the music works against the grain of the very globalised corporatism that enabled those audiences to hear the music. Lipsitz's optimistic account of Apache, and of world music in general, is echoed in later accounts of 'hybridity' in popular music (see, for example, Mitchell 1996: 61–5).

Apache Indian's moment as representative of hybridity, popular and academic, did not last, as urban British-Indian music moved in different directions. His third record, *Real People* (1996), proved unsuccessful, and the dynamics of his Indian/Jamaican hybrid music came into question. John Hutnyk, for example, reads Apache Indian's success as the populist simplification of the 'critical discourse of hybridity', 'those aspects which repackage and rein-scribe difference, juxtaposed exotica (hybrid as exotically mixed) and otherness as marketable categories' (Hutnyk 1997: 119). For Hutnyk, what happened to Apache at Island Records was what, in more influential ways, happened to Bob Marley at the same record company in the 1970s. The hybrid – in Marley's case, Jamaican reggae and American rock – was shaped by the studio to meet the perceived demand of particular influential markets. What appeared to be Bakhtin's second kind of hybridisation was in fact an example of his first. With a similar sternness, contributors to Sanjay Sharma et al.'s collection of essays on Asian music, *Dis-Orienting Rhythms* (1996), question the very processes by which Asian music can become visible and popular in a Western context. Ashwani Sharma points to the 'dangerous workings of a neo-Orientalism as it pertains to the question of contemporary Asian music cultures', and Sanjay Sharma attacks non-Asian ethnographers' location of such cultures 'squarely within an authenticity problematic that sustains a neo-Orientalist understanding of anterior Asian youth cultural formations' (A. Sharma 1996: 16; S. Sharma 1996: 36). Apache Indian, in these readings, was an amenable, manageable representative of 'Asianness' in a popular music industry cautiously interested in exploiting British 'multiculturalism' through Indian, as well as the well-established Caribbean, musical styles. His articulate analysis of diasporic problems, and radio-friendly minglings of bhangra and dancehall (with unthreatening visitors from the latter place – Maxi Priest, for example, who shares the billing on *No Reservations* despite his appearance on only one track) answered corporate problems, rather than raised them. The ragamuffin Apache became an acceptable face of hybridity, as his moment was overtaken by different music and performance styles.

The career of Apache Indian, inside and outside the academy, is open to a variety of interpretations. In one sense, it is a classic case of the necessary ephemerality of popular music. Apache's fading from notice by the time of his third record is hardly untypical of any popular recording artist. In another, it flags the dangers of an overeagerness to illustrate theory by seizing upon apparently compatible contemporary practice. The representativeness of any curriculum needs careful thought, but it is particularly important in areas like postcolonial studies that deal with subaltern cultures and their relationship with dominant economic and cultural forces. How far Apache Indian's appearances in academic literature in the mid-1990s were influenced by the convenience of his 'hybrid' strategies as illustrations of influential theoretical constructions rather than by the sustained cultural and social meanings of the performances remains at issue. It is, in part, a question of the nature of the relationship between the academy and the popular materials it selects for study, and, in part, a question of distance. The distinction between popular music that embodies the changing same of a long history of resistance and cultural redefinition, and that which is an arbitrary or artful conjunction of styles finally remains a difficult judgement of value. Some historical gap between performance and study may provide clearer perspectives, and limit the dangers of convenience swaying that process of evaluation. This is why the next case study takes a longer view of some postcolonial music in Britain. However, there is also perhaps a need to risk the kind of misjudgements that Apache Indian provoked. So, the final case study argues for the importance of the Jamaican DJ Lady Saw, and for her part in a changing same that her performances, steeped in the bio-politics of rap and Jamaican dancehall, seem to revoke.

Trinidad and Ireland Playing in England

On 22 June 1948 the *Empire Windrush* arrived at Tilbury Docks, beginning the post-war mass emigration of Caribbean workers to Britain. On board were two Trinidadian calypso singers. The elder was Lord Beginner, but it was the younger man, Aldwyn Roberts, aka Lord Kitchener, who was recorded by newsreel cameras singing a calypso that he had written specially for the occasion. 'London is the Place for Me' is an apparently simple praise song marking his arrival. Kitchener told Mike and Trevor Phillips in an interview for their book marking the fiftieth anniversary of *Windrush*, '[y]ou know how it is when a child, you hear about your mother country, and you know that you're going to touch the soil of the mother country, you know what feeling is that? . . . That's why I compose the song. Imagine how I felt. Here's where I want to be, London' (Phillips and Phillips 1998: 66). Kitchener, though, was an old-style calypso singer, and had a duty to mamguy, or to play with different masks for different occasions. In another interview he offered an alternative account of that journey to the soil of the mother country, one that emphasised the haphazard economics and migrancies of the post-war Caribbean:

> What really happened, I was sponsored to go to Curacao and Aruba and after that contract expired I went to Jamaica, on my own, I spent about six months in Jamaica, then I was looking for green pastures. I thought I could do better than just hanging around Jamaica. So I wanted to go to America really, I tried but I didn't succeed to go to America. So I tried England and I succeeded in going to England. (Ottley 1995: 14)

It is an indication that the cryptic politics of Black Atlantic performance is not limited to the blues–soul–reggae mainstreams that Paul Gilroy's work emphasises. Calypso, or kaiso, the main form of popular music in the eastern Caribbean, never maintained a strong presence in America or Britain, unlike reggae. But, in the work of Kitchener and others, it was the music that carefully articulated a transitional period in Black Atlantic culture and politics.

Lord Kitchener's career in England, from his arrival in 1948 until his return to Trinidad in 1962, illuminates both the range and adaptability of the calypso form, and the complexities of emigrant cultural life. As John Cowley has shown, Kitchener entered an already well-established black musical world in London, and one that was as much African as it was Caribbean (Cowley 1985; 1990, see also Hill 1993: 166–9). Immigration restrictions on American jazz musicians boosted the careers of musicians such as the Trinidadians Sam Manning and Cyril Blake, who played in London dance orchestras from the 1920s onwards. Jazz bands such as the Southern Syncopated Orchestra were truly Black Atlantic formations, containing Caribbean musicians alongside West African players and working with occasional visiting African-American players. This pan-Africanist musical formation was an intrinsic part of a developing anti-colonial politics, with the guitarist Manning in particular being actively involved in radical groups in a London that also included the theorists and activists of pan-Africanism, C. L. R. James, Jomo Kenyatta and George Padmore, and in which the old leader of that movement, Marcus Garvey, had lived until his death in 1940. Far from having to create a new emigrant musical culture, Kitchener was able to build upon established musical and political traditions, and his work develops these in shaping a response to the new conditions of mass emigration and the emergence of postcolonial nationhood.

The calypsos that Kitchener began to record in England in 1948 are upbeat 'roadmarch' tunes, mixing older-style kaiso arrangements, associated with the London-based Caribbean musicians, with the newer post-war calypso style imported from Trinidad. With breezy professional accompaniments, Kitch developed a repertoire of songs that fulfilled the calypsonian's duty to mask, observe and pass judgement, and exploited a new situation in which, for a period, calypso became a fashionable metropolitan form (in 1954, for example, he played in the Sunset Club, Soho, for Princess Margaret, who allegedly bought 100 copies of his 'Kitch Come Go to Bed'). Kitchener's songs, and those of other calypsonians recording in London, provide a wide-ranging commentary on the formative period of Caribbean emigration. Their narratives explore themes of emigrant disorientation, restriction and homesickness, but also point to new emergent possibilities – inter-racial sex, for one – and register awareness of and overt support for nationalist movements in Africa and the Caribbean (the CD anthology *London is the Place for Me* includes some of the songs discussed below).

A calypso like 'Sweet Jamaica' (1952) is an emigrant song in sceptical dialogue with the optimism of 'London is the Place for Me':

> Many West Indians are sorry now
> They left their country and don't know how.
> Some left their jobs and their family
> And determined to come to London city
> Well, they are crying, they now regret
> No kind of employment that they can get.
> The city of London they have to roam
> And they can't get their [passages] to get back home.

In 'The Underground Train' (1950) he is bemused by the west London tube-map and vows to 'walk the journey and avoid the misery', and in 'Food from the West Indies' (1951) he pleads for release from potatoes and Marie biscuits, and begs for rice and peas. Both these songs also encode other concerns. The woman who is feeding him biscuits and potatoes is evidently white British, and the journey on the underground involves following 'a young lady', its puzzled geography as much sexual as metropolitan. Sexual boasting, central to kaiso tradition, is restrained in these recordings, which were aimed, at least in part, at British-based audiences, but it is a persistent presence nevertheless. The calypsonian is a man 'compelled to romance', as he puts it in 'Excuse Me, Sandra' (n.d.), and Kitch's most famous song, 'Nora' (1950), is an attempt to remove himself from the results of such compulsion in England, as he begs the woman to let him return home: 'I'm going back to me country/I'm tired with London/I can't hear the steel band beating in John John'. Nora is never clearly identified, but it is implied that she is a wealthy white Englishwoman who intends to keep Kitch with the lure of material goods: 'These are the things the lady promised me/A Rolls Royce car, her father property'. Kitch, the 'born Trinidadian', rejects the blandishments, but implied in all this are the new sexual possibilities that emigration and music offered some Caribbean men in England (a theme pursued by fellow emigré calypsonian, Lord Beginner, in his 'Mix Up Matrimony' (1952)).

The same slick calypso form and accompaniment, which now incorporated Latin and bebop-influenced brass and rhythm (see, for example, 'Kitch's Bebop Calypso' (1951)), was used to develop a popular political analysis in the songs and to cultivate an African, as well as Caribbean and English, audience. Nationalist and inter-nationalist politics had been central to the debates of James, Padmore and others in the 1930s, and the ongoing anti-colonial analysis is still active in Kitchener's upbeat music. Like Mighty Sparrow in Trinidad, Kitchener maintained a sceptical view of American interventions in the Caribbean. 'The Yankees say they like my soil', sings Kitchener, 'Come and take away my oil' ('Oil and Sunshine' (n.d.)). He was also careful to mark the shifts of power in Africa. Kitchener had achieved huge popularity in West Africa with 'Nora', Parlophone distributing the recording via the old imperial routes, and he toured there in the 1950s, becoming one of the first black popular performers to complete that Black Atlantic circuit. He celebrated the new developments in West Africa with 'Birth of Ghana' (1956), a song that abandons the kaiso persona to develop a Caribbean tribute to the Ghanaian leader Kwame Nkru-mah and his work for 'us' (a telling Pan-Africanist pronoun). 'Congratulations from Haile Selassie/Was proudly received by everybody', he notes, incorporating the Garveyite inflections of Sam Manning's musical culture within a calypso that looks to a postcolonial political future.

Lord Kitchener's British recordings are little-known examples of the Black Atlantic traffic of music and people that Gilroy defines. Their deceptively inconsequential narratives are often encrypted commentaries on the consequences of that experience, its liberations as well as its privations. Their audiences were also newly international – Trinidadian, African and British. Kitchener both acknowledged and developed this network of Black Atlantic culture. His was not a migration to 'the motherland', but to a cultural nexus that allowed dialogues with other cultural migrations, African as well as Caribbean, and which, as with C. L. R. James, involved him with West Africa at a decisive point in its postcolonial emergence. A comparable process of re-encounter, absorption and change, and political implication, and one that provides different inflections to Gilroy's theory of Black Atlantic musical transmission, can be traced in the history of Irish emigrant music in the 1950s. Like Kitchener's calypsos, this is an underresearched area, and it is only recently, through the largely unpublished research of the musician and historian Reg Hall, that the complex meanings of London-Irish music in the period have begun to be understood.

The music of the Irish diaspora creates its own circular traffic in the manner of Gilroy's Black Atlantic, though its routes criss-cross the Irish Sea to and from Scotland and England, as well as coming and going across different Atlantic routes. The post-Second World War immigration of mainly rural Irish labourers from the west and south-west coincided with the Caribbean emigrations charted by Kitchener, and the two were part of the same structure of colonial economics and politics, as the metropolitan centre attracted labour, even as the external structures of colonialism retreated. However, whilst Irish and Caribbean workers competed for similar jobs, and lived in the same or contiguous areas in London and other cities, the social structures that they entered, the disadvantages and hostilities that they confronted, and the cultural contexts of musical performance that they created were significantly different. The London-Irish was an already-sizeable community in the 1950s, having been formed through earlier periods of emigration in the late nineteenth and early twentieth centuries. Whilst its social and geographical coherence had been affected by the consequences of war, its legacy in cultural and musical terms was distinct (Hall 1994: 294ff.). Unlike the politically sophisticated, cosmopolitan African and Caribbean musical environment that Kitchener entered, that of the London-

Irish was defined by generally conservative cultural traditions associated with the old nationalist Gaelic League and the Roman Catholic Church, and expressed in formal ceilidhs and dancing competitions. Whilst the popular London-Irish ceilidh bands of the 1930s absorbed some of the styles and presentation techniques of contemporary American and British jazz and dancehall music, these did not reflect a change in the essentially local structures and functions of the performances. As Reg Hall notes, 'the hybridisation of Irish rural music and dance with non-Irish forms [in this period] was in effect an uncomfortable accommodation', and one without that central flexibility of expression and mode that characterised Black Atlantic music (386).

The emigrations of the 1940s and 1950s brought a different style and conception of music to Irish London. Their musicians were mainly from rural villages, and the ceilidh-band styles of the London-Irish were unfamiliar to them. More significantly, the existing social meeting places were frequently unwelcoming to the newcomers. Hall writes that 'there was a conflict of social values and behaviours, with the immigrants generally not recognising the London-Irish as Irish, and the London-Irish often viewing new immigrants as uncouth and violent' (297). The logic of metropolitan cultural hybridity would normally be that the rural styles of the later immigrants would energise, but would also be eventually incorporated within, the economically and culturally dominant urban styles. However, one of Hall's most radical conclusions is that not only did this not happen, but that there was 'an effective popular process of dehybridisation in the 1950s' (386). Such was the critical mass of rural emigration, and such was the relative weakness of the ethnic identity of the older London-Irish, that alternative performance structures for essentially rural Irish music styles and performance codes were able to be organised in the 'new' Irish London of Camden Town and Kilburn that effectively replaced the older ceilidh model. However, this dehybridisation was not simply a return to rural roots, but necessarily entailed change and response to new conditions. As Hall notes, the creation of music sessions in urban pubs was not a straightforward transference of rural practice to the English city, but itself a social adaptation. There had been no little or no tradition of music in bars in rural Ireland; the model of the London pub session was, in fact, that of the house party. And whilst the repertoire, style and instrumentation of the music stayed the same, its agency and reception changed with its new circumstances, as it became listening music rather than dancing music, and a reminder of cultural identity within the ethnic diversities of the metropolis rather than an integrated expression of that culture (a selection of these performances can be heard on the CD *Paddy in the Smoke* (1968)).

Whilst the 'dehybridisation' of Irish music that Hall describes is a reminder that the developments of postcolonial music are diverse and respond to different social and historical circumstances, it is also important not to set up a false binary between a hybrid urban music of London-Irish ceilidh bands and a 'pure' Irishness in the music of the rural emigrants. 'Folk' is a term that is rarely encountered in discussions of postcolonial culture, mainly because of connotations of cultural purity and its complicity in the political ambivalence of early twentieth-century nationalisms, not least Irish nationalism (see Chapter 6). However, as the post-war Irish musicians made clear, their own sense of the music that they played certainly acknowledged its hybrid sources and migrant routes. The styles of the best fiddle-players of the 1950s diaspora had been formed as much by listening to the American recordings made in the 1920s and 1930s by the emigrant Sligo fiddler Michael Coleman as they had by any local 'oral tradition', as interviews with Martin Byrnes and other emigrant musicians preserved in the National Sound Archive show. The influence of modern technologies was as significant on the Irish Atlantic as it was upon the Black Atlantic, here allowing a 'folk' tradition that was endangered, at least in part, by the scale of rural emigration in the nineteenth and early twentieth centuries to be re-imported via the burgeoning emigrant recording industries of New York, and the trade and labour movements between America and Ireland, and Ireland and Britain.

The history of Irish music in post-war London, then, like that of Caribbean music, was one of movement and adaptation. It sought to preserve a particular version of Irish identity, and, whilst its aesthetics seem at first sight unexpectedly conservative, the preservation of rural music-making in the city was achieved through a radical redefinition of performance spaces and a challenge to the

Irish identities of a longer-standing London-Irish tradition. At the same time, the presence of these labourer-musicians in the city, and their own articulation of the meaning of their 'tradition', indicate a sophisticated awareness of the modernity of their circumstances, and the social opportunities that music-making provided. Whilst the music of the Irish Atlantic is not as extensively researched as its black counterpart, it offers comparable opportunities to examine cultural preservation and change, and the politics of postcolonial migration and return. Its legacies – in the growth of the popularity of 'Irish country' music in rural England, for example, and the emergence of later expressions of Irish Atlantic traditions in the work of a musician like Shane McGowan – suggest the ongoing hybridities of the tradition, including the re-importation of the urban public-house session to become a 'traditional' feature of the bars of the west of Ireland, now attuned to tourists' cultural interests and perceptions.

Case Study Three: Lady Saw

The final case study returns to Gilroy's pessimistic critique of Black Atlantic music's capacity to maintain a radical social engagement with the predicaments of late twentieth-century capitalism – predicaments similar to, though differently inflected than those described in the earlier discussion of world music. The performances and recordings of the Jamaican DJ Lady Saw are, at first sight, fully implicated in that withdrawal from the public political sphere and inflation of 'body-centred bio-politics' that Paul Gilroy identifies in much American hip-hop, and consequently remote from the deep hybridities of Bakhtin's model. The death of Bob Marley in 1981 and the coming to power of the neoconservative Edward Seaga in the same year heralded a shift in Jamaican music away from the dominance of Rastafarian-inspired critiques of neocolonialism and the resources of Afrocentrist philosophies that marked the nationalist phase of 1970s Jamaican music. These were replaced by a resurgence and rapid development of dancehall rhythms and of a 'slackness' style, a kind of toasting or chat that, in Dick Hebdige's words, 'concentrated largely on insults to women, and on themes of sex and money and the relationship between them' (Hebdige 1987: 124). The history of Jamaican dancehall music parallels that of rap in its forms and preoccupations, and in its sceptical take on the ethical and political discourses and performances of Black Atlantic traditions. Norman C. Stolzoff summarises slackness's attitude as a disavowal of any ethical position, such as those taken by Rastafarian singers. '[Its performers] claim a stance of moral neutrality', he writes, 'or a mischievous amorality, asserting that music is only entertainment, not a medium that should carry the burden of education and social reform . . . they are fully committed to the hedonistic path of individualism, sexual desire, and material consumption' (Stolzoff 2000: 163). Lady Saw's most notorious songs – 'Good Wuk' and 'Stab Up the Meat', for example – are firmly in this camp of militant pleasure-seeking, providing detailed instructions for the delivery of her sexual satisfaction. Her recordings are marked by the vocal versatility and extravagant boasting that defines the genre, and her stage shows remain controversial in Jamaica for their explicit sexuality, both verbal and performative (see Stolzoff 2000: 238–42).

The work of Lady Saw, though, also provides a means of exploring alternative resources within the revolutionary conservatism that Gilroy finds in such 'bio-politics'. For example, Saw works in the extravagantly masculinist world of Jamaican dancehall culture, the misogyny of which parallels that traced by Gilroy in American rap. Tricia Rose has argued that women rap artists in America are engaged in creating 'a relatively safe free-play zone where they creatively address questions of sexual power, the reality of truncated economic opportunity, and the pain of racism and sexism', implying that the overbearing and rhetorically (and sometimes actually) violent masculinity of rap can be reshaped and opened to gendered dialogue (Rose 1994: 146). Lady Saw's uncompromising statements on women's rightful sexual demands can likewise be seen to challenge Jamaican dancehall celebrations of cock and gun. Her physical beauty, the blatant sexuality of her movements and her unflinching sexual discourse that moves between comic extravagance and a clear elucidation of the laws of the dancehall and the bed all suggest a new place for female performance made out of the components of masculine toasting. Saw can be seen as creating a version of what the Jamaican academic Carolyn Cooper calls 'erotic maroonage' – an exploitation of a potentially misogynist rhetoric of sexuality that seeks to challenge and displace orthodoxies of gendered power from 'outlaw' bases within the established codes of statement and practice (Cooper 1995: 161).

There is a danger here, though. As Tricia Rose warns, the necessarily complex negotiations taking place in women's performances that operate in male terrains such as rap or dancehall can be dangerously simplified in analysis. Women's rap isn't straightforwardly contained within structures of Western feminism, for example. For female rap artists, Rose argues, 'feminism is a movement that does not speak to men; on the other hand, they are engaged in constant communication with black male audience members and rappers and simultaneously support and offer advice to their young black female audiences' (181). That differential dialogue cannot, then, be translated to the more easily managed definition of such rappers as 'anti-sexist' or 'feminist'. Thus Norman Stolzoff's description of Lady Saw as 'an active subject who gives voice to her own sexual desire and who thereby threatens gender norms in the society at large' risks making the DJ's radicalism something other than it is (Stolzoff 2000: 244). His assessment of her as a woman defining social agency in desire is accurate enough, but that erotic definition takes place in a dancehall economy which, as he remarks himself, 'largely functions as a microcosm of the greater system of economic inequality in that it reproduces hegemonic patron-client relations and generates its own relations of inequality' (116). Lady Saw's performances never make an overt or radical breach of that hegemony in their lyrics, though their extravagances play off the body's freedoms established in movement and spectacle, providing a knowing soundtrack for dancing that is an already-active performance of female identity on the dancehall stage (see Chapter 3).

While she repeatedly demands 'good wuk' from men, that demand is as much an appeal to a masculine confidence in an ability to fulfil the obligation as it is to the women to validate that desire in their dance. Her subject is almost always sex, but it is often hard to see in her articulation of it that 'radical, underground confrontation with the patriarchal gender ideology and the pious

morality of fundamentalist Jamaican society' which Carolyn Cooper identifies as slackness's 'politics of subversion' (Cooper 1995:
141). Sex with Lady Saw involves little carnival and much regulation. Her toasts and songs contain warnings, commands and
instructive parables, whether against oral sex or male ways or
female competition. And whilst women's desires are paramount
and physical needs must be met, they are articulated not as
libertarian performances but as acts bound by strict codes that
are never entirely – or even predominantly – at odds with the
masculine values to which they refer. The female DJ may reconfigure the agency of the acts, but, like her male colleagues, she is as
much police as sufferer, as much watchful opponent as ethical
sister. Lady Saw has finally no interest in changing the gender
dynamic; the songs are pragmatic, detailed acknowledgements of
the entailment of sex within the economic inequalities and indig-
nities of Jamaican society, even as they articulate extravagant and
militant demands from the men who define those limitations.

That Lady Saw works within the predominantly male sexual
frame of dancehall does not, however, consign her to the 'revolutionary conservatism' that Paul Gilroy finds in corporate rap, even
though she does not – cannot – overtly challenge the terms of that
framing. Within the range and styles of her performances, she also
develops that 'antiphonal' quality that Gilroy identifies as central
to the politics of Black Atlantic expressive traditions despite the
explicit lyrical addictions to the body and the wuk. Such politics
are framed in a brilliant, if fairly untypical, toast, 'What is
Slackness?' (1996), in which she defends herself from attacks by
local civic representatives that led to her being banned from
performing in Montego Bay. Debating the semantics of slackness,
the piece shifts the critique of sexual ethics as enacted by the civic
state to a critique of political efficacy and the ethics of postcolonial
power. 'Slackness is when the road wan fi fix', she chants,
'Slackness when politician issue out guns'. The morality of the
individual body, so often isolated in DJ and rap lyrics as the only,
barren centre of meaning, is here recontextualised in a witty
appraisal of the failures of the postcolonial settlement. She also
defines herself explicitly as a Jamaican, and one who has remained
on the island (unlike other star economic migrants) – a fiscally and

culturally responsible citizen, in other words. That sense of nationhood, and localness, is significant in Lady Saw's self-positioning, and not only against the civic authority of the island that is the immediate concern of the piece, but in a wider dialogue with the musical forms of America and the Caribbean and their political meanings.

As Norman Stolzoff notes, an important aspect of a DJ's authority in recent dancehall culture is achieved by verbal skill and formal variety, and Lady Saw is exceptional in the range of her performative competence (167–8). She records R&B ballads, country and western songs, gospel and Drifters cover versions alongside her better-known slackness chants. This mastery of diversity is an acknowledgement of the Atlantic currents that have always infused Jamaican music, but within her acknowledgement are tensions and contests, too, which emphasise the island status of her work. 'Ride of Your Life' (1998), for example, is an American R&B ballad structured as a telephone conversation between Saw and her lover, and seems to have no political force at all in its dramatisation of romance pitching hurriedly into explicit sexual anticipation. It begins in romantic talk, with Pancho Kryztal playing the man breathlessly anticipating his lover's arrival and moaning the chorus in the conventional American accent of such music. Lady Saw begins the piece in American, too, but when she drops the façade to enumerate the required components of the ride of her life, she shifts into the voice of downtown Kingston dancehall. Romance, typically enough, devolves into a wittily described sexual endurance contest, but in the performance of that transition Lady Saw establishes both the primacy of female demands – Kryztal can't argue – and, crucially, of the Jamaican voice to enunciate them. Whilst she occasionally records songs of romantic vulnerability ('Give Me the Reason', for example), these are performed in American stylings; the language of authority – gendered and cultured – is nation language and is Jamaican.

The range of style and form evident in Lady Saw's recordings suggests another aspect of the persistence of Black Atlantic traditions maintained in Jamaican dancehall, though not in rap. Whilst they are by no means her most popular tracks, songs like 'Glory Be to God' and 'Let Peace Reign' are church- and, to a lesser extent,

Rasta-influenced pieces. They are necessary demonstrations that Saw can perform 'culture' if required, and so part of that proof of generic competence mentioned earlier, but, more significantly, they suggest the ongoing antiphonal relationship between dancehall and 'spiritual' song in contemporary Jamaican music. Paul Gilroy's critique of rap is itself implicitly concerned with the collapse of the historical relationship between secular and sacred expression in black American music and culture, something that has been more explicitly debated in the recent work of the African-American feminist theorist bell hooks. hooks's arguments in *All About Love* (2000) and *Salvation* (2001) return repeatedly to the rhetoric, structures and history of the black church, if not to its doctrine, to restore value to African-American experience. In significant ways, despite the recent dominance of slackness, such a restoration is unnecessary in Jamaican dancehall. Protestant rhetorical traditions and their Africanist reshapings in Rastafarianism still underpin the secular sermonising of dancehall, providing not only the shape of address, but also the unlikely ethical rigour through which the sexual body is policed through slackness. The routes between dancehall and Rasta are well trodden among male DJs – Buju Banton being the most notable contemporary example – recalling, in some ways, the historically intense dialogues and exchanges between blues/soul and gospel in America. Though the gender codes of Rastafarianism make this a far more difficult route for a woman performer in Jamaica, and Lady Saw's material has none of the Africanist assertions of Banton's Rasta tunes, her rhetorical styles and rhythms nevertheless allude to religious music. She is a preacher, and whilst her sermons are secular (to put it mildly), their tone is that of low church Protestantism and her rhythmic resources, like those of much dancehall, are the traditional drum patterns of African-influenced religious traditions and the church. Reggae, partly because of Rastafarianism, maintained continuities of rhetoric and sound that survived digital changes and the coming of rap. Only in Jamaican culture, perhaps, could a record such as TOK's 'Chi Chi Man' combine virulent homophobia, a rhythm track drawn from the drum patterns of pocomania (an African-Jamaican religion) and a church-style chorus.

The case of Lady Saw allows a reconsideration of some the issues of Black Atlantic and postcolonial music. In many ways, her work, in its strident sexual concerns and unwillingness to critique the masculinist virulence of its context, reflects the neoconservative bio-politics that Gilroy laments in corporate hip-hop. In other ways, though, Saw suggests the means by which such obsessions can also articulate a changing same of black music, cryptically alert to the details of postcolonial struggles, and knowledgeable about the performative resources for engaging in that struggle through music. Ironically and tellingly, the most powerful of those resources in her development of dancehall are a keen sense of national identity, of Jamaican-ness, and the rhetorical and rhythmic traces of religious and spiritual traditions. Neither of these is present in the African-American culture that Gilroy describes, and both tend to be underplayed in a postcolonial studies suspicious on the one hand of nationalist agency and, on the other, of the subjectivities and pre-modern retrogressiveness of discourses of the spirit. Yet in Lady Saw's work, and in Jamaican dancehall more generally, they are arguably the forces that maintain the continuities of the changing same, and resist, however problematically, the depredations of final commodification.

Conclusion

The performances of Lady Saw, Lord Kitchener and the London-Irish musicians of the 1950s illustrate the distinctive qualities of postcolonial music. As Paul Gilroy suggests, it is a music that is energised by travel and encounters with other styles of performance, and is endlessly adaptable to the needs – physical, cultural and expressive – of its local contexts. Whilst the growth of globalised recording industries, and their capacity rapidly to incorporate and commodify local music, has challenged that expressive power, both in the marketing of subaltern styles and the manufacture of cross-cultural musical contacts, the changing same of Black Atlantic and other forms of postcolonial music persists. The case of Lady Saw suggests the complex encryption of religious, dance and gender traditions in a musical style that, at first hearing, seems wholly committed to what Gilroy describes as a reductive contemporary bio-politics of sex and consumption. In a different sense, the Irish musicians of Kilburn and Camden belied their music's rural, traditional connotations in their recognition of the value and importance of modern recording and communication systems, and their capacity to adapt their music to new circumstances defined by economic migrations. Such musical performances provide a means of studying postcolonial cultures at their most responsive and changeable, as they answer the demands of audiences and dancers, whilst also providing access to the histories of sound, movement and expression that shape the politics of those responses.

CHAPTER 3

Body Cultures

The body has become an important site of debate in cultural studies, and its issues are closely related to those raised by music that were discussed in the last chapter. For example, Lady Saw's insistence upon an integration of body, text and voice in the production of her meanings can be connected to some, at first sight, remote developments in feminist theoretical work on the body. Jane Gallop's *Thinking Through the Body* (1988) and Sara Ahmed and Jackie Stacey's edited collection of essays *Thinking Through the Skin* (2001), for example, offer a sustained challenge to embedded distinctions of value between a 'masculine' intellectual tradition and a 'feminine' physicality. 'An approach which refuses to privilege mind over body', Ahmed and Stacey write, 'and which assumes that the body cannot be transcended, is one which . . . emphasises contingency, locatedness, the irreducibility of difference, the passage of emotions and desire, and the worldliness of being' (Ahmed and Stacey 2001: 3) – something which Lady Saw's performances amply demonstrate. However, as the authors admit, the body produced from such a process of 'recovery' is also in danger of becoming a fetishised, and, ironically, abstracted object. Fredric Jameson, reviewing the currency of 'the body' in contemporary American cultural studies, suggests wryly that '[n]othing is more disembodied than such references to the body . . . [for] materialism is scarcely achieved by the corporeal litany' (quoted in Koritz 1996: 90). The more the body is theorised, in other words, the greater the danger of its distance from the social histories and circumstances of its formation and performance.

This danger has a particular significance in the field of post-colonial studies, which must confront the legacies of an imperialist tradition intent upon its own fetishising, through which it limited the identity of the colonised to the materiality of their bodies. From these racial markers, it produced intricate structures of racial definition, differentiation and control. The postcolonial body provokes other dangers, too. As we have seen in the previous section, Paul Gilroy has recently articulated anxieties about a damagingly 'body-centred nano-politics' in contemporary global commercial cultures which celebrates a comparable racial fetishism (1997: 32). 'The black body is a body that is no longer to be supervised by the soul which was once imagined to outlive it', he writes in an essay on the contraction of what he terms 'the black public sphere'. 'There is no longer a soul there, it has been banished by the same fatal affirmation of carnal and corporeal vitality' (26). For Gilroy, the willed reduction of black identity to become increasingly an assertion of the material body within the unchallenged conditions of global capitalist economies imperils a long history of Black Atlantic resistance and alternative cultural production. That politics was shaped by that very integrity of 'body and soul' which, in different ways, Western feminism sought to recover and reaffirm in its challenge to masculinist mind/body dualisms. Any consideration of postcolonial body cultures, then, must engage with the history of racial disparagement, intellectual and political enclosure within the 'skin-culture' of empire, and what might seem to be a contemporary abandonment of the traditionally-defined resources to struggle against such limitations.

The study of dance and sport has not occupied much space in the work of theorists of postcolonial studies, and to assert their importance might risk trivialising the often brutal legacies of empire and the body, even if it does not actively reinstate their conclusions. To study postcolonial cultures through sport, for example, is, as Chris Barker argues, to risk representing black athletes 'as primarily physical rather than mental beings', and reaffirming the masculine dominance of the most successful profes-sional expressions of sport (Barker 2000: 215). Despite these con-cerns, however, it remains true that the material and social activities of dancing and playing and watching sport have pre-occupied the minds and bodies of significant sections of postco-lonial societies. To ignore or underrepresent those fascinations has its own political risks in a complicity with the damaging body/

mind dualisms that Sara Ahmed and others have traced. One legacy of these is the relatively limited conceptual method for dealing with physical expressivity. Writers on Western 'art' dance, for example, tend to lament the lack of an agreed critical language for engaging with physical performance. It is a lack that is compounded in the less studied performances of social dances by their transformations between cultures, and in their adaptations of the detailed movements of the body to the changing circumstances of place and music. Such difficulties of transcription and analysis are also intensified by the discriminations of gender and race noted earlier. The challenge for postcolonial studies becomes one of integrating the expressive social body within its theory and its practice, even as it remains aware of the perils of that endeavour.

The strategy adopted here is intended to circumvent formal divisions between physical cultures, particularly between dance and sport. Henning Eichberg's term 'body cultures' is useful in this, as is the concept of a culture's 'serious play', famously developed by the anthropologist Clifford Geertz. Geertz's classic essay on the anthropology of sport, 'Deep Play: Notes on the Balinese Cockfight' (1972), suggests that participation in a truly popular sport, as player or spectator, is an implication in the fundamental values and contests of a culture. For Geertz, a sport that involves 'deep play' is one that demands and stages significant social and personal investment in the performance and its outcome. Such play enacts a social truth that is unavailable through other social practices. The cockfight, for Balinese men, is an 'encompassing structure', the function of which is 'neither to assuage social passions nor to heighten them but, in a medium of feathers, blood, crowds, and money, to display them' (Geertz 1993: 443, 444). The complexities that are built around and performed through the simple physical acts that compose a sport, Geertz argues, provide a 'metasocial' commentary upon those relationships and values that most fascinate and trouble a culture. In a celebrated formulation, Geertz concludes that the cockfight's function, 'if you want to call it that, is interpretive [sic]: it is a Balinese reading of Balinese experience, a story they tell themselves about themselves' (448).

Geertz's eloquent account of the dense social meanings embodied in the performances of an apparently frivolous leisure activity remains a persuasive articulation of the importance of play and sport. His formulation of sport as a 'cultural text' that works with and against other social 'texts' or performances to provide a culture with an interpretative guide to itself, a story that a culture tells about itself, allows us to take such play seriously. However, Geertz's essay also raises questions of method and context. The cockfight was a village performance working in the then intimate traditions of Balinese society. Its relevance to an analysis of sports that operate on a national or global scale, and in which spectatorship is more likely to be via television than by personal presence and participation, is problematic. The codes of, say, international football are at once potentially universal and more remote from the 'narrative' of everyday life than a village cockfight that is organised through rigorously local channels and performed to a largely homogenous spectatorship, without the intrusions of technology, commercial sponsorship and international governing bodies. Even within the terms of his own analysis, Geertz faces other limitations to the significance of the play that he describes which concern gender and politics. Whilst initially acknowledging that cockfighting is unusual in Balinese society because of the lack of any involvement of women, this skewing of gender is then practically elided as the sport becomes an 'encompassing structure'. Sport, in First World and postcolonial nations alike, is a predominantly male activity and preoccupation, raising questions about the social representativeness of its performances to a major constituency in those societies (see Hargreaves 1994, 2000). Even in the recently burgeoning sociological literature on sport, there are very few women contributors.

Geertz also denies social agency to the deep play that he describes, and this poses a further problem for its inclusion within postcolonial studies. He argues that whilst a performance displays what really matters to its participants, it cannot itself affect those matters. It 'renders ordinary, everyday experience comprehensible by presenting it in terms of acts and objects which have their practical consequences removed and been reduced (or, if you prefer, raised) to the level of sheer appearances, where their meaning can be more powerfully articulated and more exactly perceived' (Geertz 1993: 443). This has a particular relevance for postcolonial sport, of course. The involvement of postcolonial cultures in games that were introduced by colonists becomes by this token at best a conservative process, a mimicry of the concerns of colonialism, not a transformation of them. Sport, for Geertz, changes nothing, and, by implication, it might also preserve much that is in need of transformation.

If Clifford Geertz's model of deep play offers both possibilities and restrictions for a study of postcolonialism, Henning Eichberg's work on sports history and cultural geography provides some suggestive theoretical alternatives. Eichberg crucially relocates sport within a wider formulation that he calls 'body culture'. The term reflects his linkage of the institutional and regulated terrain of European-derived sport and the much more informal and much less problematically gendered activities of dance. Eichberg's concern is with the human body in performance, whether dancing, running or hitting (Geertz's cockfight narrative, of course, doesn't – can't – deal with this, except in terms of an audience response to the game or as metaphor and metonymy). Body culture, he argues, 'as a ritual of "the social body" . . . is rooted deep in the material fundaments of society, figuring patterns of work and even prefiguring revolutionary changes' (Eichberg 1998: 162). Here, the sporting and dancing body is both constitutive and dynamic, embodying cultural identities, and attuned to and instrumental in social change. A study of 'body cultures' necessarily becomes a cultural and historical study, with the details of human physical adjustments to new experiences of time and space being indices of historical change as well as of the stable social relations that Geertz's play enacts. As will be seen, Eichberg's arguments for the political agency of the sporting body had been anticipated in rather different forms in C. L. R. James's writing on West Indian cricket. However, the former's more comprehensive theorisation of body cultures allows meaningful connections to be made between dance and sport, between, say, the Australian Shane Warne's bowling in a cricket game or the performance of a Kenyan distance runner, and the popular dance cultures of the Caribbean and South America. Crucially, it accords the body a

historical and cultural agency in generating, shaping and interpreting changing meanings within the contested spaces of postcolonial societies.

The three case studies that follow develop these ideas of body
cultures and deep play by thinking about the role of dance and of
sport – particularly cricket and football – in postcolonial studies.
They discuss the methodological challenges that are posed by an
engagement with physical, rather than conventionally textual,
expression, and the relationship between that bodily expressiveness and the cultural and political histories of colonialism and
postcolonialism. The first case study will consider a range of
theoretical approaches to dance, tracing the tentative emergence
of a means of acknowledging and analysing the inscription of
cultural change within the movements of the postcolonial body.
The subsequent case study on sport will develop these readings of
body cultures within the organisations of colonial/postcolonial
sport. Using C. L. R. James's pioneering work on the body culture
of cricket as a starting point, it will suggest the ways in which that
sport was an agent for political theory and practice. James's visit to
northern England in the 1930s with the great Trinidadian cricketer
Learie Constantine is one site for this. Another is the unexpected
postcolonial body culture of the Australian leg-spin bowler Shane
Warne, which suggests an unlikely continuity in the capacity of
sport to articulate cultural change, even in the affluent global
environment of contemporary Test cricket. The third case study
concerns football in Ireland, and the way in which organised sport
reflected and initiated struggles against colonialism, and performed
an important role in the more recent shaping of Ireland as a
diasporic nation.

Case Study One: Dance, Identity and Postcolonial Politics

'The hips of tradition' is a phrase in a samba by the Brazilian singer
Tom Zé (Zé 1992). For Zé, these hips are the sensual embodiment of a
complex and developing history. Through the particular movements and stylings of samba they articulate the politics of nationhood and social struggle of twentieth-century Brazil. Transformed
from an African-derived ghetto dance that Monica Rector traces to

Angola, into a kinetic symbol of nationhood, it became both agent and emblem of modern Brazil's 'intellectual valorization of race mixing', as Hermano Vianna calls it, and of the projection of that racial hybridity as central to national values (Rector 1984: 65; Vianna 1999: 50; see also Schreiner 1993). Yet the means of tracing and writing that tradition of hips, and of understanding the relationship of their intimate movements and theatre to a wider process of cultural change and racial encounter, remain a challenge. 'Dance ethnography can never be convincing historiography', writes the samba dancer-ethnographer Barbara Browning, and yet, as Tom Zé's song argues, the body and its formalised and localised movements in dance do define some kind of alternative historiography, an account of encounter and resistance that tests the resources of cultural studies (Browning 1995: 9).

Writing in 1984, Angela McRobbie noted that '[o]f all the areas of popular culture [dance] remains the least theorised', and, though the critical literature on dance has grown, thirteen years later Jane C. Desmond was saying the same thing (McRobbie 1984: 131–2; Desmond 1997: 34–6). These difficulties are often rehearsed in more recent surveys of the field. Alexandra Carter, for example, notes the lack of a scholarly tradition in dance studies, and links this to dance's 'low social status . . . the equation of its sensual nature with its sexual potential and the difficulties of studying such a transient event' (Carter 1998: 2). Lacking an objective 'text' and a flexible critical discourse to study the body in movement, discussions of dance forms, particularly popular dance forms, frequently devolve into a consideration of the more 'stable' texts of music and lyrics. However, it is the details of bodily movement and their enaction of responses and exchanges generated by interactions of music, word, performance site and partner that disclose the most significant knowledge about what Amy Koritz calls 'the range of allowable representations of the body in motion and the policing of bodily form in a specific time and place' (Koritz 1996: 91). The means of tracing and interpreting these performances pose particular difficulties for postcolonial studies. Gay Morris's collection, for example, in which Koritz's helpful essay on dance and cultural studies appears, emphasises the practices and institutions of 'art' dance, with only one or two anthropological pieces about 'traditional' forms. In a sense, a postcolonial study of dance needs to be located precisely between these two places, between the village and the institute, in places and moments of physical transition, intimacy and hybrid formation, such as those spaces in which Hermano Vianna finds the 'mystery' of the emergence of the samba (Vianna 1999). Popular dance insists upon an attention to the entire knowledge, physical and intellectual, of the places where racial, sexual and class differences, attractions and deceptions meet in the movements of individual bodies and in their interactions. Its sites are places of shared sweat and play, the hybridity of which has little in common with the cleaner processes of its theory.

The resources for studying such places are necessarily problematic. Perhaps the most systematic study of a postcolonial dance is Monica Rector's semiological analysis of samba, which provides a detailed breakdown of the physical sign-system that works to create an apparently transcendental experience (Rector 1984). For Rector, samba is composed of social binaries embodied in that 'navel-to-navel bump': 'exaltation-retreat; pleasure-aversion; tension-relaxation . . . added to three variable attributes: intensity, quality, and imagination' (115). However, this heroic semiotics, as Rector herself admits, breaks down on these variables, and their representation in the flow and subtlety of physical movement within the structures of samba. 'The fact that it was impossible to describe some movements due to their complexity', she confesses, 'illustrates the different natures of gestural and linguistic signs.' Whilst she begins from the assertion that '[a]ll dance has purpose or intent', the process of description and structural elucidation leads to the conclusion that 'the knowledge of form does not alone reveal meaning' (117, 114). What else is required can, perhaps, be determined from some later approaches to postcolonial dance.

Recent works of dance scholarship have drawn upon the new ethnography's insistence upon an acknowledgement of and engagement with the problematic dynamic of the Western 'observer' and the Third World subject. Their study thus emerges from the problems of learning rather than the certainties of seeing, through a kind of self-conscious cultural embodiment. Barbara

Browning's *Samba: Resistance in Motion* (1995), for example, is an account of samba's sources in African-derived spirit-practices and its contemporary manifestations of the persistence of those practices. Browning's argument that 'the body is capable of understanding more things at once than can be articulated in language' underpins a discourse that defers all the time to the physical activity of her engagement with samba. 'One has no choice but to *think with the body*', she asserts, and this sceptical appraisal of the limitations of ethnography structures a study of its always unattainable meaning (Browning 1995: 13). Sally Ann Ness attempts a comparable ethnography in her essay 'Dancing in the Field: Notes from Memory' (1996). Ness's calculatedly 'unfinished' autobiographical piece is a detailed account of both her physical engagement with the disciplines of another culture's dance traditions – in this case, those of Bali and the Philippines – and the social and cultural barriers to that 'embodiment' – her teachers' treatment of her as a 'tourist', for example, and the negotiations necessary for her to be perceived as a 'dancer' in another culture. These accounts are not interested in systematic descriptions and functional interpretations of dance, emphasising instead strategies to recover the elusive process of embodying another culture.

Whilst this trend in dance studies provides an alternative narrative of physical learning to those that seek to maintain distance, describe and delineate, such autobiography, as Ness's account in particular emphasises, is in some ways limited to a personal moment of interaction. There is (and can be) little insight into the detailed practices of social transmission and change, what Jacqui Malone in her history of African-American dance calls 'the cultural history of a movement system' (Malone 1996: 1). The 'self-conscious body' of dance anthropology has much to offer in its accounts of the processes of cultural exchange between ethnographer and local practitioner. But how far this information is instructive about the informal training of dance practice that Malone alludes to, and to which Western researchers are allowed only uncertain access, remains questionable (28). The historical points of transmission and exchange, the moments of transition, that mystery of samba in Vianna's terms, remain hidden in the movements of the hips of tradition.

The deep historical play that dance performs has attracted other theorists. Wilson Harris, for example, in a characteristically provocative intervention, suggests that neglected practices of Caribbean dance represent a 'complex metaphorical gateway' between African culture and the New World (Harris 1999: 158). Harris interprets limbo-dancing not as a residual and corrupt form of African tradition, performed for hotel tourists, but as 'a curious re-assembly of the parts of the dead god or gods . . . a re-assembly which issued from a state of cramp to articulate a new growth' (159). The cramp of the Middle Passage of the slave's journey, physical and metaphysical, is released and the limbs painfully re-created within a new expressive culture, of which dance is a primary expression, not least because of the physical and intellectual repressions of slavery. Social dances consequently bear, shed and disguise the weight of that history and its re-articulation, an insight that Jamaican record producers, with their constant reconstitution of traditional dance patterns would recognise very well. Limbo, despite its apparent reduction to cliché, nevertheless retains within its disciplines and contortions an active memory – a 'living fossil' in Harris's phrase – of a traumatic and still active history.

Harris's sense of dance as active relic is hard to contain within conventional theoretical practice, yet its idea of the body performing a dialectic that is both defined by and resistant to history is one that has been taken up by some thinkers on postcolonial dance. For example, Celeste Fraser Delgado and José Esteban Muñoz discuss the failure of Dominican dictator Rafael Trujillo's attempt to harness the merengue as a populist vehicle for his regime. 'If the churning hips and shackled feet of rumba re-member the history of the African slave trade', they write, 'and the wild motion of the mambo evokes abolition, the merengue's sudden breaks into dizzying turns . . . hint at the difficulty of maintaining control through popular cultural forms' (Delgado and Muñoz 1997b: 25). Such interpretations begin the process of integrating dance within history, and perceiving its inflections as both displays and transformations of those experiences.

How this history becomes part of specific postcolonial cultural exchanges can be drawn from a more prosaic sociological account of English working-class dance practices in the 1980s. Angela

McRobbie's essay 'Dance and Social Fantasy' (1984) remains a persuasive account of the social meanings of popular dancing, and, despite its general inattention to questions of culture and race, a suggestive basis for thinking about the postcolonial formations of British dance cultures. McRobbie argues that the experience of dance – more particularly, the female experience of dance – consists of three overlapping dynamics: the creation of a social image, the expression of female fantasy and the performance of a social activity (McRobbie 1984: 130). Dance, she suggests, has been and remains a complex and powerful manifestation of young women's identity in an otherwise disempowering environment. It is one of the few activities that insists upon a public articulation of feminine identity whilst allowing a protection of that display by integration and concentration within the movement, 'a dramatic display of the self and the body, with an equally dramatic negation of the self and the body', as McRobbie puts it (144). This description can certainly be applied to the dancehall culture that Lady Saw represents in a Jamaican context, but it is also relevant to the history of the transmission of body cultures. McRobbie's sense of dance's gendered cultural and social significance is particularly suggestive for such understudied aspects of postcolonialism as inter-racial relationships with which Lord Kitchener's calypsos are perhaps the first to engage.

Dance, then, remains a potentially important resource for post-colonial studies. Despite the perception of a danger of complicity within traditions of 'physicalising' colonised cultures, its study can reveal a performative history of cultural change and hybridity unavailable elsewhere. The hips of tradition articulate the body's absorption of pasts, and its display of power and vulnerability in response to changing circumstances and influences. Whilst the difficulties of achieving a comprehensive history of the moments of encounter and change are formidable – as the wisest commentators on dance acknowledge, there is mystery as well as materiality in its processes – there is also much to be learned from, say, a study of the development of West Indian clubs in Britain in the post-war period and an oral history of their dancers, and of the reconstruction of genealogies of popular dance movements in a postcolonial context. A critical discourse of dance will always remain problematic, given the difficulties of recording and assessing the complex subtleties of physical expression and interaction. Nevertheless, the challenge is vital and inviting, and has analogues in the more developed field of the cultural study of sport. And, whilst the body culture of sport is more exclusively masculine, it has the advantage of more thoroughly documented organisational, textual and visual histories.

Case Study Two:
Cricket, Anti-colonialism and Globalisation

In 1980, Pierre Bourdieu claimed that the idea of a sociology of sport is 'disdained by sociologists, and despised by sportspeople' (Bourdieu 1990: 156). The second of his assertions probably holds true, but the first has been challenged both by a large body of sociological and historical studies, and by the establishment of specialist centres of study. Sport has become significant in postcolonial studies, as shown by the work on cricket developed by scholars such as Hilary Beckles at the University of the West Indies (see Beckles 1998). However, its presence in the mainstream of postcolonial studies remains marginal and problematic. The formalisation of the playing codes, administrative structures and aesthetics of British-derived sports such as football and cricket was contemporary with, and complicit with, the most aggressive ideological and political phase of empire in the last third of the nineteenth century. As historians of colonialism have argued, these values and laws – especially those of cricket – were deployed to shape colonial society, asserting approved codes of conduct and organising selective 'native' elites within the ethos of the game (see Stoddart 1988a, 1988b; Mangan 1992; Stoddart and Sandiford 1998; Guha 2002). Because of its popularity and its effective distance from political authority, cricket becomes what Helen Tiffin in her critique of C. L. R. James's writing on the game calls 'the most insidiously influential of all imperial cultural forms' (Tiffin 1982: 186). The rise of the 'garrison game' of football in Ireland (originally imported by British soldiers) at the expense of 'indigenous' Gaelic sports can be seen as another version of this influence, though one less carefully modulated by the class interests of imperial administration. The main political questions for a study of postcolonial sport thus become how far the games are separable from their implication in colonial history, what the agency of participants and spectators might be in effecting such a separation, and what local cultural meanings can be traced in sporting competition now defined largely by global corporate interests. The writings and performances of C. L. R. James are a useful starting point.

James was the first anti-colonial theorist to press the case for sport and other popular entertainments to be taken seriously as cultural performances alongside European canons of literature, music and – particularly – drama. Cricket was a means for James to describe and interpret what he calls in one essay 'that crowded vagueness which passes for the history of the West Indies', a history in which outlets of written record and expression, for most of the population, were scant and skewed (James 1989: 165–6). He argues that the performative struggles of a cricket match – like Geertz's cockfight translated into the humanly performed, politicised context of colonial and postcolonial sport – are complex means of engagement, expression and development. Anticipating Eichberg's sense of the sporting body and event dramatising social change, James also reads the deep play of cricket as being subtly but powerfully inflected by the shifting historical and social circumstances of the Caribbean and Europe, and as agents in that history. The conclusion of his 1969 essay on the great Barbadian all-rounder Garfield Sobers encapsulates James's extraordinary vision of cricket, and emphasises his attention to the detailed meanings of postcolonial body cultures:

> Garfield Sobers I see not as a fortuitous combination of atoms which by chance have coalesced into a superb public performer. He being what he is (and I being what I am), for me his command of the rising ball in the drive, his close fielding and his hurling himself into his fast bowling are a living embodiment of centuries of a tortured history. (James 1989: 232)

Characteristically, James sees in Sobers' physical display within the rhythms and forms of cricket, formations of and responses to the history of empire and its aftermath. His movements on the field,

like those of the dances discussed in the previous case study, are
shaped by the colonial history embodied in the game, but also by
particular inflections that are of his and his culture's distinctive
making. And James, good dialectician that he was, adds the
parenthesis that acknowledges his own – and by extension all
cricket's spectators' – implication in that performance. The great
sportsman performs minutely and extravagantly the complexities
and contradictions of his time and place, and, as in Geertz's deep
play, the spectators are not passive consumers, but constituents of
what is always in some sense a culturally meaningful drama.

James, as suggested in Chapter 1, is both a revered figure in
postcolonial studies and an underrepresented and underused one,
and his cricket writing is one reason for this. Helen Tiffin, for
example, in the essay referred to earlier (Tiffin 1982), celebrates
the radical achievements of *The Black Jacobins*, James's history of the
Haitian revolution, but suggests that his most sustained study of
cricket and Caribbean identity, *Beyond a Boundary* (1969), is limited
by a failure to revise and challenge the historical meanings of cricket
in the same way. James, she writes, 'never examines [English cricket's] values or their appropriateness in a colonial, post-slave society,
or suggests that values implicit in the game might continue to hinder
the recognition of that purely local value he strove so successfully to
establish in his earlier works' (Tiffin 1982: 187–8). In other words,
James remains trapped within the unalterably colonial structures of
cricket. For Tiffin, the social meanings of Caribbean cricket's deep
play cannot be freed from that history, and to celebrate the sport as a
means of understanding postcolonial Caribbean experience is to limit
that experience to a version, a mimicry of its colonial past. A different
critique of James's postcolonial cricket theory is developed by
Kenneth Surin, who, whilst acknowledging the importance of sport
to postcolonial studies, sees the relevance of James's work as limited
to what might be termed the nationalist phase of anti-colonial
struggles, from the 1930s through to the 1970s. What might have
been true of Garfield Sobers, Surin suggests, has less validity in a
world of globalised leisure, media-influenced sport, and of the
dissolution of those grand narratives, whether of Marxism or English
Literature, with which James was always in complicated but committed relationships. 'What cricket does more and more', Surin

argues, 'is simply to "express" its own situation as a commodity produced and consumed within a unitary and standardized flow of production and consumption that now straddles the world' (Surin 1995: 148). Cricket thus moves from what Eichberg terms sport's 'modern' phase, in which it was implicated in issues of national identity, into a phase of 'postmodernity', defined by media control and the acceptance of a multiplicity of cultural identities that precludes the kind of sporting struggle that James saw a player like Sobers as embodying (Eichberg 1998: 145). For Surin, cricket – and global sport in general – has become a form without specific cultural content.

In their different ways, these critiques of C. L. R. James's cultural study of cricket are significant for wider debates about the relevance and limitations of a concern with body cultures in postcolonial studies. By looking in more detail at James's construction of a politicised cricket writing and practice in the 1930s, and by testing the relevance of that theory to a performance in the contemporary global game, the potential for reading the politics of the body in the frame that James developed can be assessed. If the history of dance, in its popular manifestations at least, is a potent but largely inaccessible resource for understanding cultural change, the more visible body cultures developed within the imperial game of cricket, and the less prestigious, but finally more influential, sport of football provide more ample resources for study. What is needed, however, is a methodology that engages with the political challenges outlined by Tiffin and Surin, and, as in dance studies, a discourse that is adequate to defining the details of the cultural expression of the body.

Cricket, Class and Anti-colonialism

The Trinidadian cricketer Learie Constantine arrived in the Lancashire cotton town of Nelson in 1928 to play for its cricket club as a professional. Constantine had established himself as a world-class batsman and fielder on the West Indies tour of England in the same year, in a team of African-Caribbean and Indian-Caribbean players captained by a white, as all West Indian teams were to be until 1960. His arrival in Nelson was a direct consequence of the racial and economic structure of Caribbean cricket, which was itself, of course, determined by the circumstances of British colonialism in the West Indies. The son of a cocoa plantation overseer, Constantine was an educated and aspirant member of the colonial lower middle class, a social position strengthened by his cricketing success. However, despite his achievements with the West Indies team, it was impossible for him to make a living in the amateur structure of cricket in Trinidad, or to develop as world-class cricketer while playing part time. Working in Britain was his solution. In entering the domestic structure of English cricket, Constantine encountered both a reiteration of the class and racial hierarchies that controlled the imperial game in the Caribbean, and an alternative structure of the sport developed within the local conditions of English class structures and regional divisions.

The dominant force of English cricket was the county league, an institution that preserved the amateur status and class-defined values that cricket had come to represent in the late nineteenth century and which was so powerfully exported to the colonies. The county league did employ professional cricketers, but there were strict limits on their number and on the conditions of their play. Whilst many of these professionals were working class, none of them was black, a racial separatism that was, of course, reflected in the organisation of cricket in the empire. Constantine's access to English cricket, therefore, came through the Lancashire League, an organisation quite separate from the county system. League teams played one day games instead of four-day games, reflecting the leisure structure of working-class spectators, were based in the industrial towns of the north, particularly Yorkshire and Lancashire, and had a tradition of hiring 'colonial' professional players, including West Indians, though more often Australians, to captain and coach their part-time players. Constantine, then, entered Britain through a domestic faultline in cricket culture, one that in some ways challenged the structures and assumptions of the dominant class-defined values of first-class cricket. These tensions of social class and sporting organisation were to be important as Constantine and his friend C. L. R. James came to use cricket, and Lancashire League cricket particularly, in their thinking about political change in the Caribbean.

In 1928, Nelson was a town facing economic crisis due to a slump in demand for cotton during the Depression. Unemployment and labour unrest were common (Constantine arrived during a seven-week lock-out at the mills) and the cricket club's secretary, Edward Ashton, took a gamble to restore the club's own declining fortunes in signing Constantine for three seasons at £500 per year, plus travelling and living expenses. One national newspaper accused Ashton of 'introducing the picturesque transfer methods of soccer football into the world of cricket', a comment that registers the remove of even Lancashire League cricket from the working-class professionalism developing in football. Ashton, an early cricket entrepreneur, argued that cricket was primarily entertainment. 'The public demand something a little out of the ordinary', he said, 'and the mere friendly match fails to draw the proverbial three men and a dog' (*Nelson Leader* 3 August 1928: 6). Constantine was to be his out-of-the-ordinary attraction, capitalising upon a reputation already made strong in the north-west by the *Manchester Guardian* cricket correspondent, Neville Cardus. Even before he played a game, Constantine was involved with the negotiations of class, colony, race and popular theatre that shaped his and other Caribbean cricketers' careers and, eventually, their postcolonial identities.

Constantine turned Nelson into the most powerful side in the Lancashire League. However, his introduction of Caribbean body culture into the industrial north-west of England had wider consequences for postcolonial sport and politics. The arrival of C. L. R. James in Nelson in 1932 was a catalyst for this development. Constantine's successes with the West Indies and with Nelson had given him a prestige in England unlike that of any other Caribbean cricketer, and this led in 1933 to the publication of an autobiography, ghost-written by James and with a preface by Cardus. *Cricket and I* is quite anodyne in its commentary upon English and Caribbean cricket, but its significance, as James later argued in *Beyond a Boundary*, was in its rhetoric and performance rather than its content. It was 'the first book ever published in England by a world-famous West Indian writing as a West Indian about people and events in the West Indies' (James 1969: 124). Just how contested that performance was, though, is clear from Cardus's evaluation of Constantine in his foreword:

We know that his cuts and drives, his whirling fast balls, his leapings
and clutchings and dartings – we know they are the consequence of
impulses born in the blood, a blood heated by the sun and influenced
by an environment and a way of life much more natural than ours . . .
His cricket is racial . . .

His movements in the field are almost primitive in their pouncing
voracity and unconscious beauty. There are no bones in his body, only
great charges and flows of energy. A genius, and, as I say, a representative man! (Constantine 1933: xi–xii)

Cardus undoubtedly politicises Constantine's 'genius' and representativeness, but his framing of that body culture is redolent of
the primitivist iconography of race and display that had long been
part of British popular theatre and of European popular culture in
the 1920s. Edward Ashton had hired Constantine as a professional
entertainer as well as a great cricketer, and, as Cardus makes clear,
the means of reading Constantine's performance as racial stereotype
rather than political challenge was available to the huge crowds
that went to see him at Nelson.

Cricket and I was part of a developing political strategy established by Constantine and James. In *Beyond a Boundary*, James
writes of having two books on his knee when he was writing in
Nelson, one being the Constantine 'autobiography', the other being
the overtly political *The Case for West Indian Self-Government*,
published in the same year as *Cricket and I*. The two act in
characteristically dialogic relationship, the cricket book both
masking and performing, in calypso fashion, James's first extended
analysis of imperialism and argument for Caribbean independence.
Imperial cricket rests on the next knee to radical political philosophy, and the restrained discussion of the racial power structure
in West Indies cricket in the one is revisited in explicit and radical
terms in the political polemic of the other. The complex, symbiotic
relationship of the two books remained typical of James's thinking
and practice for the next sixty years, and was embodied in the
performative practice of Constantine. In both cases, it was their
experience of Nelson and the Lancashire League that was formative
in their dissident analysis of imperialism.

'Trinidad was discovered by Columbus in 1496 and by the MCC

in 1895', Constantine begins his second (and much more radical)
book *Cricket in the Sun* (1946), a neat and knowing formulation of
the relationship of cricket and imperialism (Constantine 1946: 39).
But that politics, shaped through the access sport allowed him to
Britain, was also defined by his position outside of the social and
sporting structures represented by the MCC. C. L. R. James
described Constantine as a league cricketer who played Test
cricket, and, for both, that apparently fine distinction was politically crucial. The particular features of league cricket and the
social histories that shaped them provided a way of thinking
beyond the social and imperialist assumptions of the game that
Constantine and James experienced in the Caribbean. One of the
most overtly political passages in *Cricket in the Sun* has Constantine,
en route to Trinidad, meditating on the possibilities of social
change via the distinctions between the two forms of the English
game:

> Whether it was the influence of the sea air I don't know, but an
> alarming impression came to me at times that three-day cricket matches
> are an anachronism in our hurried, workaday world. It seemed to me,
> sunning myself in a chair on the liner's deck, that the era when men
> could afford to give three whole days to one game, and then as often as
> not fail to finish it, had passed away. As in a dream, I foresaw an
> incredible world where county teams, also, played and usually fin-
> ished their games in one day, with never a wasted minute; when a
> shower did not stop play; when those thousands of fine cricketers who
> now cannot afford to turn out for anything more ambitious than a
> Saturday afternoon club got into the first-class game. (Constantine
> 1946: 39)

It is a vision of democratised play, written in the aftermath of a
socialist election victory in Britain in 1945. The experience of league
cricket, with its pragmatic attitude to match times, conditions and
team selections, becomes an alternative vision of democratic modernity to that of the class-bound and anachronistic amateurism of the
dominant form of the game, and of its imperial developments. As
such, it anticipates the more overtly radical anti-colonialism that he
would express in his later book *Colour Bar* (1954).

The politics that Constantine was able to develop through the professional game in Lancashire was a necessarily complex one in its negotiation with colonial history and his own anomalous position within British culture. Nelson was a site of intense labour struggles in the 1930s, and wartime work in Liverpool gave him further experience of industrial conflict, here with frequent racial dimensions (see his account in Constantine 1954: 146–8). Within these class struggles, however, Constantine's sporting abilities and migrant identity allowed him to redefine the status of the 'professional' cricketer. In the terms of English county cricket, the professional was marked off as socially subordinate to his amateur, gentlemanly colleagues. While Constantine was defined through race in Nelson, he was free from the class structures of the county game. With a wage of £650 per year by 1934, he was able to cultivate an English middle-class lifestyle, with a car, private education for his daughter and a social circle of doctors, solicitors, and non-conformist Christians. A biographer notes, '[h]e was a professional, entitled by his success to the attributes of the professional man', a re-appropriation of the implicitly derogatory sporting term achieved through his avoidance of English class politics, and canny exploitation of colonialist expectations (Howat 1975: 96). As the *Nelson Leader* had it in 1933, '[h]e has shown in his conduct on and off the field, that a coloured man may be a white man, and it is that side of his character that has made such an irresistible appeal to the public' (*Nelson Leader*, 22 September 1933: 6). Constantine developed radical anti-colonial politics alongside a carefully judged realisation of the material values of his skills and status in the Lancashire League that negotiated within the racial stereotypes that existed in Britain.

In a formative period of anti-colonial thought and agitation, cricket provided a frame for the development of those processes. Learie Constantine's physical performance on the cricket field allowed him to define a new body culture, a new inflection of the rhythms of the sport. 'The point about Constantine's fielding', C. L. R. James writes, 'is that you came to the ground and looked at him expecting the moment of artistic truth and were rarely disappointed' (James 1989: 236). That change to body culture, as James always argued, was a political as well as an athletic change. Constantine's cricket was part of the shift in political perception that was evident in James's contemporary intellectual work, and the possibilities offered to Constantine by the ideological fissures within the English organisation of the game. 'Constantine's cricket', writes James, 'made [the British public] aware of the Caribbean in general and of black men in particular' and his performances, like those of Sobers later, were part of playing 'the game of powers emancipating themselves in a field that needs emancipation' (278, 279). The cricketer himself exploited that recognition to achieve significant material success, even as he developed an increasingly radical political programme.

James's argument that cricket embodies the social and political history of anti-colonial resistance and postcolonial formation concentrates on the period of nationalist agitation and nation-building from the 1920s to the 1970s. As Kenneth Surin suggests in the article referred to above, there remains a question of how transferable James's analysis of body culture can be to the more recent circumstances of sport. A celebrated case might be that of a ball bowled shortly before the publication of Surin's essay in a Test match played apparently outside the struggles of race and nationhood that framed Constantine's career. On 4 June 1993, the Australian spin bowler Shane Warne delivered his first ball in a Test in England to the batsman Mike Gatting. *Wisden Cricketers' Almanack* describes it as follows:

> It set off on the line of Gatting's pads and then dipped in the air further towards the leg side until it was 18 inches adrift of the stumps; by this time Gatting was beginning to lose interest, until the ball bounced, turned and fizzed across his ample frame to clip the off-bail. Gatting remained rooted to the crease for several seconds – in disbelief rather than dissent – before trudging off to the pavilion like a man betrayed.
> (Engel 1994: 21–2)

The ball was bowled by a well-paid professional practitioner of a now-globalised game in a match between representatives of two affluent nations that are connected by rivalry through an increasingly remote colonial history. Does James's sense of body culture have any relevance to such moments?

Shane Warne is, par excellence, a product of and enthusiastic participant in the 'standardized flow' of international cricket that Surin describes, with its endless touring, the proliferation of one-day international matches (rather than five-day Test matches), and its dependence upon global television scheduling (Surin 1995: 148). But the Gatting ball was a moment of sporting theatre that seems to challenge the postmodern formalism that Surin evokes, and re-affirms the local and historical meanings of deep play, even in an apparently globalised context. As historians of the game have argued, the culture of cricket was shaped by and shaped the colonial enterprise (see, for example, Stoddart and Sandiford 1998). However, it is an imperial game that necessarily contains and retains the contradictions of the imperialism that made it, and of subsequent postcolonial histories. The meaning of Warne's ball, in other words, emerges from a specific colonial body culture, and its ritualised, but resonant aftermath.

Leg-spin bowling – a method of moving the ball off the pitch by manipulation of the wrist in delivery – had for years occupied a special place in the post-imperial imagination of English cricket. Its gradual disappearance from most Test sides, save those of India and Pakistan, in the post-Second World War period led to a discourse of nostalgia surrounding what one ex-cricketer, with characteristic orientalism, termed the 'mystery' and 'magic' of this 'very special art' (Bailey 1992: 31). The leg-spinner became an icon of an almost-disappeared quality in cricket, preserved only by rarely seen 'conjurors' in the sub-continent – a reminder of older aesthetic values gone from England, but surviving in residual form in old imperial outposts of the East. Warne's ball in the summer of 1993 startlingly disallowed such constructions. Instead of wily, myster-ious Eastern magicians came Shane, with a forename from *Neigh-bours*, brutally sunblocked, tending towards barbecue-tubby, and as remorselessly aggressive in his demeanour as in his turn of the ball. Warne inflected the okker masculinity punctiliously culti-vated by the great Australian pace bowlers of the 1970s into the forms of a body culture that had come to be associated with thinner wrists and aesthetic appreciation. In doing so, he both reaffirmed a stereotype of Australian male identity and challenged the dis-courses and representations of the imperial body that cricket, of all sports, most attentively preserves. In Warne's hands, leg-spin lost its old magic and achieved modernity. No longer an art to be preserved and cherished as an exotic, it became a devastating means of winning games.

Warne's reinvention of leg-spin went a long way to restoring an Australian cricketing dominance that had been lost after the first globalising initiative in the sport, instigated (ironically) by the Australian television entrepreneur Kerry Packer in the late 1970s. The ball he bowled to Gatting had historical and political turn as it gripped the English pitch. Whilst it hadn't the symbolic post-colonial politics of Caribbean nationalism that staged and informed Garry Sobers's performances and the later Rastafarian-inflected, warlike batting of Vivian Richards, Warne's performance never-theless suggested the potential for the body culture of cricket to develop and startle. Its compelling theatre demonstrated the capacity that Geertz identifies in play to embody and dramatise cultural contradictions. Those contradictions were displayed in the material and physical movements of play that adjusted historical expectations and assumptions embedded in the sport and made them new. And, as C. L. R. James argues about Sobers' cricket, Warne's ball was not accidental. In a startling way, it marked a change within the postcolonial theatre of the sport, even as that sport appeared to be becoming a formalised, globalised perfor-mance devoid of history. The unlikely figure of the leg-spin bowler at once re-appropriated the exotic art and made it new and definitively Australian. '[S]how me how you are running', writes Henning Eichberg, 'and I can see something of the society in which you are living', and the same can be said of leg-spin bowling (Eichberg 1998: 163).

Case Study Three: Football and Irish Nationhood

If cricket in the Caribbean achieved its influence by what Brian Stoddart terms its 'voluntary imposition by its new converts rather than from an arbitrary imposition by the imperial masters', the history of association football in Ireland is one of complex and bitter contest (Stoddart 1988b: 663). Irish nationalists were perhaps the first anti-colonialist activists to identify sport as an arena for political struggle, a strategy defined and developed by the Gaelic Athletic Association (GAA), founded in 1884. The GAA had two main objectives: to resist what its founder Michael Cusack termed 'the tyranny of imported and enforced customs and manners', and to organise and promote 'indigenous' Irish sports, particularly Gaelic football and hurling (Mandle 1987: 4). It became, in W. F. Mandle's words, 'the most consistently anti-British force in Ireland (apart from the I[rish] R[epublican] B[rotherhood]) for the last generation of British rule' (15), and its political-sporting ideology, which prevented any GAA player participating in 'colonial' sports, was to prove highly effective for the next hundred years. 'There'll be no garrison games for Ireland', said the revolutionary leader Michael Collins in 1908, referring to football and its Irish origins in the British army, '[t]hese only aid the peaceful penetration of Ireland by the British and there should be no soccer for Gaels' (quoted in Hannigan 1998: 11).

As we have seen, though, some sports embody the contradictions rather than the simplicities of a culture. The partial victory of revolutionary Irish nationalism resulted in the institution of the Irish Free State in 1922 and government backing of GAA sporting policy. However, the very indigeneity of hurling and Gaelic football that made them effective weapons in establishing a nationalist, anti-colonial body culture proved problematic after independence when the importance of international sporting contests grew in the post-Second World War period. As with American football, the only opponents were yourselves. However, unlike American football, there was a lack of scale to the national contests, and, what is more, there was significant deep play in other competing sports. Donall O'Keefe summarises the complex class and regional sporting allegiances that developed in post-partition Ireland, suggesting that 'rugby football is the urban middle-class game, soccer is the game of the working class, while Gaelic codes, with their nationalist ethos and associations, tend to be limited to rural areas and to the "pseudo-rural" section of the urban middle class' (quoted in Holmes 1994: 88). This schismatic national sporting life was reflected in the individual sporting organisations, with the Irish rugby association including both Northern Ireland and the Republic (as does that other Irish middle-class sport, cricket), the

GAA including the nationalist population of the North, and football acrimoniously split between Northern Ireland's and the Republic's football associations. The ideological dominance of GAA sport led to the underdevelopment of amateur and professional football in the Republic. Better players, who tended to come from those garrison towns such as Cork and Dublin, found employment, like many other Irish people, as emigrant workers in England.

The phenomenon of what John Bale and Joseph Maguire have termed 'athletic talent migration' is closely linked to the growth of global sports economies since the 1960s, and the exploitation of postcolonial labour by ex-colonial powers has been particularly prevalent in the wealthier European football leagues of the 1990s (see Bale and Maguire 1994). In the 2002 World Cup, for example, the Senegalese team that beat France in the opening game all played professionally in French domestic football. The history of Irish sporting emigration is unusually long (John Scally dates the first Irish professional footballer as signing for Newton Heath – later Manchester United – in the 1890s) and the consequences of wider Irish emigration are particularly striking (Scally 1998: 45). Ireland, as an international association and team, was divided between Ireland, or Eire, and Northern Ireland after 1949. Because of the Republic's claims to the six northern counties, though, all Northern Ireland citizens were entitled to hold Irish passports, and thus become eligible to play for the Irish team. The 'foreignness' of Irish players, until redefinitions of EEC employment laws, was a source of dispute within British league clubs, adding to the complicated relationships of four separate football leagues within a theoretically unified nation (Moorhouse 1996). The question of national identity only really became a part of the deep play of Irish football, though, when the Republic of Ireland started to become successful in international competitions.

Before 1988, Ireland's record was poor and its administration amateurish. The dissident journalist and former Irish international Eamon Dunphy commented, 'it was a bit of a joke playing for Ireland', pointing to inadequacies of training and organisation and a lack of ambition among those in charge (quoted in Rowan 1994: 23). A change was effected when the former English international Jack Charlton was appointed manager in 1986. Charlton implemented a new policy of exploiting to the full FIFA regulations on qualification for a national team that required only a grandparent to be a national of that country and for a player to have not represented another national side for which he might have been qualified. The effect of this strategy was to end the involvement of Irish league players, normally footballers unable to play at the standard of the upper divisions of the English league, and to populate the team with players whose link to Ireland was sometimes tenuous. This led to the Irish squads in the European Championships of 1988 and the World Cup of 1990 being the only ones in the competitions without any players from their domestic leagues. Under an Englishman, Ireland became one of the first migrant international teams (see Holmes 1994: 92).

As Paul Rowan notes of the self-advertisingly blunt Charlton, his 'mindset doesn't countenance diasporas', but, knowingly or not, that is what he was dealing with (Rowan 1994: 188). His construction of a quasi-Irish Ireland in the late 1980s and early 1990s provoked debates, both academic, drawing upon a burgeoning postcolonial theory interested in the 'constructedness' of nationhood, and popular, as a growing audience confronted this intense enactment of problematic nationhood in international competition. For some observers, the diasporic team was representative of what Benedict Anderson had famously termed the 'imagined community' of nationhood. If, as Anderson argues, the sense of being 'Irish' or 'English' or any other nationality is a powerfully imagined, emotional implication in a construction of markers and symbols, then a nation, that is, its citizens and its media of self-representation, can 'agree' to a representation that is not by other criteria 'authentic' (Anderson 1983). The revelation that the much-capped striker Tony Cascarino did not have any Irish connections at all, for example, did not lead to his popular rejection as an Irish player. Rather, the team could be seen to be a *more* authentic national representation because of its acknowledgement of migration as a dominant fact of Irish experience since the mid-nineteenth century, and its implied assertion that Irishness could be an inherited culture, as well as a settled, landed condition. As Michael Holmes noted, '[f]or emigrants, the [Irish] football team is something of a reflection of themselves, one that is perhaps closer to their experiences of being Irish than that provided by traditional notions of Irish identity' (Holmes 1994: 93). In a wonderful account of being a female Irish football follower, Nell McCafferty suggests that the team itself might also have played themselves into a previously unacknowledged identity: 'I'm sure the team didn't give a damn. They got to play international football . . . But as a result of playing internationally and with a team that was beginning to be adored, they may have discovered some kind of Irishness themselves, which by living in England they were forced to repress' (quoted in Rowan 1994: 139).

There is, though, a danger in idealising the case of the Irish team, and underestimating the problematic nature of the debate about identity that its composition raises. The FIFA qualification law that allowed Charlton to assemble his team was in some sense an institutional response to the fact of diaspora, one aimed at countering the hegemony of powerful (usually ex-colonising) nations and their football leagues. However, the regulation also led to the possibility of national identity being a commodity of transaction as well as the site of allegiance and investment, as it already was in the more lucrative world of European club football. Jack Charlton's comment on a 1993 FIFA relaxation of eligibility rules was to perceive the possibility of establishing strategic stability in nationality. 'We can make [prospective players] permanent Irishmen', he is quoted as saying in a neat statement of the arbitrariness of nationhood (Rowan 1994: 171). There were also evident limits to the relativity of that identity (despite the case of Cascarino) which suggested that the notion of celebratory (and celebrity) hybridity was in close and sometimes uncomfortable relationship with the complex colonial legacies of Ireland. Pierre Bourdieu argues that the apparent autonomy of a sporting practice is imaginary; it is always in tension with other analogous and divergent social and cultural practices (Bourdieu 1990). Thus the celebration of the Irish football team's hybridity needs to be read in direct relationship with the history of the Gaelic Athletic Association's rigorous policing of the meaning of national body culture, and as a sign of a challenge to the specific nationalist ideologies that underpinned the foundation of the Republic in the 1920s.

If, as Michael Holmes argues, the Irish team was 'the strongest

symbol of a 26-county nation that has appeared', it is not surprising
that the most complex test of the diasporic team was in international competition with Northern Ireland, a constitutionally aber-
rant 'national' side perceived by a significant minority of its
'nation' to be representative only of a factional British authority
(Holmes 1994: 95). The crucial World Cup qualifying game between
the two teams in Belfast in 1993, which took place in a context of
inter-communal violence in the north and intense Protestant
antagonism to the Republic's team from the crowd, became a
classic example of sport's disturbingly deep play. To support a
team in that match, John Sugden and Alan Bairner have argued,
was 'more than a statement of football partisanship: it was a public
declaration of national identity' (Sugden and Bairner 1994: 119),
and those political discourses constituted the issues of the game in
many ways. The manager of the Northern Ireland team, Billy
Bingham, for example, delivered a polemic on the subject of
identity in the days before the match. 'At least our team is of
Irish extraction', he asserted, 'and our players are not mercenaries'
(Rowan 1994: 163). Bingham provided a definition of sporting
representation that was, ironically, closer to the traditions of the
GAA, affirming the need for 'nationalist feeling' in a team. 'When
you feel that you're playing for the flag, you're playing for the
shirt, you're playing for these people, you want to lay down your
life for them' (168).

The story that Irish international football tells Ireland about
itself, to use Clifford Geertz's evocative definition of culture, is one
of struggle and contested identity. Nell McCafferty's account,
referred to earlier, both expresses and explores this, confirming
the reputation of Irish supporters at home and abroad for good-
naturedly carnivalesque behaviour. 'The fans were elaborate in
their courtesies, to each other and to strangers', she recalls, arguing
that the conduct of the (predominantly male) followers of the Irish
team was structured by shifting versions of Irish masculinity that
international travel both staged and encouraged, and by deliberated contrast to supporters of the English team who were noted
both for quasi-imperialist nationalism and violence (quoted in
Rowan 1994: 140). Recalling the World Cup in Italy in 1994,
she narrates a cunning anecdote of postcolonial irony that was,

perhaps, only realisable through the deep play of football: 'The English were getting harassed everywhere, God love them, with their Union Jacks. They were hounded, frightened and ashamed. We'd ostentatiously give them our Tricolours so that they could put them over their shoulders and get away from the hassle. Jesus, talk about goodbye Cromwell' (142). But just how far Cromwell and the bitter colonial history that the name evokes could be banished through the agency and cultural play of football is a moot point. The construction of the Irish team and its supporters and their national/diasporic meanings in the period have come under sceptical scrutiny from various positions, though this is itself an indication of how the discourses of identity and nationhood have proliferated around the experience of international football.

Two aspects of this debate are significant here. The first is the role of Jack Charlton and his successor as manager, the second-generation Irish, but in voice at least, very English, Mick McCarthy. Whilst there was no doubt of the popular fascination in Ireland with the team (80 per cent of the Irish population watched RTE television coverage of the 1990 World Cup games), the wider 'diasporic' meanings of the team had to be communicated by non-Irish media, particularly by the BBC. Gary Whannel argues that Charlton was a key factor here, constituting 'a linkage between the Irishness and hence alienness of the team, and the need to win a largely English audience on British television'. 'Ireland are repeatedly characterized as Jack's team', he argues (Whannel 1995: 163). This was certainly important for British broadcasters in 1994, when there was no UK team in the competition, but the implicit politics of 'English' leadership of Ireland always threatened to return the apparently sophisticated management of the outcomes of colonial history to more crudely essentialist versions of nationalist identity and struggle. Part of the reportedly scabrous tirade by the Irish captain Roy Keane against his manager McCarthy before the former's controversial departure from the 2002 World Cup resorted to just this characterisation, though within a frame of argument that actually touched on subtler political issues. Keane positioned himself against the carnivalesque construction of Irish participation and support, in which the celebration of identity – national and diasporic – is more important that preparing thoroughly, competing professionally and winning games. For Keane, perhaps imbued with the contradictory, but intense, politics of his two club managers, Brian Clough and Alex Ferguson, to acquiesce in the carnival in any way is to agree to the maintenance of a subordinate position, social (that is, class-based) and national (colonial). It is, in effect, to play up to colonial stereotypes of the stage Irishman. His critique of the 'patriotic fraud that hung around the Irish team', and 'our Third World approach to the game' in his autobiography are telling indications of this political sense (Keane 2002: 247, 258).

In his essay on football and Irish identity (national and diasporic), Marcus Free poses the question that Keane was to enact with principle or recklessness, depending on the viewpoint, in the World Cup in Japan four years later. Do Irish football 'successes' (a key term for Keane – Ireland, he argues, have never gone beyond the quarter finals of any competition, so why 'success'?) 'allow Irish people to see and ponder the contradictions of their national identity or merely reproduce them unconsciously?' (Free 1998: 221). Free's answer is a suggestive one. Whilst refusing to romanticise the carnival, and noting the readiness of 'real' Irish supporters to denigrate 'plastic Irish', that is English-accented followers, Free concludes, nevertheless, that the possibility of performing Ireland abroad has, especially for second- and later-generation migrants, created a new and real cultural force. 'To play the fool,' he argues 'is to recapture [a] romantic account of the colonial Irishman who exceeds both English discursive designations and the insular designation which persists in Ireland, despite its post-colonial pretensions . . . It is a way of metaphorically being in two places at once, imagining by re-enacting the marginality of Irish identity in Britain through its history of migration while technically being British citizens, so realising the ironic nature of that citizenship' (231).

Conclusion

Body cultures of sport and dance perform the processes of post-colonial history. Although distinctions of aesthetic value in these body cultures still persist, and although the recovery of their histories remains difficult, the movements of social dance articulate intimate and public cultural changes and exchanges. And whilst sport's more visible and commodified body cultures are in some ways limited in their social narratives, particularly by their gender specificity, their organisational histories, their mass appeal, and their accessible archives of photograph and film make them a valuable resource for postcolonial studies. Henning Eichberg's dictum, 'show me how you are running, and I can see something of the society in which you are living', is a useful one for a discipline that, in response to a pernicious imperial history as much as for reasons of taste, has been cautious in its dealings with the expressive body. But, as thinkers as different as Eichberg, C. L. R. James, and Wilson Harris have suggested, that body, in sport and in dance, is a historical and cultural body, and its 'texts' are both rich and complex.

CHAPTER 4

Film

Film is the medium most integrated within and dependent upon the practices of global capital. At the same time, though, it also remains a resolutely national medium in its descriptors, representations and consumption. Films are routinely described and assessed as representative of nationhood, despite their likely reliance upon international financing, production and distribution. The intense presence of national/local identity in a global medium makes film a particularly suggestive, and a particularly complex, part of postcolonial studies. Its potential for reaching a mass audience, and one that is not circumscribed by literacy, means that it was and is a powerful means of communicating new national identities, as with the Indian film industry after 1947. At the same time, though, the large capital investment required for film production, and the structures for distribution and marketing imperil any easy sense of film as a means of subaltern expression. Film's dependence upon substantial sources of international capital and ideologically controlled circuits of distribution means that its resources of political expression are necessarily constrained. And whilst film might consistently be interested in representing nationhood, the global exportation of that representation raises questions of audiences and their agency in creating meaning.

This chapter will consider the relationship between national and postcolonial cinemas, and the ways in which the films of these cinemas engage with key issues of postcolonialism – particularly those of history, ethnicity, diaspora and gender. The selection of case studies is particularly contentious in this field. The accessibility of video or DVD prints is even more prone to the favours and elisions of Western 'economies of value' than that of books and music. Postcolonial film-makers whose careers have developed in

America – Mira Nair and Peter Weir, for example – are far more likely to have a range of their films commercially available in the West than those who work mainly within their own national film industries. Furthermore, of the films of indigenous film-makers that are circulated in the West, questions of value and representation are sharply evident. How far that circulation is an indication of amenable, assimilable postcolonial cinema mediated by First World distributors and audiences is a pertinent question. In her pioneering academic appraisal of popular Hindi film, Rosie Thomas argued the need for an engagement with non-Western theoretical frames of genre, value and use when discussing and evaluating such cinemas (Thomas 1985: 117). Her warning still holds good, even as an apparently wider range of world film styles are available, at least in Western art-house cinemas. A study of postcolonial cinemas must acknowledge and seek to understand the specific conditions of production and reception of their films. At the same time, though, it must also seek to understand those cinemas' engagement with global film practices.

The case studies that follow will take their examples from three national cinemas – those of India, Australia and New Zealand – and from a self-defined 'diasporic' mainstream cinema. It will re-examine the meanings of postcolonialism as it is attached to the very different socio-economic conditions of production in these cinemas, as well as the generic and thematic interests that are contained in the label 'postcolonial'. Popular Indian cinema, for example, challenges the subaltern connotations of the postcolonial prefix in the very size and influence of its industry, not only in the sub-continent itself, but also in global markets that include the Middle East and the Philippines. It is also largely uninterested in issues normally associated with postcolonialism, leading some theorists of Third World film to see it as hopelessly implicated in a neocolonial depoliticising of subaltern cultures. More recent scholarship, though, has developed Roy Armes's argument that 'there exists no accepted critical methodology to handle such films', and sees a distinctive indigenous tradition at work in this cinema that need not be reactionary (Armes 1987: 65). The area is further complicated by the development of diasporic Indian film-making, whether by Indian-American directors like Mira Nair, or the makers of recent British-Asian popular films such as *East is East* (1999) and *Bend It Like Beckham* (2002). Their work necessarily negotiates a dialogue between postcolonial identity, be it 'Indian' or 'diasporic', and the demands and preconceptions of Western audiences.

National Cinema/Postcolonial Cinema

What constitutes a national cinema is a matter of dispute. One definition is that of a film industry funded, controlled and staffed within national boundaries, the products of which are intended to be consumed within those boundaries. This hardly reflects the realities of what has always been an international business (though the Indian film industry has traditionally come close to such a model). Film historians have consequently developed other definitions. These include the identification of particular stylistic and thematic traits that create a national idiom of film; a model that emphasises consumption over production, so that audiences' responses constitute films' national identities; and a sense of national cinema as a recognisably dissenting local culture set against dominant practice – films that are recognisably located outside of, and in opposition to, the conventions of Hollywood (for a summary and discussion of such definitions, see the essays in Hjort and MacKenzie 2000). All of these competing theories have in common a sense of cinema as a process of cultural engagement, definition and resistance. They are interested in the means by which film-makers and audiences can negotiate particular, localised meanings beyond what seems an increasingly homogenised global film language that has its origins in America – though how far Hollywood itself was or is a 'national' cinema is itself a point of contention.

The concept of a postcolonial national cinema requires further definition within these competing descriptions of national cinemas. As discussed in Chapter 1, the term 'postcolonial' can efface the unevenness of the developments of different national cinemas, their different generic traditions and their various audiences. If the consolidation of funding, the indigenising of production skills and the development of a mass national audience with critical knowledge of specific national film are taken as markers of a strong national cinema, significant, and perhaps surprising, divergences are evident. Indian cinema, for example, produced its first feature film in 1912, and by the 1930s had developed an industry that released over 200 films per year in indigenous languages (Rajadhyaksha and Willemen 1999: 17–21). Australia, by contrast, established a recognisably national production structure and film style only in the 1970s (see O'Regan 1996). However, this definition precludes any assessment of the content, politics or value of the films that the industry produced. Whilst Indian cinema had established itself as a powerful autonomous force in terms of production by the later phases of colonialism, the politics of that burgeoning cinema was tightly controlled by a censorship that suppressed explicit engagement with the independence movement. The censorship was maintained after independence in order to shape a cinema supportive of dominant versions of national construction and virtually silent on the most pressing and dangerous issues of that process, such as inter-religious conflict. Such a postcolonial cinema, then, apparently has none of the dissenting politics that might be expected of an emergent national industry, and it challenges its students to develop a model that can make sense of a diversity of production styles and ideological perspectives.

Roy Armes's *Third World Film Making and the West* (1987) was perhaps the first extended study to negotiate these conflicts of description and value. Armes recognises that some postcolonial cinemas meet the economic, distributive and even aesthetic definitions of a new national cinema, but can also 'fail' to be ideologically postcolonial, avoiding difficult political and cultural issues. 'Rooted in decades of low-budget artisanal production', he writes of Indian cinema, '[its films] may not be national in any true cultural sense, but they are shaped regardless of Western fashion and are largely free to adopt their own rhythms of time and to follow their own predilections in terms of narrative construction' (Armes 1987: 103–4). What that 'true cultural sense' means is the nub of the problem, of course. Whilst he acknowledges the popular cultural force of cinemas like the vast Indian industries, the focus of Armes's work is largely the traditions of film-making that confront and replace what he terms 'petty [sic] bourgeois national cinemas' failures' in constructing a formally, but not politically, independent film tradition. For Armes, the 'true' postcolonial cinema needs 'to look directly and critically at contemporary society', and he finds its most persuasive advocates in a generation of film-makers and theorists that emerged in postcolonial nations in the 1960s and 1970s (Armes 1987: 71). This 'Third Cinema' movement was the first to absorb the theoretical perspectives of radical thinkers like Frantz Fanon, and it is its version of postcolonial film, and its refinements such as Hamid Naficy's notion of 'accented cinema', that has been most influential in academic discussions of the area (Naficy 2001).

In his essay 'Towards a Critical Theory of Third World Films' (1989), Teshome H. Gabriel provides a useful summary of the analytical and polemical aspects of 'Third Cinema'. Borrowing a model of Third World development from Frantz Fanon and from Fernando Solanas and Octavio Getino's 1969 manifesto 'Towards a Third Cinema', Gabriel proposes three phases in the history of postcolonial cinema. The first is a period of 'unqualified assimilation' of a Hollywood model, and the production of films 'with escapist themes of romance, musicals, comedy, etc' (Gabriel 1989: 31–5). The second phase is a period of indigenisation, both of production and content, as film-makers engage with particular issues of culture and history that mark the various stages and environments of postcolonial experience. Gabriel's final stage, which he argues that postcolonial cinema is still struggling to achieve, is a 'combative phase' in which a 'cinema of mass participation' operates as an ideological tool drawing upon specific oral and folk traditions to create a new 'Third Cinema', a truly postcolonial world-view and narrative language unbeholden to the aesthetics or economics of dominant global film production.

This historical model is suggestive in several ways. It insists upon the political meaning of all types of postcolonial cinema, though it sees film industries not consciously engaged with that politics as collaborating with colonial processes. Much of Indian film-making, for example, by this definition, remains locked into that 'first phase' of the model. His definition of a second phase presents a cinema in transition, a state that poses as many dangers as it does possibilities. It is in this stage that indigenous film-makers can begin to represent local subject-matter and the overt concerns of postcolonial struggles. At the same time, though, they have to negotiate with the untransformed systems of production and distribution that largely control global cinema. That negotiation can lead to them courting success in markets foreign, and ultimately antipathetic, to their vision. He writes pointedly of the 'exploitative nature of some Third World film-makers who peddle Third World poverty and misery at festival sites in Europe and North America and do not approach their craft as a tool of social transformation' (32). His third stage bears the weight of the polemical demand for film as agency. 'The living expression of the nation is the moving consciousness of the whole people', Fanon wrote, and Gabriel's culminating phase of postcolonial cinema is a film-making that is expressive of just such a popular transformation, 'a cinema of mass participation', as he calls it (Fanon 1967: 165; Gabriel 1989: 33). How far such a cinema is achievable and what its relationship might be to an already existing mass spectatorship, especially in a place like India, remain difficult questions.

'Third Cinema' theory returns to the debates about cultural representation, agency and interpretation that were rehearsed in Chapter 1. Gabriel, like Armes before him, concentrates his discussion of postcolonial film on a range of radical independent cinemas that are explicit in their political critiques of colonialism and its legacies. In doing so, he relegates popular genres such as romance and melodrama to what he defines as a 'first stage' of postcolonial cinema, one shaped and ideologically compromised by colonial models. The purpose of this discrimination is to publicise and celebrate these hidden cinemas of resistance. However, such an argument also risks a restrictive structure of value that is defined by political position alone, and, more crucially, implicitly limits any sense of already-active interpretative strategies of popular cinemas' audiences. The failure of 'Third Cinema' theory to address thoroughly questions of audiences and what they do with films at particular moments in particular places leaves it open to criticisms of the very formalism that it deplores and which defines the films that are relegated to the 'first phase'. Furthermore, as Roy Armes acknowledges, the 'Third Cinema' and 'Nuovo Cinema' movements were, in formal terms at least, less independent of First World models than those, like Bombay cinema, that were economically and culturally independent of Western intervention. '[O]ne of the paradoxes of the Third World situation,' he argues, 'is that any cultural production that wishes to . . . move beyond the constraints of a production exercising a purely entertainment function in a constricted domestic market – must at the same time be influenced by yet other foreign models' (310).

The work of the Indian sociologist Ashis Nandy and the American anthropologist Sara Dickey provides a helpful counterargument to those of 'Third Cinema'. Nandy's essays on Hindi popular cinema have sought to challenge an Indian intellectual tendency, most vividly defined by Chidanada Das Gupta's *The Painted Face* (1991), that dismisses such films as degraded relics of pre-modern popular traditions. Against this, Nandy argues that they actually present a 'slum's eye view of politics' (Nandy 1998: 1). Far from being a relic, popular cinema embodies the processes of wider history, though in ways which challenge the discourses and assumptions of a dominant national or Western historiography. 'The popular film', writes Nandy, '*is* low-brow, modernizing India in all its complexity, sophistry, naiveté and vulgarity' (7). Despite the apparently apolitical narratives and their provenance in the fiercely capitalist film industries of Bombay and Madras, the meanings of popular film are ultimately negotiated with its audiences in their predicaments and through their pleasures. In her illuminating study of southern Indian film audiences and their reception of popular film, Sara Dickey describes an indigenous theory and aesthetic. The audiences in Madurai, which form a significant proportion of the city's poorer population, project a self-consciousness of their social and personal predicaments through a demand for particular genres and narratives. '[U]rban poor Tamils', she argues, 'reject movies that are too realistic, that allow too little play of the imagination', but require narratives that engage with their circumstances through fantasy and through cinematic pleasure (Dickey 1993: 174). The escape of the film is not an escape from reality, but an entry into a set of known narrative codes. Far from this leading to a passive consumption of dominant ideologies, Dickey notes the capacities of audiences for the sceptical appraisal of meanings and morals that breach their own interpretative expectations. Popular cinema cannot afford to ignore or despise this capacity for active response; as Ashis Nandy argues, 'the Indian commercial cinema, to be commercially viable, must try to span the host of cultural diversities and epochs the society lives with and that effort has a logic of its own' (Nandy 1998: 1). That logic is not one of 'Third Cinema' style education and transformation. Rather, it is one grounded in fantasy and pleasure, which is also engaged, however indirectly, with the urgent dilemmas of its audiences – and on their terms. As Western film studies has discovered through its engagement with classic Holly-wood cinema, the totalising ambitions of such an industry are challenged by anxieties within its narratives and by the changing contexts of its reception. Nandy's work on Hindi film is located in just these contradictions and changes.

Popular cinema, Nandy argues, is an integral part of what he terms, after Jai Sen, 'the unintended city', the slum that 'was never a part of the formal "master plan"', but was always and remains implicit in it (2). The slum audience was, necessarily, the primary audience of a mass cinema in India. To attract and maintain that audience, popular cinema was structured to engage with its pre-dicaments and aspirations, though through fantasy rather than realism, melodrama rather than polemic, both in the films them-selves and in the architecture of the cinemas in which they are viewed. The weakness of 'Third Cinema' theory, both as a set of analytical tools and as an ideological project, lies in its inattention to just these processes. It tends to underestimate the flexibility of popular forms for exploring (covertly and ambivalently) difficult political and social issues in dialogue with their audiences, and, by contrast, to overestimate the effectiveness of film-makers who express pre-established 'postcolonial positions'. This risks an uneasy conflation of the postcolonial film-maker as representative of an ideological vanguard, and as a creator of an undefined 'cinema of mass participation' without any relationship to an already-existing popular cinema. A critical predilection for what Hamid Naficy has called 'accented' and 'exilic' film-making also risks validating those films that meet the ideological criteria of the Third Cinema even as its spectatorship excludes the 'slum's eye view' that it ostensibly courts. The limited circulation of Third Cinema via the 'nontheatrical entry points for infiltrating the system', which Naficy defines as, among others, universities, film festivals, museums and prisons, suggests the limitations on style and politics imposed on postcolonial culture by distribution practices, but also the limitations of a critical practice that ignores popular film and popular audiences (Naficy 2001: 62).

Ashis Nandy, Teshome Gabriel and Hamid Naficy present instructively divergent examples of critical practices in postcolonial film studies. The latter pair define models of analysis and agency that draw their values and strategies from the decolonising period. They are generally hostile to mass cinema's presence in postcolonial contexts, and look to emergent cinemas to transform the depoliticised aesthetic that it purveys. Third Cinema aspires to a self-realised postcolonial film practice defined within local traditions of narrative and representation, and disregards the economic and aesthetic demands of the West. Nandy's work offers a different approach. Recognising that Third Cinema practices can present an idealised purity of aspiration that, in practice, is itself endebted to First World models (albeit avant-garde models) and their academic and metropolitan provenances, Nandy argues for the importance of mass cinema in postcolonial cultural studies. The consumption of popular cinema, he argues, is not a passive reception of dominant ideology, but an active negotiation of identity and response, though a negotiation inevitably limited by ideological, economic and cultural forces. For the purposes of postcolonial studies, the debate between these two versions of cinema offers a model of different cinematic and viewing practices in tension and dialogue, and a means to study a range of films. To 'read' Indian film, for example, it becomes necessary to think about both art cinema and popular cinema, and to see both of them as influencing new diasporic Indian formations. Similarly, the problems of including the national cinemas of Australia and New Zealand within a model of 'Third Cinema' suggest the need to develop that model to discuss those films' necessary engagement with European and American systems of production and reception, whilst exploring their local meanings within that global currency.

Case Study One: India, Realism and the Avant Garde

Sara Dickey's conclusion that poor Indians 'reject movies that are too realistic' suggests that realistic explorations of their poverty are made for other audiences. The radical Bengali director Mrinal Sen tells of a village that 'seeks political change but rejects political entertainment', electing a communist representative but preferring a cinema of fantasy to films that apparently represent contemporary social conditions (Sen 2002: 161). 'When I make these films', Sen claims, 'I make films about certain people, but not necessarily for them. I make the films for the people who understand my films' (212). Such a position obviously poses political questions, both about the structure of the relationship of film, audience and subject, and about the interpretative authority of the film-maker within this structure. They are questions that can be discussed through two films that seek to address issues of social distress and empowerment in India. Sen's *Ākāler Sandhāney* (1980) and Mira Nair's *Salaam Bombay!* (1988) present contrasting strategies for negotiating the dilemmas of representation, narrative and audience.

Ākāler Sandhāney (*In Search of Famine*) is itself an analysis of the potential pitfalls of 'Third Cinema', even as it pursues some of that movement's objectives. It tells the story of a radical film-director who travels from Calcutta to a Bengali village to make a film – also called *Ākāler Sandhāney* – about the effects of the catastrophic man-made famine in the area in 1943. Using a style influenced by the French 'nouvelle vague', techniques that Sen himself describes as 'non-narrative, a calculated mixture of the fictional and the documentary', the film deconstructs the apparent radicalism of the director as he comes into ignorant conflict with the place (Sen and Bandyopadhyay 1983: v). His desire to speak for the village, his assumptions about the meanings of its history and its relationship to the present, and the realist cinematic method that he employs are all ruthlessly exposed as the project collapses. The director (he is given no name) has an intellectual grasp of the history that he is attempting to represent, but he is unaware of the politics of his own dictatorial behaviour as he attempts to control the people when they respond to the film-making. He is also insensitive to the economic and cultural impact of the presence of the film crew, as prices of essential goods rise (a villager comments, 'they came to take pictures of a famine and sparked off another famine') (Sen and Bandyopadhyay 1983: 47). His attempt to persuade two village women to play the part of a prostitute in the film is crassly insensitive to local values, and causes disruption in the community, even as the revival of the memory of famine re-emphasises some villagers' exploitation of it years ago to buy land cheaply. As relations between urban radicals and conservative villagers deteriorate, the politics of such 'committed' film-making is revealed as a self-regarding indulgence that, in its unthinking exploitation of the rural community, replicates the very politics that the director's film is supposed to expose. The fictional film is not completed, and the crew returns to the city to construct the famine in the studio – a retreat from the actual historical and social processes to which they were committed to the fabrication of reality which is characteristic of reactionary 'conventional' cinema. The village schoolteacher, himself from Calcutta, has what passes for the last word. 'There's a gap of misunderstanding. Two worlds. You and we . . . These people with their ignorance, superstition, greed and selfishness . . . But you're not innocent either . . . you've tried to impose yourselves on them. How long can they suffer?' (78)

Sen's film is not just a satire upon the pretensions of a certain style of bourgeois political film-making. The link between the title of the actual film and the fictional film requires the audience, in Brechtian fashion, to consider Sen's and its own implication in the difficult politics of representation. The story of the failure of the film-makers to achieve a meaningful relationship with the villagers, and the reasons for that failure – political and aesthetic – have relevance to Sen's own commitments as a Marxist director. As Suranjan Ganguly has argued, 'the question he poses to the film-maker in *Ākāler Sandhāney* becomes a form of auto-critique: Is Sen the Marxist really a bourgeois filmmaker?' (Ganguly 2000: 57). The strategy of Sen's film shows how he is distancing himself from what he sees as the flawed realist assumptions of his fictional director. It constantly emphasises the constructedness of cinema and its awareness of the political dangers of presenting films' illusions as unmediated reality – something displayed in some of the villagers' absorption in the scenes that they see enacted. What Samik Bandyopadhyay calls Sen's sense of 'cinema as a mythmaking technology masquerading as a mirror of reality' has to be countered by what Sen himself describes as the film's 'confession of our incapacities' (Sen and Bandyopadhyay 1983: vi, vii).

At the same time, though, this employment of the deconstructive practices of a European avant garde sets its own political problems. It provides the means to analyse the failures of a tradition which, as Ganguly argues, is that of the dominant art cinema of India inaugurated by its most celebrated director, Satyajit Ray. However, it does little to suggest a means of reconstructing a viable cinematic practice that would allow the rural Indian subaltern to speak. Dismissing popular cinema as hopelessly implicated in a dominant class's structure of illusion, in the manner of Third Cinema's first stage, Sen shares the paralysis of his fictional director, as he admits himself. Their difference lies only in his capacity to analyse that paralysis politically. Sen can make the film about the political failure of film, but is still 'in search' of the means of addressing the terrible realities of modern Indian history and dispossession in ways which can form a dialogue with their most immediate sufferers. The danger of the knowledge of the means of that failure is that film retreats from the very aspirations that it, like Third Cinema, sets itself. Ganguly identifies in *Ākāler Sandhāney* and its cinematic dialogue with Ray a sense 'that films constantly borrow from, refer to and engage in critiques of each other, that they have less to do with life and almost everything to do with film as film' (67). It is a formalism that comes close to completely denying the social agency of cinema except as a purveyor of illusory comforts within a repressive ideology. In an interview, Sen comments despairingly about 'an audience which votes for a man who will be fighting for change, for land reform, but at the same time will flock to a film which accents a mistrust in technology and faith in miracles' (Sen 2002: 161). But, it might also be argued, such a knowledge renders its practice as politically impotent as the illusion that it apparently critiques, save perhaps as a critical tool to examine other films. Films such as Mira Nair's *Salaam Bombay!*, one of Indian cinema's most successful productions in Britain and America.

Salaam Bombay! (1988) is a drama-documentary about the life of a street child. Using mainly amateur actors, it seeks to present a narrative of vulnerability and innocence in inevitable and doomed conflict with the forces of adult irresponsibility and an insensitive social authority. Krishna, the deserted child, provides an honest appraisal of his social predicament that challenges the evasions and brutalities of the adults that seek to control and exploit him. The film's success in the West was achieved through its vivid and apparently 'authentic' portrayal of marginal lives in the slums of Bombay, particularly through the performance of Shafiq Syed in the central role. Its spare narrative and cinéma vérité techniques of shot and editing indicate its allegiances to social realist traditions, and look back to Nair's sociological training and grounding in American documentary-making that had shaped her earlier shorts *Jama Masjid Street Journal* (1979), *So Far From India* (1983), *India Cabaret* (1985), and *Children of Desired Sex* (1987). *India Cabaret* is referred to by Arjun Appadurai as an example of his projected discipline of a 'transnational anthropology' that recognised the development of a 'deterritorialized' modernity, and its demands upon new formal methods of transcribing and exploring the 'ethnoscapes' of fluid cultural identities (see Appadurai 1991). But her later film came under sustained attack from Indian critics who saw in it that calculated display of Third World distress that Tshome Gabriel identifies in the second phase of his model of Third World film, and the politically unexamined realism that Mrinal Sen had debated eight years before. For these critics, as Hamid Naficy notes, 'the film's textual and class politics are such that they sentimentalize, romanticize, homogenize and universalize the lives of Indian subalterns without analyzing the underlying causes and the specific power relations that perpetuate their poverty, prostitution, homelessness, drug addiction, and drug dealing' (Naficy 2001: 68).

Nair's public statements on the film tend to support Naficy's perception of a style of film-making being imposed upon its subjects without any acknowledgement of the political implications of such an imposition – precisely the predicament portrayed in *Ākāler Sandhāney*. For example, she stresses her struggles to make the street children 'play themselves'. 'One of the main problems . . . with the children', the liner notes to the British video release reports, 'was their tendency to copy the acting styles of mainstream Indian film stars', and strategies were developed to wean them from this imitation. 'It was impressed on them', Nair says, 'that subtlety is the essence, because the camera is capable of capturing every fleeting nuance of feeling and expression. So, slowly, "acting" became a bad word with our children'. There is little sense here of the consequences of the cultural negotiation and redefinition that are taking place. However, despite such apparently depoliticised appeals to the aesthetics of Western realism, the film itself works quite differently, and in ways that restore some sense of the cultural politics of performance and style that is missing in Nair's reported comments on her approach. The strengths of *Salaam Bombay!* lie, in part, in its implication in the very styles and strategies of popular Indian film performance that are apparently forsworn by Nair in favour of Western drama-documentary naturalism. For example, the professional actor Nana Patekar is cast as the villainous pimp, Baba, and never entirely separates himself from the conventional villain-type of Hindi cinema. As if to point this up, popular Hindi film is constantly alluded to as part of the diegetic content of the realist narrative. Dance sequences, staples of Hindi melodrama, make frequent, if fragmentary, appearances in the film, as the children dance to the radio and in the cinema. Likewise, song is integrated into the action when the characters sing relevant snatches of Hindi favourites. In this way, the excision of indigenous popular acting is by no means complete, and the film gains from an understated hybridity of performance styles which, unlike Sen's references to Godard and Satyajit Ray, locate the film in the very popular traditions that it apparently rejects.

The narrative of *Salaam Bombay!* is also a hybrid of Western realism and Hindi popular conventions. Whilst its spare, fragmentary sequencing recalls the European and American documentary influences that Nair acknowledges – the French film-makers Chris Marker and Jean Rouch, and D. A. Pennebaker – the plot itself is a staple of Hindi cinema: a child separated from his family, and driven, against his will, into criminality. It is a storyline immediately recognisable from a tradition that goes back to such classics as

Kismet (1943), a film that Ashish Rajadhyaksha and Paul Willemen describe as 'an early example of a pre-Partition "lost and found" movie rehearsing the familiar pre-capitalist fairy-tale motif of members of a family who are separated by fate or villainy and eventually are "recognised" and reunited' (Rajadhyaksha and Willemen 1999: 298). Krishna's attempts to contact and return to his mother form the emotional core of the film, along with his attempts to reconstruct family in the Bombay slums with the sister-figure Sweet Sixteen and the dealer-addict Chillum. As Ashis Nandy has argued, the rendering of the slum as an 'entity that territorializes the transition from the village to the city' is a characteristic device of popular Hindi cinema (Nandy 1998: 5–6). The evocation of 'the remembered village and the [density] of stranger-neighbours, with the former often providing a frame to cope with the latter', is implicit in many scenes here (7). For example, Krishna attempts to comfort Sweet Sixteen with a gift of a chicken, and tries to send a letter to his mother about his urban 'renaming', as the 'traditional' Krishna becomes the urban child-labourer Chaipau.

The closures – narrative and political – of the *Kismet* tradition of Hindi cinema are rejected, however. There is no reunion of Krishna and his mother, and no reintegration within social stability. In ways that look forward to the thoroughgoing critique of traditional Indian family structures in her American film *Mississippi Masala* (1991), Nair emphasises the divisive violence within family. Krishna, disturbingly in a film tradition rooted in matriarchal power, has been driven from his home by his mother until he has paid a debt to his abusive older brother. Chillum's outburst, 'Forget them all. Mothers, fathers, brothers, sisters, friends . . . lovers . . . Useless bloody lot', is the ambivalent centre of the film – a bleak articulation of the city's dismemberment of rural-derived kinship structures. The 'remembered village' remains a desperate fantasy as Krishna loses his bearings, even as he attempts to retain contact with and return to his family. He is inevitably drawn into the bleak alternative social structures of the urban criminal gang and the feared state institutions of reform – the latter a dystopic children's community that is the antithesis of the ideal village. A magical rescue, the only means of resolving Krishna's predicament, is

precluded by the realist mode of the film. But it hovers as a
narrative possibility through the fantasies of Krishna himself. This
ardent cinema-goer has absorbed that medium's desire for the
resolutions of a rural home, even as he, like Hindi film itself,
conducts on grossly unequal terms what Ashis Nandy terms 'a
dialogue with the compacted heterogeneity of urban-industrial
India' (Nandy 1998: 11).

The reception of *Salaam Bombay!* is indicative of the divisions
and contests of authority and value that frame postcolonial
studies. Its popularity in the West was, arguably, achieved
through an adept mixture of documentary techniques, and a
rather restrained authenticity that conformed to, rather than
challenged, the repertoire of images of 'Indianness'. As Rajadhyaksha and Willemen point out, there had been a far more brutal
picture of Bombay slum-life in Rabindra Dharmaj's *Chakra* (1980),
a film that remains little known in the West (Rajadhyaksha and
Willemen 1999: 445). Rajadhyaksha and Willemen's comment on
the 'idealised' India of Nair's film, an idealism disguised as
authenticity, is indicative of the second stage of Gabriel's model
which sees 'approved' versions of postcolonial film allowed
representative status in the West, even as the economics and
politics of that acceptance are elided by an appeal to what Trinh T.
Minh-ha terms 'the difference expected' (Rajadhyaksha and
Willemen 1999: 445; Minh-ha 1989: 135). Certainly *Salaam Bombay!*'s success allowed Nair the opportunities to make *Mississippi
Masala*, a far more schematic romance of displacement and hybrid
relationships that is set in America. Yet the earlier film's interest
can be said to be less in its 'realism', and much more in its
mingling of those conventions and the codes of Indian popular
film, features that Nair would return to explicitly in the Bolly-
wood-influenced *Monsoon Wedding* (2001).

Case Study Two: Indian Popular Film –
Dilwale Dulhania Le Jayenge and *Monsoon Wedding*

The Hindi film industry has traditionally been culturally conservative and insular, shaping its narratives within its national
borders and national concerns, even as it grew as a global industry

through the exportation of its products. Because of this, films dealing with the Indian diaspora tended to be produced by and seen as part of other national cinemas – the British-set social comedies *Bhaji on the Beach* (1993), *East is East* and *Bend It Like Beckham* are examples of this. Recently, however, that diaspora has become an Indian subject, too, most successfully in Aditya Chopra's *Dilwale Dulhania Le Jayenge* (*DDLJ*) (*The Bold Heart Wins the Bride*) (1995), which became the top-grossing Hindi film of all time, running continuously for six years in one Bombay cinema, and – remarkably for a Hindi film – unreleased on video until seven years after its first cinema appearance. This tale of romance thwarted by conflicts of modernity and tradition, and restored by a negotiation between those forces, was Chopra's first film. However, as the son of Yash Chopra, one of Indian cinema's most popular directors, Aditya defines in *DDLJ* a generational development of cinematic strategies to deal with new diasporic social shifts and their effects upon family and gender identities.

DDLJ begins in London, and, in the first third, focuses upon the family of the petrol-stationer owner, Chaudbury Baldev Singh, a man who longs to return to the Punjab. His means of doing so are effected by the arranged marriage of his elder daughter, Simran, to the son of a Punjabi friend. Before this takes place, he grants her wish to take a month's holiday in Europe, where she meets and falls in love with Raj, the son of a wealthy Punjabi expatriate. The final third of the film follows Singh's permanent return to his homeland, Simran's reluctant journey to her boorish fiancé's family, and Raj's inventive rescue of her from a loveless marriage. Whilst the film maintains the tonal variety of the classic Hindi film, and deploys all the popular conventions of its genre – song, melodrama, lavish action – what is intriguing for postcolonial studies is its engagement with diaspora, and its means of resolving the cultural tensions that such movement provokes.

The film begins with Baldev's voice-over stating the predicament of exile and identity: 'Everyday the street asks me my name. Chaudbury Baldev Singh? Who are you? Where are you from? Why are you here?' His conclusion is that he is, like the pigeons that he feeds, 'shackled to my bread. But someday I'll surely go to my land'. Baldev's longing for home and his maintenance of its traditions (he says after the announcement of his daughter's marriage, 'I'm not a failure. In the heart of London, I've kept India alive') are set against two versions of diasporic modernity. One is his daughter's educated desire for experience and travel in Europe, the other is the initial representation of Raj as a worthless and irritatingly immature product of a father whose material success has blinded him to the cultural possibilities of the West. Raj's father celebrates his son's expensive academic failure as a family tradition, whilst failing to protect his son from its decadence (Raj's first encounter with Baldev is when he tries to buy alcohol from his shop). The film's presentation of material wealth is ambiguous. Rachel Dwyer has argued for the importance of 'a new middle class, emerging from the lower middle classes in metropolitan centres such as Bombay [which is] actively producing and consuming a new public culture', of which *DDLJ* is a part (Dwyer 2000: 1). Certainly, this film relishes a careless and conspicuous consumption of travel, cars and clothes in its European sections, and does not seek to undermine that materialism in the opulent traditional scenes of the final sequences. Wealth is an unexamined given, part of the glamour that the genre relishes in its production values. In other ways, though, the film's narrative charts a development away from consumption and privileged mobility to an interest in the meanings of family, romance and place.

The problem that the film sets itself is that of effecting reconciliation between the traditional values embodied by Baldev and the validity of a modernity represented by the romantic love of Raj and Simran. This is achieved by a critique of archaic and absurd aspects of patriarchal tradition, and a simultaneous reassertion of the fundamental guiding principles of that tradition within an apparently diasporic context. Family is the key, because it shows itself capable of adaptation, particularly to the demands of romance, whilst maintaining a coherence of moral principle. This is reflected in formal and narrative structures in the film, particularly the parallel parent–child dialogues. Both Raj's father and Simran's mother operate as crucially ambiguous forces here. In key episodes, both appear to work outside their social and ideological functions. At the point at which Raj despairs of his love for Simran because of the cultural force of the arranged marriage, his father tells him 'The bride goes to the man who brings her home', encouraging him to stop the wedding. Likewise, Simran's mother provides an explicit critique of traditional women's roles. '[A]t every step', she tells Simran, 'sometimes as daughter, sometimes as sister, sometimes as wife . . . I went on sacrificing my own happiness', and goes on first to demand that sacrifice, then to encourage her daughter to elope in order to escape it. Both characters, however, are also instrumental in the film's assertion of the need for a reformed tradition, rather than a radical modernity, through their response to the changing Raj.

Raj's journey to the Punjab marks the key point of change in the film, as the entertaining, but aimless, tourism of the central European section becomes a journey of salvation and homecoming. In the one serious moment of the former, where Raj pretends to Simran that he has slept with her when she was drunk, he goes on to tell her, 'I'm not scum . . . I'm Hindustani. And I know what honour means for the Hindustani woman'. This Hindustani-ness becomes prominent in the final phase of the film, where the adolescent silliness of the character is shaped into a purposeful charm and strategy, and his diasporic shiftlessness is formed into a rooted Indian manhood that gains respect from all. Raj changes from representing Western consumer to re-articulating traditional values of family and honour. So, whilst his father and Simran's mother encourage a breach of those traditions through an elopement, Raj rejects this means of resolving the film's central dilemma. 'You can only run from strangers', he says. 'From the ones we call our own where could we run away to?' His insistence that he marries Simran through traditional processes – 'I haven't come here to steal you', he tells her, 'I might have been born in England. But I am Hindustani. I've come to take you back as my bride' – requires his father and prospective mother-in-law to make their own resolutions of tradition and modernity through their responses to his dilemma. The new Raj is an articulator of wisdom to his elders, as well as a figure that discovers traditional cultural identity within his own apparently diasporic condition, a reversal of generational dynamics that yet confirms the structures of family and gender in which those dynamics are formed.

Rachel Dwyer, in her study of sexuality and romance in modern India, reads films like *Dilwale Dulhania Le Jayenge* as part of a wider cultural project to 'revive a form of the feudal family romance in a new, stylish, yet unmistakably Hindu, patriarchal structure which . . . is connected to their contribution to the resurgence of the politics of Hindutva in the 1980s and 1990s' (Dwyer 2000: 100). Raj simultaneously rescues Simran from the consequences of a thoughtless application of tradition, and reshapes that tradition to be one that is able to compass diasporic change and morally aware individualism, what Rajadhyaksha and Willemen call 'a feudal patriarchy where young people may aspire to a kind of watered-down version of modern subjectivity represented in consumerist terms before "returning to the fold" ' (Rajadhyaksha and Willemen 1999: 528). Certainly, the unresolved tensions of the narrative concern the female characters. Simran's educated, critical, but respectful perspective on Hindu tradition is defused as the film develops, even as her mother's articulation of their predicament develops to her statement '[the Indian woman] is born to be sacrificed for their [sic] men. For their women, men will never make sacrifices'. Raj's revival of tradition is paralleled by Simran's retreat to passivity, as the sexual discourse of the earlier European dance/fantasy sequences, in which she can sing 'I feel like making love to you', is replaced by an increasing tendency to weeping and physical collapse. 'Now Simran isn't your problem', Raj tells her mother, '[s]he's my headache', a statement indicative of the transformation of a romance initiated in what Dwyer terms the 'liminal spaces of leisure, travel/tourism and nature' being formalised and regularised as patriarchal duty in the family domain of the Punjab (Dwyer 2000: 13).

It is instructive to set the debates of *Dilwale Dulhania Le Jayenge* beside those of Mira Nair's *Monsoon Wedding*, a film that tackles similar issues of diaspora and gender roles from a self-consciously 'diasporic' perspective. Unlike *Salaam Bombay!* and *Mississippi Masala*, *Monsoon Wedding* is explicit in its debts to Hindi popular film, engaging in a debate with neo-romance films like *DDLJ*, and acknowledging the fashion for Bollywood films that marked the art-film end of the British cinema in the late 1990s (the video release contains advertisements for a Channel 4 Bollywood season, and

Andrew Lloyd Webber's musical *Bombay Dreams*). Nair's film is concerned to achieve a balance between Indian popular styles and the narrative realism customary in British-American film. Hand-held camera shots create a cinéma vérité feel that recalls *Salaam Bombay!*, whilst knowing stylistic references (the Bollywood breeze in stars' hair at emotional moments, for example) reclaim the film for Indian romance. Like *DDLJ*, *Monsoon Wedding* is interested in a negotiation between modernity and tradition. As in the earlier film, the emotional focus is upon an arranged marriage and its effect upon participants experienced in Westernised life-styles – the bride-to-be returns briefly to a married lover on the eve of her engagement, and the groom is resident in the USA. The solution to this dilemma is significantly different from Nair's earlier treatment of a comparable cultural-ethical dilemma in *Mississippi Masala*, and from that of the Hindi films to which the film is stylistically closer. Whilst *Mississippi Masala* suggested the ne-cessity for the abandonment of family for the success of inter-cultural romance, the later film, superficially like *DDLJ*, restores the family as a structure capable of integrating modernity whilst reaffirming traditional values. However, the dynamics of this accommodation are different, and their implications are as much concerned with the projected audience of the film as they are with the Delhi context that it evokes.

Like *Dilwale Dulhania Le Jayenge*, Nair's film devolves the moral and cultural decision about marriage and its social codes from the female protagonist to the initially passive male suitor as the relation-ship is imperilled by transgressions of sexual custom. The nature of these challenges, like the processes of their resolution, is very different, however. In *DDLJ*, Raj has to negotiate a way to intervene in an already-arranged marriage; in *Monsoon Wedding*, Hemant has to deal with the disruption of his own arranged marriage by the catastrophic infidelity of the bride-to-be on the night before the betrothal. In the former case, the male protagonist wins through by effectively restating traditional values of family, going through a process of the social courtship of his prospective relatives, defining his masculine responsibility, particularly to Simran's mother, and, in a climactic scene, rhetorically deferring to Baldev's decision. *Monsoon Wedding*'s transgression is altogether unthinkable in the moral

world of neoconservative Hindi film – in *DDLJ*, Raj affirms in Europe
the primacy of female sexual honour, and it is part of the innovative
ironies of the film that it is the 'traditional' fiancé who announces to
Raj's father his intention to be unfaithful to his future wife. The one
moment of Simran's sexual self-expression is the song-fantasy scene
in Switzerland, but, significantly, that elicits Raj's first expression of
Hindustani seriousness, and from then on Simran's sexuality is
clearly increasingly (self-)constrained. Anupama Chopra states that
the film suggests that the 'great struggles of redefinition' it alludes to
'of Indianness, of individual selves, of the nation-state – can and will
be easily resolved if women are properly controlled, if their sexuality
is constrained'. 'The paradox', she continues, 'is that Indian women
are now more unwilling than ever to be controlled or constrained,'
and this also seems to be the paradox that Nair makes the narrative
crux of *Monsoon Wedding* (Chopra 2002: 87). The sexual and cultural
politics of Nair's resolution of that predicament are not straightforward, however.

Aditi's resistance to the arranged marriage takes the form of her
return to the affair with one of the film's figures of Indian
modernity, the television presenter, Vikram, who hosts talk-shows
on globalism and telephone sex. However, the police's interruption
of their monsoon lovemaking in his 4x4 exposes his 'traditional'
male responses of anxiety about his social position and his dependence upon marriage – he deserts Aditi to call his wife. Aditi's
confession of the infidelity to her prospective husband the following day allows him to render the apparently 'archaic' or residual
form of arranged marriage 'emergent' in its capacity to encompass
the very anxieties that Chopra argues that *DDLJ* avoids. After
righteous indignation, he makes the following speech:

> I really appreciate you telling me about Vikram. That honesty means a
> lot to me. I know it's a risk but what marriage isn't a risk? Or whether
> our parents introduce us or we meet in a club what difference does it
> make? I know we can put this behind us . . . I believe this can work. I
> believe we can be happy.

Here the Houston-based Hemant effaces the division between
tradition and modernity, arguing both the randomness of 'modern'

romantic choice, and the flexibility of the apparent strictures of arranged marriages. If Raj in *DDLJ* finesses romantic chance into the pre-ordination of tradition by refusing the option of elopement, so, in *Monsoon Wedding*, Hemant renders that tradition itself potentially romantic by renouncing its other side, the stigmatising of the 'unchaste' bride. The reintegration of community in the final dance – another of Nair's nods to Hindi narrative style – then becomes an affirmation of the capacity of family and culture to negotiate the pressures of diaspora and modernity.

Dilwale Dulhania Le Jayenge and *Monsoon Wedding* can be read together as a popular cinematic dialogue concerning the conflict of tradition and modernity as it develops through pressures upon female sexuality. Both the Indian Hindi and the diasporic Hindi film reach a similar, apparently optimistic, conclusion about the capacity of Indianness to survive physical and ideological distancing. In other ways, though, they suggest the different audience cultures that they are aimed at. *Monsoon Wedding* significantly revises the presentation of family in Nair's first American film, *Mississippi Masala*, in which the Ugandan-Asian emigrée Mina has to leave her parents in order to continue her relationship with her African-American lover. *Monsoon Wedding*, reflecting the art-house popularity of 1990s Bollywood cinema in Britain and America, is able to retain and celebrate a family reintegrating its diaspora into India. The emphatic modernities of that family, however, resist any appeal to a residual cultural stability. The Delhi that is portrayed is affluent and sophisticated, and mobile telephones are everywhere. *DDLJ*, as we have seen, also borrows from the world-view and material concerns of the emergent Indian metropolitan middle class. As Anupama Chopra suggests, films like *DDLJ* and the earlier romance *Hum Aapke Hain Kaun* (1994) shifted popular cinema away from a preoccupation with violent melodrama by reshaping the social constituency of its audiences – in part, by raising ticket prices in new, high-quality cinemas (Chopra 2002: 13). Nevertheless, such a limited, if growing, audience could not sustain *DDLJ*'s success. Aditya Chopra was also careful to appeal to provincial values – the family returns to the Punjab, not to Delhi or Bombay – and to the experiences of diasporic audiences. Unlike *Monsoon Wedding*, the families in *DDLJ* embody explicit ethical and traditional values, rather than representing a network of individual contacts, and the romantic narrative is bent to meet the demands of those values rather than vice versa. In *Monsoon Wedding*, Hemant's relationship-speak is much closer to the language and psychology of contemporary Hollywood romance, and is foreign to the world-view of *DDLJ*, in which, by the end, it is tradition and the social relationships, not an individual relationship, that bear the cultural meaning of the film.

Case Study Three: Australasian Film in the 1990s

The film industries of Australia and New Zealand are young and small. Unlike that of India, they only began to have a significant national and international presence in the 1970s and 1980s, and, again unlike India, they retain only a small market share of their national audiences. Even with two significant successes in *The Adventures of Priscilla Queen of the Desert* and *Muriel's Wedding*, Australian films' box office share was only 10 per cent in 1994, and the huge success of *Once Were Warriors* (1994) lifted New Zealand cinema's home share from 1 per cent to 7 per cent in the same year (Couling and Grummitt 1998: 7, 59). The traditional dominance of Hollywood cinema meant that the dynamics of an emergent national/postcolonial cinema in these countries was very different to that of India. There, the effective dominance of an indigenous industry, albeit one developed under colonialism, produced distinct performance styles and narratives that, at an early stage, had incorporated elements of traditional cultures, and were consequently resistant to any wholesale importation of Hollywood genres and methods. In Australia and New Zealand, by contrast, a distinctive 'national' cinema emerged largely through European-influenced art cinema, state-sponsored production initiatives and national television programming. The shared histories and the English-language medium also made the international distribution and acceptance of the cinema much easier for Australian and New Zealand feature-film-makers.

The two films discussed here define sharply distinct versions of Australasian cinema. Jane Campion's *The Piano* (1993) was her first large-budget feature, funded by French backers and with an

established international cast in a postmodern version of a historical colonial romance. Set in Campion's native New Zealand in the
mid-nineteenth century, the film tells the story of Ada, an elective
mute, and her young daughter's journey from Scotland to New
Zealand to pursue an arranged marriage with Stewart, a colonial
developer. It traces their unhappy and ultimately violent relationship, and her strange love affair with the overseer, Baines, both of
which relationships are developed through Ada's passionate
attachment to the piano that she brings from Scotland. Lee Tamahori's *Once Were Warriors* is a contemporary urban melodrama set
in South Auckland. Using a predominantly Maori cast, it tells the
story of the violent Jake, his initially submissive wife, and their
children who are in different ways affected by their parents'
destructive relationship, and by the social and cultural deprivations that shape their lives. Fast-paced, with a loud soundtrack and
emotive and violent sequences, Tamahori's film deploys the techniques of music video and the stylings of 1990s African-American
ghetto films such as *Boyz N the Hood* (1991) in postcolonial cinema.

Jane Campion's film tends to be studied as a definitive, if
problematic, feminist film which formally deconstructs the male
gaze of traditional cinema as it tells the story of Ada's strange
combat with the forces of patriarchy that see her bartered from Old
World to New to become the silent female observer of insensitive
colonialist expansion. The surface narrative is that of her rebellion
against this erasure of female agency and against the reckless
destruction of land and indigenous culture that the colonial project
entails. In this reading, there is a structural correspondence
between the silent Ada and the Maori characters whose language
and traditions Stewart neither knows nor respects. Ada's salvation,
sexual and social, comes through Baines, whose illiteracy is countered by – and perhaps enables – his understanding of the Maori
language and his apparent integration within their culture. His
moko, or tattooing, marks this physically, and signals his difference from the introverted and sexually repressed Stewart. The
film's sexual romance can, in this way, be read as a politically
utopian reconsideration of the possibilities of New Zealand history
at a point of cultural indeterminacy before nationhood is established (crucially, in this language-obsessed film, no character has a

'New Zealand' accent). Baines and Ada combine his quasi-indigeneity and her proto-feminism to imagine the possibility of an alternative history of colonialism, one that avoids the material, ethnic and gendered violence that the dour Stewart perpetrates. But this utopianism, as various commentators have argued, belies difficulties of representation within the film, and questions about its reception and marketing return us to wider issues of postcolonial film, its agency and its audience.

The Piano's most problematic element for feminist critics tends to be its eroticisation of the material transactions between Baines and Ada – he trades her the piano, key by key, if she meets his increasingly explicit sexual demands. Her (aesthetic) longing for the piano is thus counterpointed by his fetishising of her body. Far from passing judgement on this, the film uses its tensions to establish the sexual energies of the story, to suggest Ada's growing sexual self-realisation through Baines's attentions, and to construct that utopia of passion that ultimately restores her music and voice – though not without physical cost. Such is the fascination of the story of seduction that the racial and ethnic elements of the gothic romance can be marginalised in a way that is reminiscent of the very nineteenth-century colonial fiction that the film both draws upon and pastiches. 'The Maori', Lynda Dyson argues, 'are located on the margins of the film as the repositories of an authentic, unchanging and simple way of life; they play "nature" to the white characters['] "culture"' (Dyson 1999: 112). While this to some extent underestimates the complexity of Campion's use of the Maori characters as knowing parodists of the settlers' ways, and as obstructive, as well as enabling, presences, it is nevertheless true that they tend to serve the purposes of the film's main (European) protagonists. Baines's sexuality and his stubborn marginality that allows the anticipated romance to take place are dependent both upon the presence of the Maori, their non-English discourse, and their bawdy sexual talk that subverts the repression of the colonists. But in the narrative of the film, these qualities serve not to initiate an exploration of the Maori cultural condition in a period of violent cultural change for them, but to expedite the European sexual romance and a vague articulation of a utopian projection of postcolonial politics.

This politics needs some further consideration. Anna Neill and Bridget Orr, for example, see the film as a highly crafted intervention in a contemporary New Zealand postcolonialism that seeks to restate white New Zealand identity as distinct from its colonialist history whilst depoliticising the very Maori cultural presence that is its means of doing so. Neill suggests that the film presents a 'dreamtime' vision of the 1850s that in one way troubles a dominant history of New Zealand multiculturalism, but in another way borrows from its most pernicious strategies. 'Scenes of contact', she writes, 'are limited to . . . moments of cultural inscrutability, stripped of any sense of political conflict, as if by the 1850s the Maori had no political strategies at all for challenging the radical alienation of their land which had been going on for at least twenty years, and as if questions of land ownership had not already been articulated in New Zealand at the level of political sovereignty in 1840' (Neill 1999: 138). The radical restatement of colonial history as female history, with its suggestion of other possibilities beyond the determinism of Stewart's cultural and ecological brutality, becomes what Orr describes as a strategy 'to absolve [Ada] from settler guilt by linking her through an erotic metonymy to Maori, and to focus colonial culpability on the male pioneer's sexual and territorial possessiveness' (Orr 1999: 149).

This critique also demands a consideration of Campion's postmodernist narrative strategies. In one sense, the film's anachronisms, formal intrusions (the brief cartoon episode, for example) and inventive camera positions are part of a deliberated destabilising of a realist historical narrative, and, more particularly, of a normative colonial narrative. The knowing pastiche of historical romance allows the viewer to resist absorption in determined conventions, and recognise alternative possibilities in narratives and history – something registered by the multiple endings. Ada's New Age improvisations on the piano (scored by Michael Nyman), rather than appropriate and 'realist' nineteenth-century parlour conventions, for example, are calculated anachronisms that at key moments in the film wrench her from colonial doom to modern possibility. But these strategies have their perils, too, providing a formal rationale for the political elisions that Neill and Orr identify. If the concept of an ordained historical narrative is in question in the film, other narratives are equally relativist in their implications. So Campion uses the narrative conventions associated with 'male' eroticism to create the sexual and cinematic tensions of the central sections of the film, as Baines trades piano keys for glimpses and touches of Ada's body. Whilst various cinematic devices, such as point-of-view shots and knowing, ironic editing, suggest a parodic version, and undermining of these techniques, it is also that narrative strategy which energises the film, parody or not. Its commitment to a playful consciousness of cinematic method, rather than what 'Third Cinema' theorists might term a political consciousness of cinematic potential, means that it has no interest in revoking those conventions. In that play of the signs of power lies the film's actual power, and it was precisely such political equivocations that were exploited in the American and European marketing campaigns that bolstered the film's global success.

Whilst much of the academic discussion of *The Piano* and postcolonialism deals with the narrative strategies that I have just described, the contexts for the reception and interpretation of the film are equally important. Campion's film was taken up, after completion, by the American production and distribution company Miramax, and, as Dana Polan has argued, *The Piano*'s compatibility with that company's innovative strategy of film marketing suggests a further context for examining postcolonial cinema (Polan 2001: 16–19). Miramax, a subsidiary of the Disney Corporation since 1993, was instrumental in identifying art-house films that could be sold to a popular market. The company was interested in creating what Alisa Perren calls the 'indie blockbuster', that is, a film whose style and narrative construction 'aspired to the status of "art"' and which dealt with 'unconventional subjects and styles', but which, in its treatment of – particularly – sex, violence and controversial subject-matter, could 'replicate the exploitation marketing and box-office performance of the major studio high-concept event pictures' (Perren 2001–2: 31, 30). *The Piano* was a highly successful mixture of just these elements, with the additional 'niche market' of 'radical woman's picture'. As with other elements of the film, there is an ambivalence about this. In one way, the postmodern strategies of pastiche and archaism enabled a serious and challenging examination of a moment of colonial formation to be seen by huge audiences. In another, those very strategies that attracted a company controlled by Disney inevitably compromised the politics of those issues, allowing it to be shaped and consumed as a subterfuge historical romance about sexual expression. It presents, as Cynthia Kaufman argues, 'an appeal [that] rests in its promise of white female liberation existing comfortably within the structures of colonial domination' (quoted in Polan 2001: 48).

If *The Piano* poses difficulties in its evasions of ethnicity and modernity, the challenges of Lee Tamahori's *Once Were Warriors* emerge in the very stridency of the presentation of those issues. Like *The Piano*, *Once Were Warriors* represents a significant moment in Australasian cinema. Following on from the success of the controversial novel by the Maori writer Alan Duff on which it was founded, it became New Zealand's most commercially successful film. As with *The Piano*, this was based upon an international success that began at the Cannes film festival. However, the narrative, cinema and strategy of *Once Were Warriors* are very different from those of *The Piano*. Whereas Campion uses Maori characters as a chorus to a colonial/historical romance, Tamahori, like Duff, grounds the narrative in the contemporary dysfunction of a Maori family in Auckland. White New Zealanders barely exist in the claustrophobically violent story of Jake Heke, and his self-destructive struggle to maintain 'mana', the Maori concept of pride that Duff describes as 'standing in the eyes of your peers' (Duff 1993: 28). As the film goes on, however, the focus shifts to his wife, Beth, and her responses to Jake's alcohol-driven abuse. The romance of Jake and Beth, fleetingly but necessarily established in the film, is distorted by his brutality and the wider context of a Maori culture that has lost its ethical traditions in the city, even as it maintains a residual travesty of its communal structures and values in destructive codes of honour and violence. Their sons drift into petty crime and urban gangdom, and their daughter, Grace, is raped by an 'uncle' who Jake brings into his house, and to whom he affords misogynist protection. The rape provokes Grace's suicide and Beth's break-up of the nuclear family at the end of the film when she takes the surviving children to live in the rural home of her extended family.

Once Were Warriors was remarkable in its establishment of an indigenous production base – director, writer, stars and many of the crew were Maori – and its initiation of a national and international debate about Maori modernity. Its own engagement with issues of Maori culture, urban disaffection and domestic violence remains controversial, however. Like Campion, Tamahori and writer Rowena Brown use a popular genre – in this case, a family melodrama – to tell a postcolonial story. Brown changes the narrative structure of Duff's novel, which worked through Jake's inarticulate and troubled consciousness as well as that of his wife, to make Beth story's the film's ethical centre. Beth endures Jake's self-regarding shiftlessness and, in a disturbing scene, his violence, whilst remaining complicit in maintaining the family structure that hosts such aggression. Grace's rape, and subsequent suicide, initiates a change. Beth's estranged family comes to the city to perform traditional funeral rites, and Beth is reintegrated within Maori spiritual traditions. She renounces her husband, in a climactic speech that gives the film its title, revoking the decadence of ghetto Maoridom, and affirming the reconstitution of premodern family structures as she leaves the city with her children. It is a melodramatically satisfying closure, but one that poses problems in its postcolonial politics.

Beth's recovery of tradition is structured through a woman's 'coming-to-consciousness' narrative familiar from American/British traditions, arguably leaving her, in Geoff Mayer's terms, 'a recognisable stock character [with a] predictable transformation from victim to one who takes control of her world' (Mayer 1995: 5). The specifically Maori elements in this gendered transformation are hazy and problematic. Beth retreats into a largely unseen, unexamined and essentially pastoral version of Maoriness. It is a world that has been ironically undercut in the film's first shot, in which an idyllic New Zealand natural landscape is revealed as an advertising hoarding sited in the urban squalor of the South Auckland ghetto. The agents of Beth's traditional redemption are as marginal in the narrative as Campion's Maoris, appearing at Grace's funeral, performing no function except that of a means of closure. Jake and the city are left untouched and untouchable by this restatement of supposedly traditional identity. The film thus risks both a return to an essentialist romance of pre-modern Maori virtue, and the concomitant abandonment of Maori modernity to the condition of Jake's violent impotence. In a sceptical appraisal, written soon after its release, the journalist Denis Phelps argued for both the eva-siveness and implicit conservatism of the film's apparently radical agenda. 'Maoris are now a mainly urban people', he writes, 'and their problems call for political action. It suits the New Right to hear the answer is with the individual . . . And Maori activists and white liberals will like the idea that the answer is in "culture", from which not a few already make a living' (quoted in Mayer 1995: 4).

Other aspects of Tamahori's film contribute to the political unease that its conclusion engenders. Beth's narrative apparently defines a recovery of ethical tradition in opposition to an urban corruption signified by alcohol, violence and social purposeless-ness. However, the film's cinematic qualities draw upon visual and aural strategies deeply implicated in the very urban moder-nity that finally seems to have been rejected. There are calculated references to MTV-style video, American rap stylings and the imagery and tone of George Miller's *Mad Max* series. These reference points, developed with a youth audience in mind, might tend to contradict the politics of Brown's narrative. For example, the film's portrayal of Jake as an emblem of self-regarding masculinity and unmanageable violence is offset by its fascination with his physique and the body art of the Toa, or urban street gang that his son Nig joins. In Duff's novel, this gang, like Jake, is a brutalised and brutalising representation of a decayed warrior culture, committing rape as well as the ritual violence portrayed in the film. The film, however, presents the Toa both as a striking example of *Mad Max*-style postmodern youth culture – facial tattoos, leather and shades – and as a reconstruction of communal tradition within the city, one that is ultimately validated by Beth herself (and therefore necessarily misunderstood and despised by Jake). The issue here is how far the Maori moko, the public signifier of genealogy and traditional identity, maintains specific cultural meaning in this 'Maori' popular film. In urbanising that tradition through reference to black American style, the danger is that such meanings are subsumed within a repertoire of exotic imagery familiar from

advertising and music videos, and compliant to a global construction of largely unspecific 'otherness'. Jake's body poses
similar problems. Whilst its violence is clearly evident and
overtly rejected by Beth and his family, it is also fetishised by
the film in ways that relate to the reductive 'bio-politics' that
Gilroy notes in the contemporary African-American culture (see
Chapter 3). But it is, nevertheless, in these presentations of the
body, as well as in Beth's articulation of a message of cultural
retreat and retrieval, that the film can be said to challenge its own
potentially reductive version of ethnicity.

The melodramatic/feminist narrative of Beth's coming to consciousness is complicated by other counter-narratives that centre
upon Jake. For example, the climactic act of violence in which Jake
savagely beats Uncle Bully is staged by Beth herself as she reveals
to Jake the identity of Grace's rapist. Beth's position is ambivalent
here – she knows what Jake's reaction will be and watches and
relishes the rough justice, even as she goes on to implicitly
denounce its savagery in her parting speech about the deculturation of Maori masculinity. This ambivalence is shared by an
audience which is also complicit in an act of violence that is both
an anticipated dramatic climax and a disturbing representation of
Jake's pathology. In this scene, Tamahori and Brown bring together various conflicting elements of Jake that have been developed earlier in the film. Throughout *Once Were Warriors*, the
cinematography lingers on the body of Temuera Morrison, the
actor who plays Jake, as it does on the tattoos and ritual violence of
the Toa. The camera aestheticises Morrison's musculature, as well
as showing Jake's violence in the beatings of Beth and of Bully.
This attraction to physical conventions of masculine aesthetics is
compounded by a local extra-narrative reference point noted by
Geoff Mayer in his observation of the lack of total negativity in
New Zealand's audiences' responses to Jake (Mayer 1995: 6).
Morrison played Dr Ropata in the country's popular soap opera
Shortland Street, a 'positive' representation of Maori achievement
that is played against type in the feature film. One of Jake's few
considered speeches also adds complexity to audience response,
and provides a link to Duff's original exploration of Jake's interior
consciousness. Commenting on Beth's nostalgic account to the

children of her rural past as they look at the family's burial
grounds, Jake sullenly insists on articulating the aspect of that
culture that led to Beth's alienation from her family on their
marriage and, implicitly, her relocation to the city. This is an
accusation of racism within Maori culture, past and present, that
treated his blackness as a marker of lower-caste status and slave
history, and hence a barrier to a relationship with the higher-caste
Beth. Ironically, it is a version of this same 'accusation' of slavery
that Beth re-articulates as she leaves Jake in the city to return to the
ancestral family lands.

Once Were Warriors, despite its apparently populist deployment
of melodrama and ethnic stylisation, can also be seen as a film that
is interested in the processes of ethnic representation. Whilst the
challenges of Alan Duff's representation of urban Maori (not
'Nanny Kuia down on the beach gathering kaimoana for her
mokopuna . . . but . . . hard drinking men, and not a few women,
who were appalling parents, who were wife beaters, child rapists,
beer-sodden low-lifes') are softened in Brown and Tamahori's
narrative to the extent that Beth returns to 'Nanny Kuia' in the
end, this is not the whole story (Duff 1993: ix). In *The Piano*, there
is a self-consciously double ending, with Ada's drowning and her
survival to lead a genteel colonial life with Baines posing stark
historical choices for the viewer of the narrative. Ada's fate can be
that of a doomed romantic idealist or of a fully colonial woman,
both of which effectively close off any dialogue with the Maori
culture that underpins the earlier narrative of emancipation. The
apparently far more emphatic closure of *Once Were Warriors*,
whilst providing Beth with a means of retreat to tradition, leaves
Jake in the city as a diminished presence, but also as an unsolved
problem. His 'mana' is publicly removed from him by his wife and
sons, even as he performs its last violent ritual in the beating of
Bully. Yet it is Jake's performances of the degraded fragments of
that virtue – his bringing home of the fish at the beginning of the
film, his defence of the bar singer, his own song with Beth – that
carry more force than the styles of 'moral' street gangs or the social
worker's lecture to Boogie on Maori martial traditions (one of the
least convincing scenes in the film). The film strives for positive
closure through Beth's retreat to family and tradition, and Boogie

and Nig's encounter with residual and emergent forms of that tradition. However, the film's most urgent and interesting conflicts are arguably played out in the uneasy politics of the body. The clash of the film's final cultural assertion articulated by Beth with the urban energies of cinematographic and generic resources and with the ethnic conflict and problematised masculinity embodied by Temuera Morrison suggest an unresolved engagement with the politics of postcolonial film-making.

Conclusion

The films of Mrinal Sen, Mira Nair, Aditya Chopra, Jane Campion and Lee Tamahori illustrate a cross-section of postcolonial cinema's industrial, cultural and generic range. They suggest the irregular histories of postcolonial national cinemas, the diversity of audiences, the cultural tensions within those cinemas and their different engagements with global funding and distribution structures. Each of the films discussed here develops particular narrative and cinematographic approaches to issues important to postcolonial studies. *Ākāler Sandhāney* and *The Piano* are both films about the politics of particular moments of historical change, and about the means of cinema to engage with such histories. Chopra and Nair present comparable, though very different, responses to the challenges of Indian diaspora. Campion and Tamahori articulate contrasting approaches to the representation of indigenous cultures. The films also illustrate dilemmas and decisions in issues of representation and audience. Nair, Campion and Tamahori, in different ways, exemplify a cinema attentive to both local and international audiences, developing localised films that also draw upon First World cultural and economic resources. That negotiation of postcolonial politics and global commerce has diverse consequences. For Nair, for example, it can be seen to problematise the politics of her representation of Indian social crisis in ways critiqued by Third Cinema theorists and by Sen's *Ākāler Sandhāney*. In *Once Were Warriors*, on the other hand, stylistic and generic dilemmas arguably articulate the deeper politics of the film's representation of postcolonialism in Hollywood-influenced cinema. Sen's film both poses stark questions about film's capacity to articulate and intervene in the struggles of postcolonial subalternity, and represents the limitations of such articulation and intervention in its own self-referentiality and indifference to popular spectatorship.

CHAPTER 5

The Irrational
and the Postcolonial

Issues of rationality and irrationality are particularly compelling aspects of wider questions about the practices of postcolonialism. Postcolonial studies, as was seen in Chapter 1, is committed to tasks of questioning and challenging embedded assumptions of colonialism in the economic, social and intellectual practices of the First World, and of understanding emergent cultural formations. At the same time, it also has to confront the complicity of its own methods of analysis in the universalist assumptions of European Enlightenment rationalism that lie behind them. Eighteenth- and nineteenth-century humanist convictions of the ultimate comprehensibility of the world through rational means underpin the academic endeavour of human sciences and the humanities, just as, in other, darker forms, they underpinned the practices of colonialism itself. Books like this, courses in postcolonial studies and the establishments of learning in which they both operate, implicitly and explicitly, accept secular procedures of evidence-gathering and argument, deploying empirical processes of assembling and analysing knowledge to arrive at their conclusions. Cultures that often form the objects of those studies, however, can work through very different principles and through systems of belief, whether these are institutional religions or local practices that involve spirits and magical beliefs.

How secular rationalism deals with such 'irrationality' is problematic. In fact, the very term 'irrational' carries pejorative implications because of its negation of the perceived 'good' of reason. Whilst religions and other, less structured, bodies of supernatural belief have long been acknowledged by anthropology and sociology as significant parts of living structures of social organisation, interpretation and experience, the content and agency of their beliefs do not – cannot – inform the methodology of study. What Clifford Geertz calls the 'inherent moral asymmetry of the field-work situation' in anthropology concerns this unequal confrontation of world-views (Geertz 2000: 33). To understand cultures predicated upon 'other' systems of causality and consequence, the anthropologist, the cultural critic and any other observer-interpreter translate those cultures' materials into terms with which secular discourse is comfortable, and – more problematically – to which its perceptions of the world correspond. That act of translation cannot be innocent, of course. Its process changes its materials. And how far that change of people's beliefs into the dominant secular concepts of Western social science and humanist scholarship is itself an act of power, rather than an act of under-standing, is central to the concerns of postcolonial studies. 'Looking into dragons, not domesticating or abominating them, nor drowning them in vats of theory is what anthropology has been all about', writes Geertz, optimistically (63–4). But, in the end, anthropologists, like postcolonialists, don't normally believe in dragons.

The 'moral asymmetry' of the encounters of many postcolonial ethnographers and cultural commentators and their subaltern subjects have led to sceptical examinations of the ideological processes of the 'objective' practices of Western sciences (see Chapter 1). However, this scepticism is itself controversial in postcolonial studies, particularly with regard to religion. The Indian scientist Meera Nanda, for example, has written critically of the 'epistemic charity' that some apparently radical Western theorists have granted non-Western belief-systems. In a recent collection of polemical essays, Nanda challenges postmodern critiques of Western science as ideological, rather than objectively rational productions of knowledge. Reflecting upon what she sees as the ruinous de-secularising of Indian politics in the last twenty years, Nanda insists upon the political potential of science for Third World liberation struggles. 'The only option for the friends of the oppressed in the postcolonial world', she writes, 'is for them to recognize that the interest of the oppressed in secularization and demystification of traditional ideologies is best served by the naturalism and skepticism of modern science' (Nanda 2002: 91). For Nanda, the Western romanticising of indigenous belief-systems and postmodern relativisms of world-views support continuing repressive social practices of religio-political regimes. Nanda makes particular reference to the rise of Hindu fundamentalism in the secular state of India, and its support for the enforcement of caste laws against dalits, or Untouchables, and gender discriminations, traditions opposed by Gandhi during his anti-colonial struggles. 'Far from experiencing the objectivity and value-freedom of science as a "rude and brutal intrusion"', she writes, 'important dalit-feminist intellectuals have *celebrated* the contents and methods [of] modern science as a source of demystification of the Brahmanical Hindu understanding' that has led to their own 'double' oppression as dalit and woman (36).

Nanda's sense of the political efficacy of Western science is based upon its capacity to allow groups oppressed by indigenous systems of value and authority to think beyond those terms, and to work towards an equality defined by the essential democracy of biological description. However, she pays rather less attention to the political means and consequences of the importation of those values, and to other possible meanings of the persistence of the irrational beyond their roles in systems of political and social control. Her critique of the relativist tendencies of Western intellectuals in their countenancing oppressive belief-systems because of their indigeneity rather than because of the efficacy or generosity of their practices can be complicated by the more equivocal arguments of thinkers like the American-Ghanaian philosopher Kwame Anthony Appiah. Appiah's essays in *In My Father's House* (1992) explore the possibilities of constructing an intellectual middle ground on which a Western-trained African intellectual can engage with the belief-systems derived from pre-colonial African cultures without denying the agencies that energise those systems. 'The world of the intellectual *is*, I think largely disenchanted', he writes, but that 'disenchantment' leads to the 'question of how much of the world of the spirits we intellectuals must give up (or transform into something ceremonial without the old literal ontology)' (Appiah 1992: 234–5, 219). Appiah articulates the dilemma of a thinker trained in a Western rationalist tradition, unable and unwilling to work beyond that tradition, who, at the same time, recognises both the troubling implications of its complicity in colonial histories, and the need for a considered assessment of the continuing hold of other systems of belief and interpretation in African and other cultures.

In My Father's House warns against a convenient translation of African religious systems into readily comprehensible Western terms, a process that he describes as treating 'traditional believers as reassuringly rational only because they deny that traditional people mean what they say'. 'It is peculiarly unsatisfactory', he goes on, 'to treat a system of propositions as symbolic when those whose propositions they are appear to treat them literally *and* display, in other contexts, a clear grasp of the notion of symbolic representation' (Appiah 1992: 187). For Appiah, the challenge of an engagement with the postcolonial 'irrational' is one of resisting the restoration of Western rationality by covert means, whilst also conducting a meaningful dialogue that draws upon – rather than seeks to abandon – the resources of Western intellectual endeavour. To shed the latter tradition is as ineffective as it is dishonest, part of the 'epistemic charity' deplored by Meera Nanda. Appiah himself cites the Ghanaian philosopher Kwasi Wiredu's dismissive critique of celebrants of an imaginary 'pure' African past, 'observing that people die daily in Ghana because they prefer traditional herbal remedies to Western medicines'. '[A]ny inclination to glorify the unanalytical cast of mind', Wiredu argues, 'is not just retrograde; it is tragic' (Appiah 1992: 166). Yet, as Appiah himself argues, there also needs to be an attempt to deal with elements of experience and thought that differ fundamentally from those that underpin the disciplines that attempt such engagements. One means of doing so is to consider contrasting approaches to areas of individual and cultural experience that remain problematic within Enlightenment traditions of rationalist analysis and treatment. One such area is that of mental illness. As the psychoanalyst and literary critic Jacqueline Rose suggests, 'it is in relation to madness that universality shows its most dubious Euro/ethnocentric colours as it spreads its diagnostic certainty across the globe' (Rose 1994: 402).

The management of the irrational personality was central to the European Enlightenment project of the eighteenth and nineteenth centuries. Analysing and treating madness as a medical condition was an assertion of a broader secularist philosophy that removed supernatural causes from the analysis of such states, and established social, therapeutic and chemical means of treating perceived psychological aberrations (for this history, see Foucault 1971; Porter 1987, 2002). However, the application of psychiatric theory and practice to colonial and postcolonial contexts raises particular problems. The development of psychiatry during colonial times was limited both in its range and efficacy. As Jock McCulloch notes, '[a]s late as 1944 the annual reports on asylums for British West Africa . . . appear as a subheading under prisons' (McCulloch 1995: 3). Even when psychiatry was developed within colonial contexts beyond those of the pragmatics of order and control, it tended to be in ways that corresponded easily to racist assumptions about the relationship of a dominant and rational European culture to 'primitive' societies and psyches. The projection of primitive irrationality became embedded in biomedical traditions of thought. Colonial Africa, in particular, became an outpost of residual nineteenth-century pseudo-sciences, drawing on eugenics, crude measurements of the cortex and other distortions of evolutionary theory aimed at showing the inadequacy of Africans in dealing with 'modernity' (see McCulloch 1995). Psychoanalysis was similarly burdened with a conceptual framework that implied a universalist description of human development, and a metaphorical language that denied that very universalism. The binaries of colonial order – self/other, civilised/primitive – were exchangeable with the developing discourse of psychoanalysis as childhood and neurotic states were routinely linked to earlier, 'primitive', stages of human development, analogies that find their classical expression in Freud's psycho-anthropological work *Totem and Taboo* (1919) with its revealing subtitle, 'Resemblances between the Psychic Lives of Savages and Neurotics'.

Two main developments provided challenges to the practices and discourses of colonial psychiatry: the development, in a variety of forms, of ethnopsychiatry intent on emphasising cultural difference in the causation and effects of mental phenomena in psychiatric practice; and the influence, intellectual if not practical, of the work of the Caribbean psychiatrist and revolutionary Frantz Fanon. These different strands of theory and clinical practice are complemented by other texts that are concerned with the con- structions and encounters of the rational and the irrational in colonial and postcolonial contexts. The work of Wilson Harris also provides a provocative challenge to the assumptions and discourses of colonial and postcolonial cultures alike. Harris's critique of colonial rationalism and its legacies can be linked to Fanon's determined deconstruction of psychiatry in *Black Skin, White Masks* (1952), though each develops a position from apparently different premises. Harris also links his critique to the practices of postcolonial fiction. Setting himself against what he sees as the damaging limitations of a Western realist tradition, he both devel- ops himself and celebrates in others fictional discourses that are attentive to world-views that have been suppressed or eradicated by the historical practices that the false objectivity of realism represents. How this is demonstrated in the wider field of post- colonial fiction will be examined through a discussion of the works of three writers: Jean Rhys, Bessie Head and Erna Brodber. Coming from different postcolonial contexts, each nevertheless is interested in the conflict of Western reason and local world-views, and each develops a distinctive stylistic and narrative practice in which the culture of the 'irrational' is explored.

Case Study One:
Psychiatry, Ethnopsychiatry and Postcolonialism

The history of ethnopsychiatry, like that of ethnography in recent years, is one of a coming to self-consciousness of the ideological implications of self-proclaimedly objective practices of description and analysis. Ethnopsychiatry begins from the assumption that mental illnesses are, to varying extents, 'culture-bound' – that is, their causes, symptoms, effects and cures may be different in different cultural contexts. What Byron J. Good calls the 'empiricist theory of [European] medical language', based upon an assumption of a universal description of the natural order, can be challenged by a serious acceptance of other discourses and analyses of mental disorder (Good 1994: 5). Such a challenge to the dominance of biomedical descriptions of disease becomes particularly acute in regard to severe mental illness. In this case, as Roland Littlewood and Simon Dein write, 'Western psychiatry remains unable to offer its own patients any understanding, technical or moral, in terms of everyday knowledge (or, indeed, even of biology)' (Littlewood and Dein 2000: 23–4). Mental illness and its irrationalities, as Michel Foucault famously realised, form a significant faultline in dominant empiricist practices of medical science and psychology. Ethnopsychiatry, rather than seeking to maintain a unified field of analysis and category across cultures, instead acknowledges Western psychiatry's implication in its own culturally bound definitions of mental health. In response, it develops strategies for interpreting psychological phenomena through systems of classification and treatment embedded within the traditions of the cultures in which the phenomena appear. In Roland Littlewood's words, 'ethnopsychiatry offers us an alternative to psychoanalytic or biological determinism by regarding psychopathology, not as a particular individual's state of mind at a given time or as Nature thinly disguised, but as a cultural datum with complex linguistic, political, and historical determinants' (Littlewood 1998: 36).

Ethnopsychiatry's reconfiguration of psychiatric practice challenges empirical definitions of psychiatric normality. It is a challenge that has recently been acknowledged even by the standard analytical tool of American psychiatry, the *Diagnostic and Statistical Manual of Mental Disorders*, or *DSM*. In 1994, it introduced a brief section on 'Culture-bound Syndromes', noting that a 'clinician who is unfamiliar with the nuances of an individual's cultural frame of reference may incorrectly judge as psychopathology those normal variations of behavior, belief, or experience that are particular to the individual's culture' (*DSM-IV* 1994: xxiv). The authority of symptom-categorisation thus becomes, to some extent, culture-bound, though the discourse and systems of the manual nevertheless retain a formidable force of scientific objectivity. Such tentative admissions of relativist uncertainties in psychiatric diagnosis and management disguise radical differences in those descriptions and treatments. The American ethnopsychiatrist Richard J. Castillo provides an example of this:

> In societies in which people regularly hear the voices of their dead
> ancestors, hearing voices is a normal and normative experience. In
> contrast, in those societies that conceptualize hearing voices as the
> attack of evil spirits, they will understand the interview questions [of a
> psychiatrist] in those terms. Yet the typical western diagnostic inter-
> view schedule conceptualizes hearing voices as a symptom of psycho-
> sis. (Castillo 1997: 74)

For Castillo, and for other ethnopsychiatrists, a 'diagnostic ethnocentrism' that automatically defines phenomena such as hearing
voices as symptoms of psychotic disorders has to be reshaped
through a negotiated clinical reality that acknowledges other
possible provenances and meanings of the phenomena (69).

The premise of a negotiated clinical reality raises its own
difficulties, both theoretical and practical. For a psychiatrist to
accept a person's belief in, say, spirit-possession is one thing, but at
some point in the clinical process that belief-system will necessarily
be seconded to the dominant interpretative frame of psychiatry. In
other words, the spirits will have to be recast into more normative
discourses of psychological affect, even if that translation is
not made overtly. Psychiatrists ultimately remain psychiatrists,
'ethno-' notwithstanding; they are not shamans or Tswana healers,
nor can they be. The American psychiatrist Raymond Prince
finesses the issue tellingly in his foreword to a pioneering study
of spirit-possession. The formulations of 'spirit systems' can have
therapeutic value, he admits, but 'they have less truth value than
Western psychoanalytically oriented theories' (Crapanzano and
Garrison 1977: xv). For Prince, 'therapeutic value' can be acknowledged, but spirit systems hardly challenge the empirical resolve of
the true science of psychiatry, whether they are therapeutic or not.
Openly or covertly, these arguments imply, the psychiatrist must
behave like a psychiatrist and interpret like a psychiatrist because,
as Roland Littlewood writes, '[p]rofessional intervention in sick-
ness involves incorporating the patient into an overarching system
of explanation', a system which is, almost inevitably in a postcolonial context, one that is not entirely his or her own (Littlewood
1998: 247). The ideological power necessarily embedded in such a
system is deployed in analysis and treatment, the only question

being the intensity (and the degree of clinical success) of that deployment.

This is an impasse that is familiar in many forms of cross-cultural studies, of course, and the power inherent in the act of translation is something that has been noted earlier in the discussions of academic postcolonialism and of Appiah's philosophical work. Recent thinking in both ethnopsychiatry and anthropology has suggested responses to this. In his essay 'From Vice to Madness', Littlewood argues that the central difficulty of 'category translation' in ethnopsychiatry developed from an earlier translation within the history of Western medicine that caused a limited system of explanation for various mental phenomena to emerge. '[T]he professionalisation of health care in Western medicine', he argues, 'has endorsed naturalistic explanations: the influence and resources of biomedicine are reflected in the extent to which the notion of *madness* becomes transformed into *psychopathology* or *mental illness*'(Littlewood 1998: 68). The implication of this is that ethnopsychiatry requires not only a cultural unpicking of the categories of psychiatric illness assigned to non-Western contexts, but also a thoughtful revision of the concept of 'mental illness' itself as it is conceived in the West. Clinical definitions of psychosis, depression and so forth can be entered into dialogues with broader therapeutic and non-pathological discourses of other cultures, even recovering a looser, more mysterious state of 'madness' for a West that has found it perhaps the least tractable of pathologies. In such exchanges, the seemingly untranslatable conditions of psychosis and spirits enter into a constructive dialogue.

Anthropologists attempting to deal with cultures structured through spirit-based experiences have developed comparable strategies to those of ethnopsychiatry. Classical anthropological approaches to magical practices discriminated between empirically verifiable phenomena and phenomena that were imaginary but served an identifiable social purpose. As Sir Edward Evans-Pritchard pithily expressed it, '[w]itchcraft explains unfortunate events' (quoted in Kenny 1996: 151). The approaches of more recent ethnographers and anthropologists like Joan Dayan, Jeanne Favret-Saada and Michael Taussig are much less secure in their arbitration between the real and the functional imaginary. Taussig, in his study of devil-beliefs in contemporary South America, reads the proliferation of devil narratives as intimately bound up with, but not wholly determined by, the intensification of modern capitalism in the region. 'Magic', he argues, 'takes language, symbols, and intelligibility to their outermost limits, to explore life and thereby to change its destination.' In the end, Taussig makes no essential distinction between the spirit world of South American agrarianism and that of an encroaching commodity capitalism which, as Marx himself suggested, created its own powerful ghosts and fetishes even as it abolished those of others (Taussig 1980: 15). Joan Dayan's study of Haitian spirit-possession likewise sees its practices both as constitutive of and constituting particular historical and social experiences and changes. Far from being residual African elements, she argues, the most powerful spirits in Haitian voudou are intimate with colonial history itself. 'A historical streak in these spirits', she writes, 'entirely this side of metaphysics, reconstitutes the shadowy and powerful magical gods of Africa as everyday responses to the white master's arbitrary power. Driven underground, they survived and constituted a counterworld to white suppression' (Dayan 1995: 36). It becomes impossible, therefore, to extract the 'truth' from the 'magic'. They are the same inextricable phenomena. For an ethnographer to study such spirits, argues Jeanne Favret-Saada in her study of rural witchcraft in France, he or she has to enter the discourse of spirits, and not try to translate it into something else. The startling implication of this is that, when faced with conditions of mental extremity beyond its cultural borders, Western psychiatry be-comes just one of many 'official theories of misfortune', albeit one embedded within powerful institutions (quoted in Good 1994: 13).

The depathologising of some versions of 'madness', the aware-ness of various cultural frames for psychic phenomena and an emergent relativism of analysis and treatment suggest other means of negotiating diversities of mental experiences than those asso-ciated with traditional biomedicine or psychoanalysis. However, ethnopsychiatry runs it own dangers, particularly those of re-forging colonial links between the postcolonial and the irrational/primitive, and of understating the political effects of colonialism and its aftermath in structuring psychic disorders in the first place.

All of the sites in which ethnopsychiatry is practised are in complex dialogue with the legacies of colonialism and the various global cultural and political systems that followed. As Michael Taussig argues, they cannot, therefore, be analysed as wholly beyond the influence of the ideology and structures of Western psychological experience – as wholly 'other'. The conjunction of different ways of perceiving the world, often within the kind of debilitating economic and social conditions that Taussig and Dayan describe, can also be seen as a causal factor in mental distress. Moreover, the power-laden relationships of colonialism and neo-colonialism can be replicated in the structures of medical treatment, even in those that seek dialogue with other cultural frames of interpretation. This political aspect of madness isn't much addressed in textbooks of ethnopsychiatry. However, it provides a link between the recent revisionist practices of anthropology and ethnopsychiatry and the earlier writings of the psychiatrist and revolutionary theorist, Frantz Fanon. Fanon's work has had more influence on academic postcolonial theory and polemic than it has upon the developments in his own profession, but it is grounded in his medical practice and interest in the psychology of colonisation. His clinical work in hospitals in France and Algeria, and his early book on the relationship between colonialism and psychiatry, *Black Skin, White Masks*, explore the relationship between socio-political and psychological conditions, and question and probe the limits and possibilities of a new psychiatry and a new psychiatric discourse to deal with emergent postcolonial experiences.

Case Study Two: Frantz Fanon and the Politics of Postcolonial Psychiatry

Frantz Fanon, was born in the French Caribbean colony of Martinique in 1925, trained in psychiatry in Lyon in the early 1950s, and began work in mental hospitals in Algeria during the beginnings of the independence struggles against French colonialism. His growing involvement with Algerian nationalism led to his departure to Tunis, where he combined revolutionary political activities with his practice of psychiatry. During his period at Blida hospital in Algeria, from 1953 to 1957, Fanon confronted the cultural disjunctions between European clinical practices and the world-view of his Arab-Islamic patients. In response, he initiated styles of treatment and institutional life aimed at making connections between the hospital and the surrounding social structures, even as he experimented with chemical treatments. His biographer David Macey describes his commitment to a 'social therapy', the goal of which was to 'create a neo-society within the hospital' (Macey 2000: 325). Fanon's profession of psychiatry has only recently come to be studied as a significant element of his work as a political theorist (see McCulloch 1983; Vergès 1996). However, the pragmatic and visionary politics of that developing clinical practice offers an intriguing counterpoint to the anti-colonial thinking of *White Skin, Black Masks*, perhaps the most influential of his works for recent postcolonial theory.

Written before he began psychiatric practice in Algeria, and therefore drawing upon experiences in Martinique and in mainland France, *Black Skin, White Masks* forms what he terms 'a clinical study' of colonialism (Fanon 1986: 14). Fanon presents colonialism itself as neurosis, a force that shapes and develops pathological responses in individuals and their social relationships. Such relationships are destructive to both colonised and coloniser, but are utterly destructive to the colonised, who, he argues, are forced to define themselves in the terms of the coloniser. 'The black man wants to be white', he writes, and colonialism structures identity in such perverse relationships, creating unrealisable desire whilst denying the possibility of contact beyond the markers of skin. 'The white man is sealed in his whiteness./The black man in his blackness' is Fanon's characteristically aphoristic description of the condition (11). Such dynamics make coherent human identity impossible, '[f]or not only must the black man be black; he must be black in relation to the white man' (110). The psychological result of the colonial enterprise is an unmanageable fracturing of identities and an endlessly failing attempt to achieve resolution. For Fanon, there is no possibility of 'curing' this double-bind except by first understanding and then destroying the political, economic and psychological transactions of colonialism that underpin it. Only after these are gone can health – individual and social – be restored under conditions that he defines as those of a 'new humanism' (9).

Fanon's 'case study' is important in a number of ways. Crucially, it politicises psychology and psychiatry by questioning the emphatic divisions between the sane and the mad in colonial society, and the causality of mental illness. Nobody can be 'sane' in a society structured through the relationships of colonialism, he argues, and psychiatric science must, therefore, look beyond a narrow concern with 'objective' clinical diagnosis and traditional institutional treatment to wider socio-political environments. Fanon's concern with identity was also to become influential. Blackness and whiteness become for him damaging processes of simultaneous definition and limitation that necessarily deny completeness to those that engage with them. His exploration of inter-racial sexual relationships as fundamental to this process of construction was a startling innovation, and remains a radical consideration of a fraught topic. Perhaps most startling of all, though, is Fanon's discourse and mode of writing in the book, strategies that he was to abandon in his later work. *Black Skin, White Masks* is a strange 'case study' because it refuses the consistently analytical approach implied by that term, despite its constant reference to contemporary psychiatric and sociological materials. In places, it seems to trust to the efficacy of a psychoanalytical solution to colonial psychopathology only for such affirmations to be called into question through an alternately poetic and testy dialogue with such a project. At one point, for example, Fanon famously denies the existence of the Oedipus complex in black people, effectively abolishing the fundamental process of Freudian identity formation and its claim to universal validity (151–2). Such apparent inconsistency of theory is reflected in the fragmentary, aphoristic and allusive mode of a writing that mingles scientific analysis with narrative, anecdote and pithy assertion.

Rhetorical strategy and social/scientific analysis exist in a calculatedly uneasy dialectical relationship in *Black Skin, White Masks*. As with C. L. R. James's work, the distinctiveness – the oddity – of the form and style is a constitutive part of the political meaning of the writing. The contradictions, arguments, poetic formulations and conjunctions of textual material and apparently improvised commentary – according to David Macey, the book was in part orally-composed and dictated to Fanon's wife – never allow the text to settle into explicatory rationalism (Macey 2000: 134). At the same time, however, it resists any studied irrationalism. Whilst the discourses of Négritude – that poetic celebration of an essential 'African-ness' expressed in the work of Caribbean and West African writers and political theorists such as Léopold Senghor and Aimé Césaire – is an important source for Fanon, the book is also critical of its illusory political trajectory (Macey 2000: 180–6). The Caribbean doctor in Arab Africa recognised that there was to be no simple return to lost identities.

Fanon's book performs its own dilemmas, restlessly probing between skin and mask. It demonstrates the limitations of European-derived concepts and practices even as it affirms the necessity of confronting and using those ideas, rejecting any fantasy of a return to an imaginary pre-colonial cultural purity. Typically, accounts of the philosophical and psychiatric theory that underpin the text are interrupted by pragmatic, curt interventions that reroute the discourse. Octave Mannoni's psychoanalytical analysis of the violent dreams of his Madagascan patients during the period of French rule as being linked to childhood trauma, for example, is summarily dismissed. These dreams, Fanon suggests, are starker engagements with the actual violence of colonial power and the French deployment of West African troops in Madagascar: 'The enraged black bull is not the phallus . . . The rifle of the Senegalese soldier is not a penis but a genuine rifle, model Lebel 1916' (106). Such brusque assertions of the potential for political naivety in psychoanalysis and psychiatry are characteristic of the work's own insurgent critique of its discipline.

Black Skin, White Masks is a complex study of colonial pathology that recognises its own theoretical tools as complicit in the experiences that it seeks to analyse and defuse. Its stylistic and formal strangeness is a means of destabilising the certainties of Eurocentric science, creating instead an inquisitive, tonally shifting mixture of psychiatric methodology, autobiography, anecdote, polemic and poetry. Like C. L. R. James, Fanon seeks to occupy a strategic position beyond boundaries of colonial discourses, but in necessarily intimate dialogue with those discourses. His writing performs a persistent self-questioning, distancing itself from the universalising and totalising implications of the psychiatric and psychoanalytical paradigms from which it draws some aspects of its method. It forms a bridge to a conception of postcolonial writing that is interested in reshaping the discourses of colonialism and revoking the assumptions of inherited categories of writing and thought. *Black Skin, White Masks*, like James's *Beyond a Boundary*, works outside normative classifications such as that of 'scientific text' or 'autobiography'. The performance of an emergent post-colonial world-view, it implies, requires both a dialogue with the condition of colonialism and its intellectual resources, and a redefinition of its categories and discourses. To be a postcolonial psychiatrist, for Fanon, is also to be a political revolutionary and a writer who reconstitutes the discourses and methods of psychiatric expression.

Case Study Three:
Wilson Harris, Postcolonial Fiction and the Irrational

Fanon's early work, like the ethnopsychiatry that followed it, is a challenge both to the persistence of colonialism as a mental, as well as political and economic, force, and to the intellectual means of analysing and changing that condition. It is not enough to translate the psychological experiences and distresses of the colonial subject into the conceptual language of a psychiatry that is itself a product, however benevolent, of that universalising project. Instead, it is necessary for an analyst of that condition, in Wilson Harris's words, to 'breach the uniform pavement that we tread on earth' (Harris 1999: 62). For Harris, as for Fanon, that pavement is a deceptively solid ground of rational description, understanding and exploitation of the world that belies the intellectual and actual violence of the colonialism that constitutes it. 'We tend to read the world in a uniform kind of way, a uniform kind of narrative, a uniform kind of frame', Harris writes. 'That kind of thing may very well be one of the consequences, one of the deprivations we endure in the light of the traditions which we have apparently lost' (Harris 1999: 77). But the processes of uniformity are also processes of destruction and repression, and of the remorseless denial of alter-native world-views and expressive resources. Like the Fanon of *Black Skin, White Masks*, and like ethnographers such as Jeanne

Favret-Saada and Michael Taussig, Harris is interested in destabilising the apparently secure boundaries of the rational and the
irrational, of the scientific and the imaginary.

In his fiction and his essays, Harris deploys a disconcerting
rhetorical strategy that itself embodies his urge to 'breach the logic
of cause-and-effect realism' (62). Locating his narratives in extre-
mities of psychological and physical experience, he re-imagines
them outside of the securities of both empiricist science and a
European tradition of realist fiction predicated upon the stable self
and the capacity of an author to deliver a coherent narrative of
rational cause and effect. Harris insists upon the necessity for
engaging with energies that have been excluded and controlled by
modernity, particularly those of the apparently erased histories of
pre-colonial societies (in his case, those of pre-Columbian Central
America and the Caribbean). Not to do so is to live within the
'dogmatic exactitude' of a closed, if avowedly globalised, world.
The 'numinous inexactitudes' that he celebrates are those of a
world of knowledge achieved by 'civilization's arrival upon
bridges from one closed mind to another, from one closed world
to the other' (194). The aim of the postcolonial intellectual, he
argues elsewhere, is 'to transform claustrophobic ritual by cross-
cultural imaginations that bear upon the future through mutations
of the monolithic character of conquistadorial legacies of civilisation' (Harris 1983: xv). In other words, the legacies of 'knowledge'
defined by imperialism (the 'conquistadorial legacies') must be
challenged, not by destroying them, but by entering into (a
necessarily traumatic) dialogue and hybrid transformation. Only
in such dangerous moments of encounter, vulnerability and change
can the desolate condition of a modernity that has denied itself
histories and closed off its resources for survival be recovered.

Harris's difficult ideas, argued as they are in a version of the very
discourse that they aspire to, one that lies outside of the norms of
either fiction or rationalism, nevertheless provide a significant
resource for thinking about the issues of the chapter and the
remaining case studies. He argues the need to recast fundamentally
the terms and dynamics of apparently empirical descriptions and
assessments of cultures and individuals within the circumstances of
colonialism and postcolonialism. Whilst resisting the 'epistemic

charity' that Meera Nanda deplores – Harris is certainly no primitivist or romantic – he also asserts the necessity for an inclusive recovery of the energies and experiences that any colonial system of political and cultural control must seek to reshape or suppress. That recovery, however, requires an entry into the very places and discourses most despised, misunderstood and dreaded by those systems. This 'regeneration of oneself through the furies one has long feared', as Harris terms it, is a central preoccupation of his work, and one that is, in its discourse and assumptions, at odds with the methodologies and traditions of the human sciences, let alone traditional psychiatry (Harris 1999: 226). His insistence that such a transformation requires the crossing of what he calls 'unsuspected bridges', and his radical questioning of closures of disciplinarity certainly make life difficult for postcolonial studies (242). Nevertheless, that difficulty is lodged at the centre of the discipline's concerns and its attempts to make sense of and to transform conditions of personal and cultural crisis and loss. It also invites the meeting of its different worlds of endeavour and understanding, challenging the habits and suspicions that keep them apart. The unsuspected bridges that will form the final case studies here are those between the psychiatry and ethnography that have preoccupied the first two sections of the chapter and four works of fiction.

Jean Rhys, Bessie Head and Erna Brodber approach the description and analysis of postcolonial experience through the irrational in ways that are analogous to the thinking of Harris, Fanon and some of the ethnopsychiatrists discussed above. Their writing is marked by formal and narrative strategies that are, in many ways, outside the realist traditions that Harris suggests are themselves implicated in the world-views of colonialism. Each confronts the reader with predicaments, both psychological and political, which resist translation into the language and ideas of conventional criticism, postcolonial or not. Their various presentations of madness and spirits are not ones that can be easily resolved into metaphor or fantasy, or limited to a discrete literary world. As Harris and the ethnographer Jeanne Favret-Saada argue, the Western tendency to see language and the irrational as areas for rational limitation and interpretation belies the performative power of both in cultures in which questions of belief in magical agencies and performance are irrelevant. 'Language is not a set of neutral propositions about the world, which the ethnographer judges to be more or less empirically valid', writes Byron Good with reference to Favret-Saada's work, 'but the medium through which vicious and life-threatening power struggles are engaged. The world of illness and witchcraft only opens to the ethnographer as she enters the discourse' (Good 1994: 14). The same can be said about Jean Rhys's *Wide Sargasso Sea*, Bessie Head's short story, 'Witchcraft' and novel *A Question of Power*, and Erna Brodber's *Myal*.

Four Narratives of the Irrational
Wide Sargasso Sea, *Obeah and the Asylum*

Jean Rhys's novel *Wide Sargasso Sea* (1966) is a postcolonial rendering of Charlotte Brontë's *Jane Eyre* (1847), though Rhys hardly refers to the story of the English Jane and her circuitous path to marriage with Mr Rochester. Rhys's concern is with the 'other' woman in Brontë's novel, Bertha Mason, Rochester's Caribbean first wife, whose violent insanity has led her husband to incarcerate her and to deny her existence to Jane. *Wide Sargasso Sea* recentres the narrative of *Jane Eyre* by figuratively liberating Bertha from the English attic in which she is confined for much of the original story. Rhys thereby releases and examines the hidden colonial forces that underlie the central romance of *Jane Eyre* and, by extension, the wider world of nineteenth-century British literature and society. Part of this project of recovery concerns Bertha's madness. In the original story, the madwoman's insanity is a fearsome, inexplicable force of violence; in *Wide Sargasso Sea*, it is an irrationality structured through intense forces of colonial power – economic, sexual and racial – and their conflict with the indigenous world-views of the Caribbean.

The traumatic life of Antoinette Cosway is shaped by the conflicts of early nineteenth-century Jamaica. Her psychological and sexual vulnerability, for example, is intensified by the relative impoverishment of her family after the collapse of the Caribbean sugar economy and the end of slavery. These factors lead to the duplicitous bargain by which Antoinette is traded as sexual capital in an arranged marriage with the naive Englishman, (the unnamed) Rochester. Simultaneous with these changes within the colonial economy and its social organisations is the emergence of a volatile black Caribbean population ready to challenge the weakened autonomy of the plantation autocracy in the wake of emancipation. Antoinette's family home is destroyed by a mob of former slaves, and, in these economic and social reversals, Antoinette finds her identity both threatened and complicated, confusions that are to be at the core of her subsequent 'madness'. Instead of Brontë's representation of Rochester's wife as a monstrous, animalistic version of the foreign 'other' – the threatening 'madwoman in the attic' – Rhys establishes the process of her mental collapse within a discourse of political causation. Antoinette's personal chaos is intimately related to the disorders of colonialism of which she is an unknowing part. The destruction of her privileged identity as the daughter of a powerful slave-owning family is rapidly followed by her marriage – or sale – to Rochester. Rochester, finding himself in a world that he neither understands nor controls, and with a wife who is trapped disastrously between an apparently English whiteness and an emergent Jamaican identity, rejects and then confines her. In the confused world of their colonial marriage, slavery is privately restored, and Antoinette – renamed by Rochester, in slave-owner fashion, as Bertha, and unacknowledged as a wife – is transported across the Atlantic to England as chattel and madwoman. Bertha/Antoinette becomes a white slave completing a parodic reversal of the Black Atlantic passage until she, like the slaves on her own plantation, rebels with fire.

The central section of *Wide Sargasso Sea*, which describes the disastrous honeymoon of Rochester and Antoinette in a place called Massacre on an unnamed Caribbean island, is Rhys's most sustained examination of the structures of colonial and postcolonial madness. Mainly narrated by Rochester, it describes the collapse of the marriage, as the initial intensity of the sexual relationship gives way to his equally intense questioning of Antoinette's cultural identity. Rochester, displaced from even the residual colonial securities of Jamaican society, endures a disintegration of his own certainties of interpretation. He finds himself without any cultural markers, and begins to float free in a narrative full of gaps, unexplained actions and failures of communication. 'There are blanks in my mind that cannot be filled up', he writes, and his perception of Massacre becomes increasingly incoherent as he begins to doubt both the sanity of his wife and his own role as masculine and racial authority in a social context that he doesn't understand (Rhys 1966: 76). These uncertainties are intensified by what he perceives to be a confrontation with the supernatural, forces that he is unable to control by summoning the norms of early nineteenth-century Enlightenment values. His failure and the emotional chaos that ensues lead him to cross into the shadow side of that Enlightenment. He begins to re-enact the codes and practices of slavery, ironically on Antoinette, the slave-owner's daughter. In a brutally intimate domestic context, he creates a relationship and a material environment that conjoins the conditions of slavery (officially abolished, of course) and the emergent environment of the insane asylum.

Rochester's encounters with Antoinette's black Martiniquean servant Christophine are central to the complicated dynamics of change in this section. Christophine operates in the text as a point of security for Antoinette, as a mediating figure between Antoinette and her husband, and as a dangerous, mysteriously powerful force in Rochester's eyes. The encounter between the three after the first night on the island is characteristically ambivalent: 'Antoinette was leaning back against the pillows with her eyes closed. She opened them and smiled when I came in. It was the black woman hovering over her who said, "Taste my bull's blood, master" ' (85). Here, Christophine is at once the 'good servant', positioned alongside her mistress, and a 'hovering' presence who displaces the sexuality of the moment from the silent new bride to her own imposing body, forcing Rochester to the reluctant admiration of her hands as 'thin and beautiful, I suppose' in the next sentence. Christophine's first words challenge the racial and sexual securities that a marriage between two whites should have sealed. The coffee that she offers is '[n]ot horse piss like the English madams drink', and the masculine implications of the offer of 'bull's blood' is characteristic of a woman who more than once challenges her mistress to have more 'spunk'. The tableau here draws upon the fearful discourses of inter-racial sexuality which Fanon studies in *Black Skin, White Masks*. Rochester, white master and husband, is being sexually challenged by the black servant. As the sexual pleasures of marriage intensify, Rochester becomes disturbed by the unexpected physicality of the white wife, and at this point the 'otherness' – racial and cultural – of Christophine begins to be displaced on to Antoinette. She quickly becomes 'a stranger to me, a stranger who did not think or feel as I did', a process intensified by the suggestions of miscegenation and con- genital madness made by Daniel Cosway, a character who claims to be the mixed-race half-brother of Antoinette (93). As Christophine is reluctantly persuaded by Antoinette to practise obeah, an African-derived system of magic, to restore her estranged husband to her, Rochester becomes disorientated and paranoid. Beginning himself to interpret his experience of Antoinette and of Christo- phine through an irrational screen of magic derived from his reading of pseudo-anthropological accounts of the Caribbean, he loses control.

Rhys's presentation of the irrational, and of obeah in particular, is in some ways a problematic one. Judie Newman, for example, argues persuasively that the novel's treatment of African-Carib- bean magic is closer to Hollywood horror films of the 1940s than to a developed anthropological sense of the practice's place in the culture that she describes (Newman 1995: 13–28). However, the novel is also alert to, and interested in such distortions. For example, Christophine and obeah are described and interpreted through the perspectives and discourses of the two white char- acters, Antoinette and Rochester, and it is their sense of the efficacy or otherwise of the practice that is represented. And Christophine is not defined by the irrational alone, as, ironically, both Antoinette and Rochester come to be in this section. Christophine's thinking and behaviour are rooted in her evaluation of the viable economics and social possibilities of the post-emancipation moment when she can choose to leave Antoinette's employment and advise her former mistress to abandon her marriage (109–10). When pressed, she apparently performs the obeah that Antoinette desires and Roches- ter fears, but its results are ambiguous, and tell us more about the psychological predicaments of the white characters than the agency of African traditions. The estranged husband returns to his wife's bed, but he is now confirmed in a belief of his wife's essential 'otherness'. His response is to fuck a young black servant. This is simultaneously an act of cruel revenge, performed in his wife's hearing, a restoration of the sexual privileges routinely exercised by slave-owners such as Antoinette's father, and a realisation of the unacknowledged cross-racial sexual desire that has been present in Rochester since he first contemplated Christophine's beautiful hands on Antoinette's bed. In Rhys's narrative, obeah becomes a force that is not only a stereotyped magic in the way that Judie Newman describes, but, as ethnopsychiatry has come to recognise in different ways, an active dynamic operating within and without the discourses of rationalist understanding. Christophine's practices – secular and supernatural – show Rochester what he wants, and his rationalism is unable to sustain those desires. Its revelations are the reason that he reintroduces the practices of slavery to Massacre, and are what he has to turn the key upon when he returns with Antoinette/Bertha to Thorneyfield Hall.

Wide Sargasso Sea has become a text central to postcolonial literary studies. This is partly because it seems to offer a relatively easily assimilable guide to the relationship between postcolonial thought and a colonial past, and partly because of its alliance with the revisionist reading of the canon of English literature initiated by feminist critics in the 1970s (Sandra M. Gilbert and Susan Gubar's influential study *The Madwoman in the Attic* (1979) uses *Jane Eyre* as its centrepiece). Rhys's novel has become a classic case of a postcolonial narrative 'writing back' to the imperial centre. It reshapes a canonical text for its own purposes, revealing power structures secreted within apparently apolitical discourses, and redefines the previously despised and abject colonial object – the now-celebrated 'madwoman in the attic' – as a complex figure misshapen by colonialism and in difficult revolt against its power. The three later texts of 'mental illness' that I will discuss have a less secure place in the postcolonial canon, and this might be because they dwell more consistently in the colonial/postcolonial subject's mental world, and are consequently less amenable to translation. Whilst they are necessarily in literal dialogue with the discourses of colonialism and its aftermath – they are written, published texts that are knowing about colonial pasts and postcolonial presents – they also disallow the explicatory readings of patriarchal-imperialist power structures that *Wide Sargasso Sea* invites. Bessie Head's *A Question of Power* and her short story 'Witchcraft' and Erna Brodber's *Myal* locate the reader in what might be termed untranslatable postcolonial consciousnesses, and challenge the reader to enter the discourse of spirits in quite different ways.

Psychosis and Spirits

In Bessie Head's short story 'Witchcraft' (1977), set in Botswana just after independence, a villager, Mma-Mabele, is struck down with a strange affliction that is characterised by hair loss, headaches, lassitude and the presence of voices. It culminates in physical attacks by an apparently supernatural presence. The debilitating illness threatens Mma-Mabele's new-found economic security as a housekeeper, and the story describes her struggle to continue her life and understand the physical and psychological attacks that she is undergoing. Head presents this struggle as a contest between two interpretative systems. On one side is the traditional Tswana medicine that interprets such disorders as malevolent spirit attacks, the consequence of the witchcraft of the title. On the other are the 'colonial' systems of analysis represented by Christianity and the Western medicine of the hospital that diagnose her condition as the product of a dietary disorder. The relationship between these two systems of interpretation and treatment and the world-views that they imply is then played out in the struggles, mental and social, of Mma-Mabele as she seeks to understand her affliction and cure it.

Head's text treads a cagey line between the two approaches to treatment. Lekena, the Tswana healer in the story, is a cunning and proprietary presence, whose proffered treatments are always carefully priced and whose concern for Mma-Mabele is strategic rather than communal. The narrator notes the 'repeated failures' of Lekena's treatments, and suggests that Mma-Mabele's own sympathies are with the '[c]oldness and logic' of the 'Western' analyses of her condition (52). However, those tools are also shown as inadequate in dealing with the violence of her illness. The hospital's prescription of a change in diet fails to cure her, and the appeal to Christian salvation does not work. It is, in fact, Lekena who offers her the most sustained dialogue about her affliction and the most coherent cultural analysis of its progress. 'The trouble comes from Tswana custom', he tells her, 'and it is only Tswana medicine that can help you' (52). It is Lekena, too, who is the most acute and flexible interpreter of Mma-Mabele's symptoms, analysing the most extreme manifestations as a 'new thing' and intriguingly linking its appearance to the new political and social conditions created by Botswana's political independence in 1966 (55).

The ending of the story offers neither a choice between the opposing therapeutic practices, nor a synthesis of them:

> Just when everyone expected news of her death, she suddenly recovered and began to eat voraciously and recover her health. She was soon seen about the village at the daily task of drawing water and her friends would stop her and query: 'How is it you aren't sick any more, Mma-Mabele? Did you find a special Tswana doctor to help you, like the rich people?'
>
>   And she would reply angrily: 'You all make me sick! There is no one to help the people, not even God. I could not sit down because I am too poor and there is no one else to feed my children.' (55–6)

Here Mma-Mabele moves outside of the conflicting paradigms of psychopathology and spirits in an angry assertion of economic necessity as the dominant force of both suffering and cure for the African villager. Her condition remains inexplicable. The odd, disjunctive effect of this is characteristic of Head's work, and points up her sharp articulation of the challenge of the irrational for postcolonial studies. In most fiction, discourses of the irrational – madness, dreams, magic, spirits – are set within a dominant, normative narrative that frames and guides the reader's interpretation of its strangeness. The third section of *Wide Sargasso Sea*, for example, is written in the voice of the now-mad Antoinette/Bertha who is confined in Rochester's house in England. However, the reader is able to make sense of her irrationality by reference to the narrative, images, characters and locations of the previous sections and to the precursor text, *Jane Eyre*. Whilst Antoinette's monologue is itself disturbed and inconclusive, as readers we understand the condition of the narrator and know that the section is leading to her firing of the house because we can read it in unspoken relation to the earlier novel. Antoinette's madness is sanctioned, and ultimately redeemed, by a master narrative that can explain the causes and meanings of her apparent derangement. As in popular psychoanalytic practice, irrational narratives can be made to signify beyond themselves; they can be made to mean. In Bessie Head's fiction, though, this narrative and ideological pact breaks down. Her most radical exploration of this irrational space and bridge between, in Wilson Harris's terms, is the novel *A Question of Power* (1974).

A Question of Power concerns two years in the life of Elizabeth, like Head, a mixed-race South African living in exile in a village in Botswana. There is very little linear narrative. The novel veers between an evocation of Elizabeth's marginal life in Motabeng, particularly her participation in a village agricultural project, and an account of her inner persecution by the spirit projections of two village men, Sello and Dan, and a female spirit, Medusa. There are no explanatory transitions between the 'realism' of the village sections and the fantastic inner dramas, and no sustained attempt to interpret those dramas by the third-person narrator. Readers are pitched into what appears to be the raw material of mental extremity without guidance, as Elizabeth battles to survive the 'hard conflict of good and evil in arid terrain [that] crashed down into her consciousness as soon as she closed her eyes in the dark' (Head 1974: 61).

One response to the detailed and troubling descriptions of Elizabeth's disturbances is suggested by the Southern African context of the discourse and of Head's own history. Elizabeth's mental collapse and the aggression of the Dan and Sello spirits towards her are sustained through her and their preoccupation with certain categories of identity. As Fanon's later work on psychiatry and politics suggests, the political pressures of colonial regulation prey upon fundamental conceptions of self. 'Because it is a systematic negation of the other person and a furious determination to deny the other person all attributes of humanity', he writes in 'Colonial War and Mental Disorders', 'colonialism forces the people it dominates to ask themselves the question constantly: "In reality, who am I?'' (Fanon 1967: 200). The apartheid state in which Bessie Head and Elizabeth grew up had crude answers to that question. Since 1927, sexual relationships between black and white had been illegal, with mixed-race children therefore criminalised from conception. Elizabeth fractures along the lines of fissure within post-war South Africa, as sexuality, race and her relationship to a notion of 'African-ness' become sites of struggle and torment. '[T]he evils overwhelming her were beginning to sound like South Africa from which she had fled', the narrator comments, as Elizabeth's self-dissolution is 'organised' by strong interior presences which assault 'this loosely-knit, shuffling ambiguous mass which was her personality' (57, 62). Ironically, the psychosis/spirits work through the discriminations and tactics of terror established by the apartheid state: the Population Registration Act (1950), which required each South African to be racially registered, and the Mixed Marriages Act (1949) and Immorality Act (1950), which extended state power over sexual relationships. This political psychosis is complicated by the identities of the spirit agencies of her turmoil, however.

If Elizabeth is trapped in a violent psychic contest whose terms and anxieties are those of the puritan-racist state from which she is exiled, her chief tormentors are not South African, but projections of 'real-life' Motabeng cattlemen. The novel's laconic beginning, 'It seemed almost incidental that he was African', proves bleakly ironic, as African identity and Elizabeth's precarious social identity in Botswana become central to the mental theatre of the novel (11). Her racial hybridity and uncertain exile status are exploited by the spirits in their mockery of her exclusion from the rituals and argot of village life, and from the wider collectivities of the pan-Africanism that developed through the period of postcolonial nation-building. The main female spirit-tormentor, Medusa, lectures Elizabeth on both of these topics. 'Africa is troubled waters', she tells her, 'I'm a powerful swimmer in troubled waters. You'll only drown here. You're not linked up to the people. You don't know any African languages' (44). Far from opposing the rigorous fixtures of racial identities characteristic of apartheid, the African spirits exploit Elizabeth's displacements, disparaging her 'non-blackness' as an indication of sexual and mental weakness. Motabeng is, in one sense, a place of 'beauty and harmony', as she terms it, qualities associated with the market garden project that occupies much of the 'realist' parts of the novel (157). However, as in 'Witchcraft', the village is also identified with a cruelty and an ungenerous inwardness that becomes, in the spirit-figures of Dan, Sello and Medusa, active hostility.

Elizabeth's displacement of apartheid racial categories and per-secution on to Motabeng can be read in Fanon's terms as her ruinous internalisation of colonial practice, as past disturbances first intrude and then restructure her place of safety as one of further repression. Such a reading, though, needs to be set beside other aspects of Elizabeth's experience. As in 'Witchcraft', the positive aspects of Motabeng's community are offset by a sense of that society's exploitation of supernatural 'terror tactics' against each other (21). In a letter written after the publication of *A Question of Power*, Head is explicit in her localisation of the experiences in the book:

> It might simply be local African horror and I might have put my grand and faulty imagination into something I don't understand. Because all I have left is the horror and perhaps people don't know anything about how Baloi [Botswanan spirit-operators] work and how they go on and on behind the scenes . . . it might simply be local and African and something I don't understand at all. (quoted in Eilersen 1995: 150)

Here she shifts interpretation away from categories of psychosis and paranoia, and from the dynamics of Fanon's colonial trauma, insisting instead upon the possible local cultural meanings of her and Elizabeth's experiences. The narrative, she suggests, might be out of its author's control, touching, as Wilson Harris argues postcolonial discourses must, upon unknown local resources that are beyond the reach of universalising categories of psychology and political affect. If so, there is an irony here. Discussing her predicament with the South African director of the market-garden project, Elizabeth tells him, 'They have a saying that Batswana witchcraft only works on a Motswana, not an outsider. I like the general atmosphere because I don't care whether people like me or not. I am used to isolation' (56). The attack of the spirits could, strangely, be an acknowledgement of a (problematic, but growing) intimacy between Elizabeth and the Batswana culture of her exile. The vicious process of realignment with her new place, in which she is made to face 'African destiny, African circumstances', as she puts it at the end of the text, is also evidence of growing engagement, as well as disease (191). Perversely, the war of the spirits and her self can be read as a ceremony of integration as much as it is a theatre of cultural hostility. 'People . . . began to tell me of things that I had lived through in *A Question of Power*', Head wrote after her research for her history of Serowe, 'which are normal everyday events for black people' (quoted in Sarvan 1990: 15). Trauma can also be understood as enculturation, and the disintegration of Elizabeth might also be a process of integration of sorts.

A Question of Power, like 'Witchcraft', finally havers between interpretations of the experiences of its protagonist. The spirits might be those of psychotic episodes, those of the collapse of coherent self-identity in the aftermath of colonial/apartheid sociopathology, or the Batswana baloi. At the end of the novel, Elizabeth, like Mma-Mabele, just stops having the attacks. She 'left the story like that, unresolved', neither destroyed nor cured, neither despairing nor renewed (Head 1974: 201). Part of the wager of the novel, as Jacqueline Rose has argued, is that the reader is displaced, and left without secure tactics, 'feeling oneself go a little bit mad', as she puts it (Rose 1994: 404). The interpretative irresolution, in which Fanonian colonial psychopathology, clinical psychosis and malevolent baloi compete for meaning, is actually Elizabeth's own battleground of personal and cultural competence. The reader's minor derangement within this battle forces acknowledgement of the untranslated and untranslatable local experience of postcolonial extremity. As Rose suggests, *A Question of Power* forces the issue of ethnocentrism in discourse and interpretation. '[T]he boundaries between reality and hallucination are culturally specific *and* historically (as well as psychically) mobile', she writes, and Head's novel operates precisely on this strange border (407). In this way, to 'accept' its spirits, rather than rendering them psychosis or trauma, is not to depoliticise the experience of madness, but rather to re-politicise it, acknowledging in the process a range of interpretative possibilities that includes local functions of experience and analysis. South African apartheid and Motabeng baloi are not mutually exclusive agents of distress, nor is Western psychiatry either blind or true. The postcolonial critic, in other words, must keep his or her interpretative options open. Such a suspension of or pause in interpretation becomes even more critical in a reading of the final text of postcolonial mental distress, Erna Brodber's *Myal*.

Spirits, History and the Postcolonial Novel

Myal is set in the first twenty years of the twentieth century in the village of Grove Town in St Thomas parish in the east of Jamaica. It tells interwoven stories of two mixed-race adolescents. Anita is the victim of a 'spirit-theft' initiated by a neighbour, the landowner, Baptist and obeah-man, Mass Levi, in order to cure himself of sexual impotence. Ella, married to an American entrepreneur, Selwyn Langley, endures another version of spirit-theft when her husband uses her stories of her early life in the Jamaican village as the basis for a commercially successful minstrel show. Langley's cultural theft, like Rochester's behaviour in *Wide Sargasso Sea*, is also connected to anxieties about cross-racial sexual relationships. In the crises of both of *Myal*'s stories, the two young women endure mental and physical sufferings that resemble the symptoms of psychotic and psychosomatic illness, but which, in the discourse of the novel, are presented as the result of spirit attacks. They are both cured by the combined forces of other characters in the village who operate, like Dan and Sello in *A Question of Power*, both as social beings of different class and racial groups, and as the embodiments of local spirit powers (in this case, beneficent ones). This group is culturally diverse, including a Baptist preacher, an African bush-doctor, an elderly woman adherent of the Jamaican kumina cult, and, ultimately, the white English wife of the local Anglican minister. Together they perform the healing process of myal, to which the book's title refers. This work, drawing upon both inherited African tradition and emergent Jamaican belief-systems, combats the exploitation of girls made vulnerable by their age, by their mixed-race identities and by their engagement with British colonial education systems and the nascent neocolonialism of the USA.

More than *Wide Sargasso Sea* or *A Question of Power*, *Myal* places spirits at the heart of the story. In those other texts, Christophine's obeah and the Motabeng baloi allow a reader a degree of inter-pretative freedom. While they resist an easy translation of cultural experiences, and problematise the power relationships between African mental suffering and a Western psychiatric analysis of that suffering, the possibility of a 'rational' understanding of the distress is never explicitly denied. In *Myal* it is. The bush-doctor, Ole African, provides a key refrain in the story. 'The half has never been told', he declares, a biblical quotation that also states the limitation of the Western critical processes that have reached the island through colonialism (Brodber 1988: 41). *Myal* confronts that unknown half on its own terms. It is not interested in describing or analysing rural Jamaican belief-systems for the reader ('myal', for instance, is never defined or even mentioned in the text itself other than in the title). To explain would be to replicate the condition of the colonial Jamaican schoolgirl Anita, whose Western-style of studying 'splits the mind from the body and both from the soul and leaves each open to infiltration' (28). Anita's rigid education in exclusively colonial ways leaves her open to attack. Implicit in this is the suggestion that the postcolonial novel itself is always in danger of perpetrating the kind of theft and parody that Selwyn Langley effects through his exploitation of Ella's local experience and his presentation of that culture to a foreign audience. If a culture explains itself in the contexts of colonialism, it becomes complicit in that colonialism. Instead of explaining, *Myal* performs. It insists upon a reader's abandonment of the destructive certain-ties that debilitate its central characters, and upon his or her acceptance of the discourse of spirits. The book can't be about myal without denying the very principles of myal's practice. Instead, it aspires to be myal. This is why the term itself is never defined or even mentioned in the story. To define, categorise and analyse is to create the very threat that the process seeks to solve.

There are obviously difficulties for the humanist-trained reader in this demand, let alone for a harder-nosed cultural theorist. Brodber, though, is aware of these. A sociologist by training, her academic analyses of postcolonial women's conditions in Jamaica are securely within the secularist traditions of the field (see Brodber 1975, 1982). In *Myal*, though, she implicates the reader in different discourses and traditions of political analysis. Myalism is normally seen as the first pan-African religious movement to develop in the Caribbean. It emerged as a popular challenge to tribal divisions exported by slavery, thus initiating a distinctively Caribbean tradition that was in transatlantic dialogue both with the African past and a developing colonial modernity (see Chevannes 1998). Such discourse and practice result from new hybridities brought about by displacement and resettlement, and represent a system of interpretation and management that is resistant both to reductivist Afrocentrist appeals and to the co-options of 'colonial' systems of analysis. Myal is a force that is at once metaphysical and earthily political. It works through communal resistance to the individualisation and manipulation of power both from within a community (Mass Levi combines the different powers of preacher, policeman and obeah-man) and outside it (Selwyn Langley embodies the economic and cultural threat of a nascent globalising America). Whilst readers have no other choice than to take the spirits seriously as agents of change and reconstitution, their practice is never devolved from socio-historical struggles.

A long Jamaican history of rebellion and cultural invention is both summoned and prefigured in the places and events of the text. The setting of St Thomas recalls the Morant Bay rebellion of 1865, an insurrection over post-emancipation land rights. Its leader, the Baptist preacher Paul Bogle, lies behind the figure of Simpson in *Myal*, also a Baptist preacher, suspicious of collaborationist sects and able to maintain a co-existence between radical non-conformist political theology and African tradition. Simpson is also aware of new political manifestations. He speaks with qualified approval of the 'fellow in St Ann', a reference to Marcus Garvey, the Jamaican pan-Africanist who argued for the return of Caribbean and American ex-slaves and their descendants to Africa (see Brodber 1987). Simpson is critical of Garvey's literalist approach to the recovery of African identity, however, regarding it as a distraction from the immediate and local concerns of Jamaican culture. For Simpson, it is a misreading of the labile, Black Atlantic qualities of African identity that are always-already there in the densely specific culture of Grove Town and in the myal – spiritual, psychological and political – that the villagers make for themselves.

Myal, then, is a text that reassesses the descriptions and discourses of mental distress in a colonial/postcolonial context. It is, perhaps, the most radical of the literary texts discussed in this chapter because it requires an acceptance of and immersion in the non-Western conceptions of spirit-theft and the means of recovery. At the same time, though, it refuses to divorce such a world-view from a continuing postcolonial struggle for worldly political autonomy and social improvement. The spirits here are embedded in the body-politic of the individual and his or her society. They are sensitive to attempts to disrupt that local connection, and also attuned to wider political and cultural connections and threats, whether it be then-emergent political movements like Garveyism, old African traditions, or new colonialisms from beyond the Caribbean. Writing in the 1980s, Brodber had absorbed Fanon's arguments about the psychologically damaging power relations created by colonialism, and, in *Myal*, creates a text which, like *Black Skin, White Masks*, questions the appropriate strategy for describing and assessing that damage. The discourse of spirits becomes for her neither a reductive nor a sentimental return to African pre-modernity, nor a knowing exercise in a postmodern fiction. Rather, it is a means of exploring particular contexts of mental distress without recourse to concepts that are themselves implicated in the ideologies that contribute to that distress. To accept the spirits is as risky in its tendency towards the unconscious Other that Appiah warns against as it is in its confrontation with biomedical analysis. But not to do so, as Wilson Harris argues, is to eradicate existing resources of interpretation and change.

Conclusion

The fictions of Jean Rhys, Bessie Head, and Erna Brodber, in their different ways, press at the questions of the postcolonial agency and meaning of non-rational world-views. Whilst postcolonial studies, as an academic discipline, is committed to a secularist and rationalist programme of intellectual endeavour, works like *A Question of Power* and *Myal* confront the disjunction between such methods of study and indigenous systems of the interpretation of mental distress. Fiction, in some ways, is a special case; it is a discourse that accepts and allows some free-play of fantasy and the irrational. But, as Wilson Harris argues, it is also a discourse that is deeply implicated in European Enlightenment world-views at the expense of other narratives of explanation and expression. Harris's idiosyncratic demand for the acknowledgement of pre-colonial resources of understanding in a postcolonial context is significant beyond the limits of literary criticism. As the work of Frantz Fanon, ethnopsychiatrists like Roland Littlewood and anthropologists like Michael Taussig has shown, the unequal encounters of European-derived systems of analysis and interpretation and non-European contexts of experience are often problematic. The acts of translation and explanation implicit in these encounters are particularly ambivalent in those difficult areas of experience, such as madness and supernatural beliefs, which most fiercely challenge rationalist models of the world. As Meera Nanda has argued, there is the potential for dangerous indulgence in relativist positions that deny the efficacy and truth-values of Western rationalism. At the same time, though, it is necessary for practitioners of postcolonial studies to question the limitations and implications of their methodologies, and the politics of their encounters with other means of description and interpretation.

CHAPTER 6

Memory

One of the ways by which colonialism maintained power was by writing its own histories. These histories, like the imperatives of the colonial project themselves, were conceived within grand narratives of progress, expansion and enlightenment. Inevitably, they both systematically and accidentally recast, ignored and silenced other competing histories from the places and cultures with which they came into contact. Postcolonial studies has consequently set itself the task of examining and challenging those narratives, developing other ways of telling histories, and re-evaluating other ways of remembering. 'The desire of today's anti-colonial historian', writes Robert Young, 'is to retrieve a subaltern history that rewrites the received account both of the colonizing academics and of the native ruling elite, a history of the excluded, the voiceless, of those who were previously at best only the object of colonial knowledge and fantasy' (Young 1995: 162). Such processes of retrieval face formidable challenges of method, however. The pervasiveness of Western historiographies is, in fact, the central concern of the book that inaugurated academic postcolonial studies. Edward Said's *Orientalism* is not that new history of the 'voiceless' to which Young refers, but a demonstration of the scope and depth of the resources of historical representation developed and deployed by European and European-influenced narratives — scholarly, personal and imaginative — to produce its Others. It also demonstrates the complex investment of those narratives within the systems of political and economic power that conceived and administered empires and colonies. The history of that historiography, Said implies, is the history of the power to narrate. Any attempt to reconstitute the history of the colonised requires not only a questioning of history's subjects, but also a questioning of the methods and audiences of its narration.

Pessimistic assessments of postcolonial history suggest that there can be little or no escape from the enmeshments of colonialist historiography and 'narrativity'. Dipesh Chakrabarty, for example, argues that histories of colonised cultures, whether or not they style themselves postcolonial or subaltern, inevitably reproduce, if only by mimicry or allusion, structures and concepts implicated in the colonialism that they seek to reverse. 'So long as one operates within the discourse of "history" produced at the institutional site of the university', he writes, 'it is not possible simply to walk out of the deep collusion between "history" and the modernizing narrative(s) of citizenship, bourgeois public and private, and the nation state' (Chakrabarty 1992: 19). For Chakrabarty, postcolonial history, even in its most radical manifestations, necessarily works on the terms set and in the narrative patterns defined by dominant colonialist traditions. Whilst it may contest the latter's material and interpretations, and seek to represent experiences of subaltern groups, at a profound level it inevitably accepts their most powerful predicates – such concepts as nation, politics, progress. Said's *Orientalism* is shaped by the intellectual method and steeped in the details of the very scholarship that it seeks to re-interpret. Likewise, the Indian Subaltern Studies group, with which Chakrabarty is associated, may recast the priorities of Marxist history, but does not challenge the ultimately Eurocentric tenets of Marxist analysis itself. The very force of colonialism's presence in the lives and educations of those who seek decolonisation through the academy assures its influence in the later narration of those dissenting histories.

A more positive assessment of the potential of postcolonial historiography might point to the latter's contribution to a wider challenge to the grand positivist narratives of historical progress in the late twentieth century. Robert Young, for example, argues that experience of environments struggling against colonial legacies was crucial to the work of Michel Foucault and Jacques Derrida and to its challenge to what Foucault called the 'Western episteme', or system of knowing, just as it was in Frantz Fanon's more self-consciously political writings (Young 2001: 395–426). One of the ironies of the development of postcolonial literary studies in the Western academy, in fact, is that at the point of its celebration of the former colonies 'writing back' to the centre, the old imperial centres of knowledge, influenced by Foucault and Derrida, were busy writing themselves off as centres at all. The attack on the grand narratives, whether in the Western academy via deconstructive and postmodern theory, or through the political consequences of the collapse of Cold War certainties after 1989, or through new ethnographies and interests in localised, methodologically diverse conceptions of the past, produced a diversity of histories. These 'memory cultures', as Andreas Huyssen calls them, work outside or in sceptical dialogue both with the disciplining structures of knowledge that Said describes, and with those of their classical counter-narratives that were established through Marxism. 'The geographic spread of the culture of memory', Huyssen argues, 'is as wide as memory's political uses are varied, ranging from a mobilization of mythic pasts to support aggressively chauvinist or fundamentalist politics . . . to fledgling attempts . . . to create public spheres of ''real'' memory that will counter the politics of forgetting, pursued by postdictatorship regimes either through ''reconciliation'' and official amnesties or through repressive silencing' (Huyssen 2003: 15). As Huyssen's description suggests, though, this legacy of alternative history is a politically ambivalent one for postcolonial studies.

The dissolution of 'History' as a universal descriptor, and the emergence of 'histories' or 'memory cultures', as local, competing descriptors, can be seen as positive for postcolonial cultures. The pluralisation of histories encourages a recognition of subaltern groups' voices previously elided from historical narratives, and challenges the implicit hierarchies and progressive dominance of Eurocentric principles and practice. Capitalised 'History' becomes only one of a number of ways of telling a story that might take as its centre a range of different social formations. Moreover, these postcolonial histories need no longer necessarily define themselves through a struggle against a dominant 'master narrative', shaping their practice through an attention to the silences and gaps of imperial discourse. Subaltern histories can now be in dialogue with other subaltern histories outside of a once-dominant colonial paradigm, rather than with the old centre of empire. Australian historians, for example, could begin to explore the long history of the contacts between Aboriginals on the north coast of Australia and other maritime cultures, and the pre-Columbian cultures of the Caribbean can take a greater prominence in its cultural histories (see, for example, Baker 1999). The absence that was the so-called 'pre-colonial' could begin to take a more material shape, as the modern foundation myths of imperial 'contact', be it 1492 or 1788, were challenged, and indigenous social formations became more significant as historical sites and stories. Europe and its 'Others' was no longer the only significant axis of investigation.

Yet there is room for sceptical debate here, too. Andreas Huyssen himself poses the question as to whether the recent proliferation of 'memory cultures' 'can be read as reaction formations to economic globalization' (2003: 16). Rather than being signs of the collapse of History, memory cultures might instead be an indication of History's transformation into other, more insidiously totalising forms. They can be seen as histories that are both allowed and belied by an economic and political transnationalism that no longer needs an openly capitalised History to sustain it. Global capitalism can afford for local contestations of the past to take place because they provide no significant political challenge to its activities and powers. In fact, in many ways, such pluralism provides welcome distractions from the development of any such challenge. If nationalisms, and the 'imagined' histories that underpin them, proliferate without gaining significant economic and political power through that proliferation, a new global order can benignly tolerate and encourage cultural diversity as it pursues an old project of developing and consolidating its power and influence. In this way, History has not been broken up by the endeavours of Western intellectuals, by postcolonialism, or by the end of the Cold War. Though it has retreated from its old stages, it continues to develop its narratives by other means. As Edward Said has repeatedly argued since the first publication of *Orientalism*, the capacity for imperial narratives to reinvent themselves, barely disguised, in the political and economic executives of globalism and new world orders should be a constant source of concern and attention (see, for example, 'Preface' to the most recent edition of *Orientalism*: Said 2003: xi–xxiii).

The motives and practices of the pluralist histories themselves also need some cautious consideration. Instinctive sympathy for the recovery of subaltern voices has to be offset by a wariness of the intolerance and violence encoded in some of the expressions and effects of that recovery. Cultural histories, subaltern or not, are not necessarily benign, as the new nationalisms that emerged in the post-1989 Balkans clearly demonstrate. And the challenge to a universalist, positivist narrative of Western historical development through the acceptance of a variety of more localised histories need not come only from subaltern positions. Arif Dirlik notes that 'Disney these days justifies its constructions of the past or of the Other on the grounds that since all pasts are invented or constructed, their [sic] constructions are as valid as anyone else's' (Dirlik 1998: 225). In other words, an apparently pluralist sense of different experiences, conceptions and narratives of the past also needs to take into account the cultural and economic power deployed in creating and communicating those different constructions, and their consumption and use by different audiences. Using the logic of postmodernist relativism, the Disney corporation can argue that a film like *Pocahontas* offers a complementary, rather than a false, sense of history, one to be set beside, rather than against, Native American traditions or historical scholarship. Such an argument does not, of course, take into account the economic, technological and social contexts of the performance of these narratives. Disney's means of displaying and selling its narrative skew notions of relative validity in their exploitation of its power in a global economy. The resources of totalising forces can easily be deployed in the guise of relativist cultural transactions.

Despite these dangers, the challenge to History and the development of memory cultures, in particular, do present opportunities for postcolonial studies. In everyday usage, memory tends to be associated with individualised recollection that serves to constitute personal identity within a society, as opposed to the wider sweep of an objective narrative of cause and effect evoked by the term 'history'. But, as recent work in ethnography, psychology and cultural studies has suggested, memory can also provide a provocative critique of historical practice, and a flexible means of exploring postcolonial pasts. So, whilst the term 'memory' has more subjective connotations than 'history', its practices can also be related to wider social and cultural narratives. Paul Antze and Michael Lambek, for example, argue that memory can be conceived as social performances 'of commemoration, of testimony, of confession, of accusation' (Antze and Lambek 1996: xxv). These performances, Lambek proposes, should be 'understood as moral rather than simply technical, intellectual or instrumental', offering interpretations of historical experience rather than objective evidence (Lambek 1996: 235). Such material offers an opportunity to work outside the limits of textual authorities that underpin the traditional practices of European historiography, but which prove extremely problematic in dealing with predominantly oral cultures and in postcolonial contexts in which access to necessary documents is impossible or written evidence hopelessly contaminated. Filip De Boeck describes 'a generalised *memory crisis* and the breakdown of the production of history' in his study of the recent history of Congo. 'Congo/Zaïre's "factual" history of the past century is no longer available', he writes, and new postcolonial strategies are needed to confront this lack (De Boeck 1998: 26, 31). In such circumstances (and apartheid South Africa is, in some ways, a comparable example) the role of memory and its narratives becomes crucial. Postcolonial historiography has to develop methods of dealing with memory performances and their textless histories.

There is an obvious problem here in a potential loss of rigorous attention to empirical data, and this in a field in which such data has been previously ignored or difficult to access. However, memory cultures are only isolated oral records in extreme cases, such as that of the Congo to which Filip De Boeck refers. More usually, memory and orality can and do work in dialogue with written evidence, expanding and challenging the materials and practices of conventional history, and acting as an alternative version of those critiques of colonialist discourse initiated by Edward Said and Homi Bhabha. The emphasis upon memory as a performative practice may include a range of material and oral resources that can broaden postcolonial studies' textual emphasis to include other ways of framing historical narrative. These include such colonial 'performances' as museum displays. The case studies that follow discuss the 'Translantic Slavery' gallery in Liverpool, the work of the Irish storyteller Eddie Lenihan and the Truth and Reconciliation Commission in South Africa. The first traces transformations in the classical mode of staging and narrating colonial knowledge, the metropolitan museum, as it confronts postcolonial challenges to its methods of historical display and interpretation. Using as an example the 'Transatlantic Slavery' gallery in the Merseyside Maritime Museum in Liverpool, probably the most sustained attempt to renegotiate colonial history in a public context, it examines the strategies of its memorialising and the controversies these provoked. This is followed by a discussion of the relationship of orality, textuality and history in two contrasting postcolonial cultures. Beginning with a consideration of the implications of the Internet for cultural diversity, it will look at two contrasting cultures of performances of memory and orality. The first concerns Irish orality, nationalism and modernity, using the work of the contemporary storyteller and folklorist Eddie Lenihan to examine the problematic position of orality in a developed postcolonial state that is eager to distance itself from some aspects of its revolutionary nationalist past. The second assesses the significance of oral testimony in the postcolonial politics of South Africa, discussing the historical and political debates about memory that were raised by the work of the Truth and Reconciliation Commission in the post-apartheid settlement.

Case Study One:
Museums and Postcolonial Public Memory

The most striking material expressions of the power and meanings of colonial historiography were the great nineteenth-century metropolitan museums of Europe. Their monumental architecture and central locations are public assertions of a political and intellectual confidence in the management and control of history and geography. Within those monuments, the organisation and display of their artefacts are statements of a dominant culture's capacity to order and interpret the materials of others' cultures. To tour a Victorian museum was to enter a controlled world of the past and of a 'developing' present. There, the visitor could enjoy rightful access to and intellectual ownership of any of the material products of others that were considered meaningful. The museum became the site of a performance of knowing, an active translation of signs of 'otherness' into an emergent universal taxonomy, or grammar, of the past and of the known world. Specialist museums of natural history, archaeology, national history and ethnography housed in their displays objects that combined to create intersecting disciplinary narratives that established, in Tony Bennett's phrase, an 'evolutionary itinerary' of nature and culture (Bennett 1995: 181; see also Shelton 2000). The civilisational apex of that evolution was, implicitly or explicitly, expressed in the museum itself, in which all else could be displayed and known.

This process of universal knowing was also a process of selection and erasure. Even as displays organised their materials into a cultural grammar of description and interpretation, they effectively denied knowledge of the political, military and economic activities that underpinned that knowing. How an object moved from its place of production and use to its place of display and classification was elided, as were the material and social contexts of their previous use. The museum cleansed the artefact of the processes of empire even as it implicitly confirmed the extent and force of the resources of that empire. The involvement of nineteenth-century museums in the politics and trade of imperialism, and their public display of that imperialism's tendency to loot places of the goods that it found interesting, inevitably led to them being important to debates involving postcolonial history and ethnography. The role of the museum in former colonial centres and former colonies came into question. Curators had to engage not only with the history of the artefacts in their charge, but with the colonial history of the capture, transmission, display and interpretation of those artefacts. The ethnographic museum, in other words, had to confront its own past, and consider new dynamics of representation and use.

The recasting of such powerful ideological and material formations in a postcolonial context took two main forms. The first was an acknowledgement of the museum's historical implication in the processes of colonialism and revision of methods of exhibition, purpose of displays and expectations of visitors' responses. The second involved the inclusion of new kinds of materials, the restoration of absent histories of subaltern cultures and the retelling of the stories of artefacts with attention to the cultural histories and interpretations of their producers. More broadly, and most urgently in a postcolonial context, ethnographic museums sought to redress their role as archivists of dying cultures, a function in a 'science of disappearance' assigned to them by the positivist narrative of the European civilising process (Hallam and Street 2000b: 2). Their task of 'salvaging' materials from 'disappearing' cultures had helped shape a self-fulfilling prophecy, of course, as the artefacts – sometimes sacred objects – were removed from cultural sites to museums for 'preservation', thereby leaving indigenous cultures without cultural materials central to their identity. How this process could be reformed without abolishing the very concept of the museum has been one of the most testing theoretical questions of recent museum studies.

One response to this predicament was the development of the ideas surrounding the concept of the ecomuseum, an institution originally designed to aid the recovery of subaltern cultures within European nation states. The ecomuseum, in its presentation of history and its relationship to its sources and visitors, is strategically critical of the power structures of classical museum practices. 'Rather than serving as a storehouse or a temple, both of which isolate objects from ordinary people and require professional assistance for access and understanding', Nancy J. Fuller writes, '[it] recognises the importance of culture in the development of self-identity and its role in helping a community adjust to rapid change' (Fuller 1992: 328). In this influential reconception, the institution of the museum materially and ideologically spills over into, and itself hosts, the everyday activities of a living place, instead of standing physically and intellectually apart. As a contributory part of a living locality, rather than a withdrawn, objectifying collecting place for dead and dying cultures, the ecomuseum recognises and explicitly seeks to address the diversity of people that are nearby. Just such an intention is implicit in the development of the Liverpool gallery exploring the history of slavery and Merseyside (see below). To do so, it must disrupt the nineteenth-century codes of museum practice, both in its attention to the provenance and cultural meanings of its exhibits, and to the variety of visitors' possible responses to those materials. The most sanguine accounts of such 'postcolonialisation' of museums describe the emergence of new contact zones where 'co-presence, interaction, and inter-locking understandings and practices' between the previously divided cultures of displayers and displayed can create new dynamics of memory (Bray 2001b: 3). Museums become permeable, active institutions, rather than agents of cultural authority and recorders of inevitable destruction, and spaces for the performance of cultural encounters, rather than for the covert performance of colonial power. The display of items in a museum with the agreement and the participation of their cultural owners in their presentation and interpretation, James Clifford argues, can make exhibitions 'sites of a historical negotiation, occasions for an on-going contact', and museums places of communication and of social validation for a wide range of 'tradition-bearers' (Clifford 1997: 194; see also Simpson 1996; Kavanagh 2000).

The challenge, then, in James Clifford's words, is for '[m]aster narratives of cultural disappearance and salvage [to] be replaced by stories of revival, remembrance and struggle' (Clifford 1997: 109). Museums have to find ways to disrupt power structures embedded both in their own histories and in the material details of their 'ordinary' practices – their architecture, exhibition style, demands upon and expectations of visitors and their signage. Competing conceptions of the 'artefacts' by their original producers and owners need to be acknowledged and integrated within ideas of display and interpretation - if, indeed, such integration can be achieved at all. Michael Baxandall, for example, argues that there is an 'issue of exhibitability' in the very process of cultural display. 'A viewer looking at an artifact that is not designed for looking at', he writes, 'but that is exhibited as culturally interesting, culturally telling, or indicative of cultural or technical level is hard put not to be a voyeur, intrusive and often embarrassed' (Baxandall 1991: 40). And embarrassment is an understatement of that effect when objects are not only not meant for display, but are – on their own cultural terms – damaged by that display. Edmund J. Ladd gives an example of a dilemma produced by consequences of the Native American Graves Protection and Repatriation Act 1990, which returned significant rights of ownership of 'museum stock' to Native American groups. In Zuni culture, certain sacred objects, now displayed in museums, realise their sacred power only 'through the process of disintegration' (Ladd 2001: 110). The basic cultural imperative of the museum – that of preservation – comes into direct conflict with the cultural practice of what it was preserving. To preserve the object, in such a case, was actually to destroy it as part of its own cultural process. In such conflicts, the postcolonising endeavour of museums confronts other practices of cultural memory, meaning and use, and its own ideologies of preservation and display.

James Clifford's vision of cultural inclusiveness in a reformed postcolonial museum also faces competition from other contemporary developments in museum theory and practice. To read training materials for museum work, such as Timothy Ambrose and Crispin Paine's *Museum Basics* (1993), is to enter a very different world to that of academic ethnography, a world rooted in theories of post-industrial capitalist leisure, rather than theories of cultural difference. 'Museums in all parts of the world are in competition', they write, 'not simply with one another, but with all the other calls on people's leisure time', and their concern is with the display and marketing best able to manage that competition (Ambrose and Paine 1993: 17). Significantly, issues of culture, race or ethnicity are hardly mentioned in the textbook. Intense interest in the forms of display is balanced by a proportionate lack of concern with the politics of its representation or past. In a competitive environment, such as that defined by Ambrose and Paine, the development of clear narrative strategies and of historical 'experiences' that correspond with those other forms of entertainment are priorities. '"[T]he museum for a global village"', suggests Iwona Irwin-Zarecka, 'is a multimedia experiment in the engineering of feelings', and the relationship between the forms of that experiment and the cultures and histories that are being represented and 'felt' are politically as well as commercially significant (Irwin-Zarecka 1994: 106).

A postcolonial museum practice, then, aspires both to a self-consciousness about the implication of 'traditional' museum display in the politics and ideologies of colonialism, and to a reconfiguration of the relationship between the institution of the museum and subaltern cultures. Instead of rescuing fragments of dying cultures or celebrating a totalising historical and ethnographic system, the postcolonial museum seeks dialogue with living cultures, complementary practices of display and explanation, and the contextualising of its objects. Against these aspirations, however, are pressures of commercial competition and funding that encourage the replacement of older exhibitions with display practices that pose their own dangers in a postcolonial context. Museums that represent 'living' indigeneity, however sensitively they develop those representations, still confront the ideological difficulties of display and preservation that underlie the institution of the museum and its history in European Enlightenment thought. The very act of display itself, no matter how sensitively achieved, as Barbara Kirshenblatt-Gimblett has argued, removes the activity being displayed from its 'living' environment: museums and festivals 'share a performance discourse that often stands in contrast (if not in opposition) to the ways communities stage themselves' (Kirshenblatt-Gimblett 1991: 429). To create such a performance risks social practice against institutional memory, as participants 'become signs of themselves', in Richard Kurin's phrase (Kurin 1991: 338). And even where the experience is in some ways distanced by the past, there can remain severe difficulties in the politics of that representation. The history of slavery is one example of this.

The permanent exhibition 'Transatlantic Slavery: Against Human Dignity', housed in the Merseyside Maritime Museum at Albert Dock in Liverpool, remains the most significant and sustained attempt to address directly issues of colonialism in a British museum. Opened in 1994, and funded by a grant from a local charitable foundation, it aims to examine transatlantic slavery and 'seeks to increase understanding of what has happened to people of African descent in the modern world' (*Transatlantic Slavery* n.d.: 1). This ambitious undertaking was unprecedented in Britain (save for the more limited display in Wilberforce House in Hull) and in America. Its compact galleries, housed in the basement of the museum, thus embody the dilemmas and decisions of a new metropolitan museum attempting to achieve a critical postcolonial perspective on its own city's disturbing colonial history. The controversies that those decisions continue to provoke also suggest the volatility of its representational and political processes.

'Transatlantic Slavery' is organised as a chronological and geographical narrative of the slave trade. Beginning with presentations on West African life before transatlantic slavery, it goes on to describe the processes of enslavement, offers a brief assessment of the role of slavery in Liverpool's early development, before re-presenting the development of American and Caribbean plantations, and the various struggles against slavery that culminated in the ending of the trade and eventual emancipation. There are a variety of displays: artefacts, such as African cultural objects, dioramas, video installations of West African slave forts, audio material such as readings of extracts from slavers' and slaves' letters and memoirs, and some interactive elements – Liverpool street-signs that lift to reveal the slave connections beneath, for example. The most striking – and controversial – aspect of the gallery, however, is the darkened room that represents the ship's hold during the Middle Passage. Here, the visitor walks through a low, empty space, with video projections of blurred human forms, which provides a transition between the African sections and the New World gallery.

The decisions taken in the construction of the sequence of galleries all concern the difficult politics of representing an extreme racist history to a varied group of visitors in a place implicated in that history. Two issues are immediately evident in the display strategies. The subtitle of the exhibition, 'Against Human Dignity', alerts the visitor to the explicit principles of the display. It seeks to offset any objection to a voyeurism or tastelessness in presenting such a history, an objective that is also emphasised in the signage. The second issue is one of representation and perspective – who is telling whose story to whom. The exhibition has to prevent a sense of the exhibition appropriating the subaltern histories of Africa and the Caribbean for its own purposes. One strategy for achieving this is a fictional narrative of an African family whose personal experiences of the slave trade attempt to provide a subjective element to the exhibition. There is also a particular highlighting of an African agency in resisting slavery throughout its history in order to counter any sense of complicity or passivity among slaves, and to prevent a depiction of the white anti-slavery movement as the ultimate deliverers of black freedom. This issue of agency is also a constant concern in the signage of the exhibition. In her account of her part in the writing of display commentaries, Helen Coxall emphasises the difficulty of establishing a discourse that avoided implication in the very processes of the history it sought to relate (Coxall 1997). She describes the detailed assessment of the political implications of vocabulary and syntax in these areas, including the use of the word 'slave' as a generic term that itself enforces the deculturation and anonymity embedded in the systems of slavery. The narrative voice of the signs also runs the risk of asserting an institutional command of an 'other' history. For example, the temptation to use passive verb constructions when discussing 'what was done to slaves' implicitly removes all agency from the enslaved Africans. In the very articulation of the meaning of its exhibits, signage can reveal the complex enmeshment of the avowedly postcolonial museum and its discourses in the colonial histories that it seeks to describe and critique.

The most pressing political arguments about the transatlantic slavery exhibition have concentrated on the representation of the slave ship. Anthony Tibbles, the exhibition's curator, writes that 'a walk-through experience was essential, visitors needed to experience the dislocation, but we did not want something that frightened people (particularly children) and we did not want to sensationalise' (Tibbles 1996: 99). This difficult equation suggests fundamental political problems of postcolonial representation. Whilst the room attempts a roughly accurate reconstruction of the hold of a slave ship, it is also, with stark irony, subject to contemporary Health and Safety legislation (which required the elevation of the ceiling), and addresses the sensitivities to which Tibbles alludes. The spare order of the contemporary space certainly contrasts with the displayed quotation from a contemporary witness, Alexander Falconbridge, who reports that the 'floor of [the slaves'] room was so covered with blood and mucus which had proceeded from them in consequence of the flux that it resembled a slaughterhouse'. The room's stylised allusion to such horror is, as Tibbles himself admits, a compromise between the risks of exploitative representation and those of complicitous excision. In his critique of the gallery, Marcus Wood argues against the very necessity for the experience that Tibbles emphasises. 'The models and installations', he writes 'have been evolved out of a curatorial theory emphasising "consumer involvement" and "client participation" . . . [y]et, surely, there are subjects and objects which cannot fit within the educational framework of current museum culture' (Wood 2000: 300). For Wood, the experiential aspirations are necessarily compromised by the institutional means of their delivery, the concomitant ironies of health and safety in a reconstruction of a slave ship, and the wish not to alarm. How far such ironies endanger the political effectiveness of the exhibition's narrative for its visitors remains a key question, as does the appropriateness of a museum gallery for the memorialisation or explanation of such a subject.

These questions about the politics of memory are sharpened in the final part of the exhibition. After the gallery that gives an account of the abolitionist struggles and successes, the exhibition concludes with a video-display of African-Caribbeans in Britain talking about the importance of history to their identity, and the different ways in which that history informs their lives – individual and collective. The final sign, as the visitor exits, is a poem: 'My history is of Afrika/my past is of the West Indies/my present is of England/my future is of the world'. Whilst the interviews seem intended to emphasise the continuing relevance of slave history to Black British experience, that Britain, like the poem, is shaped to an emphatic message of self-determination, multiculturalism and development. 'My future is the world' might seem an awkwardly gestural closure to the topic of slavery as the visitor leaves, and heads towards a consideration of the less problematic diaspora of the 'Emigrants to a New World' in the next gallery. However, it is also one that poses again questions of the function of the memorialisation. Is the museum intended to record the complex implication of the history of Liverpool in slavery, narrate a history of resistance, or articulate a positive political message of emergent multiculturalism?

The arguments that continue to surround 'Transatlantic Slavery' are not just about the strategies and decisions of the exhibition itself. Rather, they concern wider questions of the meaning of the memorialisation of traumatic histories, the representation of colonised cultures, and the relationship of postcolonial memorials to their location in a place like Liverpool and to their various visitors. The gallery remains the only substantial attempt to engage with these questions in the context of a free public museum. The continuing critiques of its decisions, now over ten years old, suggest that, while they remain controversial, the museum still acts as a site for the performance of debates about public representations of slavery, as well as a site for those representations themselves. The literature surrounding 'Transatlantic Slavery' is only one aspect of this. More difficult to describe and assess, but in many ways more significant, are the responses of non-specialist visitors. My (anecdotal) evidence of listening to conversations in the gallery during several visits over the last five years is that of hearing exactly the debates about the propriety, strategy and relevance of the displays that have been described above. These informal discussions of historiography are, of course, performances working outside the carefully calibrated narrative and signage of the gallery itself, but they touched on the central questions of the representation of postcolonial memory, nevertheless. Listening to them suggested the possibility that the exhibition itself might have acknowledged and integrated its own problems of strategy and design in its signage, creating what Dipesh Chakrabarty describes as 'a history that deliberately makes visible, within the very structure of its narrative forms, its own repressive strategies and practices, the part it plays in collusion with the narratives of citizenships in assimilating to the projects of the modern state all other possibilities of human solidarity' (Chakrabarty 1992: 388). Chakrabarty's model of a self-critical museum that would integrate its problems of representation within its displays, rather than present solutions to them, is an appealing response to the critiques of the 'Transatlantic Slavery' gallery. And yet the risks of overcomplication, and of defensiveness and evasion in such a self-reflexive strategy, are also present. Whilst the museum might aspire to some kind of closure of meaning, the performative debates of its visitors – difficult to record or quantify – nevertheless suggest that its active processes of memorialising lie (necessarily) elsewhere.

Case Study Two:
Information Technology, Orality and Postcolonialism

If the 'Transatlantic Slavery' gallery provides a case study for the 'postcolonialisation' of European museum traditions, developments in digital technologies for preserving and communicating knowledge suggest new strategies for thinking about postcolonial memory. At the same time, the debates around information and communication technology (ICT) also return to older questions about memory cultures, their forms, audiences, access and involvement in wider structures of political power. This section will outline some of the debates surrounding ICT's potential for preserving and disseminating 'minority' cultures, before discussing the structure and significance of one of those residual 'minority' cultures within a developed postcolonial nation. Both concern the relationship between text and orality.

'[A]ccess to information and knowledge increasingly determines patterns of learning, cultural expression and social participation', writes the Director-General of UNESCO, Koïchiro Matsuura, 'as well as providing opportunities for development, more effective poverty reduction and the preservation of peace . . . knowledge has become a principal force of social transformation' (UNESCO 2003: 1). UNESCO's promotion of 'knowledge societies', which led to its World Summit on the Information Society held in Geneva in 2003, is based upon the premise of an expansion of ICTs throughout the developing world. Such an expansion would allow remote communities to have access to and participate in the creation of knowledge, and to deploy it to change their economic and cultural circumstances. As the UNESCO website also makes clear, though, there are significant obstacles to this participation, not least the existing access to such technology (7.8 Internet-connected computers per 1,000 inhabitants in sub-Saharan Africa, for example, compared to 400 per 1,000 in the West). A second is the level of literacy essential to Internet use. UNESCO records a world non-literacy rate of 20.3 per cent in 2000, with that of Africa standing at 40.2 per cent, compared with America's 6.9 per cent. 'How can we build equitable information societies or thriving democracies', asks Koïchiro Matsuura, 'if so many remain without the tools of literacy? How can intercultural dialogue and mutual understanding prosper when the literacy divide is so great? And how can poverty be eradicated when the roots of ignorance are left undisturbed?'

UNESCO's placement of information technology and literacy at the centre of its development project raises questions for postcolonial studies as well. It is predicated upon the Internet allowing not just an improvement in Third World access to knowledge, but in that access achieving a significant shift in global relations of power. Instead of older forms of 'one-way' cultural technology, such as television, which transmits the images and voices of dominant cultures, digital technology potentially allows a dialogic, 'two-way vehicle' of communication. There is an economic dimension to this as well. Television depends upon large-scale capitalisation and complex production technologies to produce products for domestic consumption and then export. The absence of comparable culture industries in developing countries inevitably made those cultures consumers rather than producers. Drawing on the work of Dan Schiller, the UNESCO report sees the possibility of more reciprocal cultural relations through new technologies. 'Trans-national cultural production', it argues, 'is shifting towards commercializing local cultural content on a global scale, which means that the foreign cultural influence on products sold to people in the U.S., for example, is greater than had been the case in previous decades' (UNESCO 2003: 3).

UNESCO's optimistic interpretation of the Internet's capacity to preserve and promote cultural diversity and address imbalances of cultural distribution is contentious, however. Dan Schiller himself argues that there is a strong link between digital communication systems and neoliberal globalisation policies, noting that a 'lengthening series of social practices through which we play, educate, and generally provide for one another are more or less rapidly being annexed by capital' (Schiller 1999: 206). Another source for UNESCO's proposals on ICTs is equally sceptical. Armand Mattelart argues that the 'contemporary universalization of a productive and techno-scientific system remains, more than ever, marked by the inequality of exchanges' (Mattelart 2000: 109). These 'logics of exclusion', as he calls them, affect not only the economics of unequal development, but also the very cultural identities that UNESCO is so sanguine that ICTs can help to sustain. The argument for the use of the Internet as a resource for the storage and communication of cultural diversity tends to rely upon assumptions of a cultural equality within its users and of the form of its storage and communication being ideologically and politically neutral. However, access to the 'universality' of the Internet depends upon the local availability of its portals.

As well as the low figures of access in the developing world, cited earlier, the UNESCO report also points out the dangers of rapid technological obsolescence in digital technology, with obvious implications for retrieval by cultures that are, at best, outside the vanguard of digital evolution, and dependent upon cheaper imported technologies. Mattelart also challenges 'the recycled myth of the neutrality of technology', arguing for the cultural specificity of the Internet itself. 'Systems for structuring meaning through digitization of knowledge', he writes, 'underlie a specific geocultural model. The risk is that it may impose as a criterion of universality a particular mode of thinking and feeling, a way of "organizing the collective memory"' (Mattelart 2000: 120, 118). If diverse cultural memories are to become reliant upon ICTs, in other words, the storage of and access to those memories are, at best, socially and economically negotiated processes, and the form and content of that memory will be affected by the 'invisible' culture of the communication system itself. This is something that is particularly evident in ICTs' encounters with predominantly oral cultures.

Orality, as was noted earlier, has a marginal place in recent postcolonial studies. Indeed, re-inflected as illiteracy, it remains a problematic element in cultural exchanges, as the UNESCO report on International Literacy Day indicates (UNESCO 2002). In that report, illiteracy is an unequivocal social wrong, a barrier to knowledge and progress, and a badge of cultural and economic backwardness. Whilst there are certainly powerful arguments for relating political progress with the growth in literacy, there are also dangers in eliding the complexity of the relationships between written cultures and spoken cultures that the concept of 'illiteracy' disguises. For whilst cultures can be (pejoratively) illiterate, they can also be (more positively) oral. The non-negotiated development of literacy can, in fact, have a deleterious effect upon the integrity of oral cultures, just as much as it can make those cultures 'players in the knowledge-based post-industrial era', as the UNESCO report has it. In a recent review of the state of the complex oral art of Wolof griots, or Senegalese praise singers, for example, Samba Diop sees them as 'doomed to disappear altogether because of new forms of entertainment such as cinema, radio, television, and videotape, but most of all because of the impact of schooling and literacy' (quoted in Kaschula 2001b: xv). These cultures of orality should never be romanticised (a nostalgia that can only be developed through the means of literacy, of course), nor should the social and political benefits of literacy be understated. Nevertheless, the place of orality for postcolonial studies, not least in its complex relationships with literacy and memory, remains a significant, if under-represented, one.

Postcolonial studies is rooted in textual materials and textual criticism. Consideration of orality tends to be concentrated upon its influence upon writing or limited to specialist disciplines within a broader field of ethnography such as 'oral literatures', a contradictory term that suggests some of the conceptual difficulties in addressing the topic (see Finnegan 1988, 1992). But orality, like memory itself, insists upon the possibility of a de-textualised, performative history that works on different principles from those of conventional historiography. In his classic study *Orality and Literacy* (1982), Walter J. Ong has a chapter entitled 'Writing Restructures Consciousness', a summary of the book's main argument. Writing is not just a transcription of sound, but is a technology that produces fundamental change in conceptions of the world, its meanings, and the recovery of knowledge through its establishment of an 'autonomous discourse' (Ong 1982: 78–116). The technology of writing is rapidly naturalised in a textual world, Ong suggests – cultures come to write and read without thinking about the actions as processes of transformation. However, in cultures where orality remains a powerful influence, this shift of consciousness is incomplete, and powerfully residual and even dominant forms of remembering persist. The 'psychodynamics of orality', as Ong terms it, depend upon situated performances of meaning (31–

77). Telling and remembering are dialogic acts that cannot be displaced into the remoter privacy of writing. Oral communication of memory is, therefore, always socially based, constructed within a given moment of performance and, theoretically at least, open to response, debate and challenge. The 'privatisation' of history and narrative in a text limits such possibilities, and accrues a power to itself as a text, a silent code of knowing that is quite different from the inevitably social acts of the public speaker of memory.

The arguments that are generated by these different structurings of history/memory concern the value and meaning of narratives. The empiricist tradition of Western historiography is dependent upon the establishment of material and textual sources and their interpretation, and the development of a linear narrative that appeals to objective criteria of historical truth. These criteria cannot be applied to oral narratives or 'social memory' as James Fentress and Chris Wickham have termed it. 'Facts are typically lost quickly at early stages of social memory', they write, and this means that historical meanings are expressed by other rhetorical strategies and narrative conventions (Fentress and Wickham 1992: 73). In these circumstances, stories remain the primary means by which social memory operates. As John D. Niles argues, '[s]tory-telling helps the members of a group maintain an awareness of how the present is a result of past action. It can thus help groups maintain their identity without institutional amnesia, thereby relating their past history to the present state of things and preparing the way for an imagined future that may be a more blessed state' (Niles 1999: 54). For Niles, history/memory in oral cultures needs to be analysed not only by reference to verifiable facts – that is, textual sources – but through its performance and its efficacy within particular social contexts. History as oral performance is removed from the remote objectivity of text and re-placed in the immediacy of dialogue.

Orality and social memory have been subject to contradictory evaluations by text-based cultures. In terms of empirical historiography, social memory can only be of 'a lower order of reliablity', as one historian puts it, and oral history still tends to be a supplementary activity to mainstream (textual) history (Vansina 1985: 199). As Ong and Fentress and Wickham argue, the processes of memory cultures are in many ways antipathetic to the values of 'historical narrative'. Such testimony is prone to factual 'error' and to forgetting. Memory, particularly in strongly oral cultures, works uncomfortably within the structures and processes of historical research, interviews and source-evaluation, where different values of sequential order and narrative value tend to apply. The performative aspect of oral memory also renders the recording of its narratives problematic, as they have, in some way, to be translated into 'texts'. Yet the performance itself – its body and its moment – is necessarily part of the act of memory. To remove the body is to limit the performance is to recast the memory.

This unequal relationship between apparently 'secure', easily transmittable text, and the fragile momentariness of memory-performance has also led to various ideologically driven valuations of orality. Nationalist movements, particularly those engaged in struggles against colonial powers, were able to appeal both to the endangeredness of oral traditions, threatened by colonial imports of literacy and education, and those traditions' embodiment of pure cultural values. The collection, preservation and revival of those traditions, as in Ireland in the late nineteenth century, became a political process of anti-colonial resistance and nation-building. Orality, based, in Diarmuid Ó Giolláin's words, 'on the ideal notions of a past completely dominated by tradition and of a present and future completely antithetical to it', becomes a political construct as well as a social and cultural practice (Ó Giolláin 2000: 173). Typically, this romanticising of traditional cultural purity elides or distorts a long-standing and complex interplay of literacy and orality in so-called oral cultures. This has ironic results. Orality, rendered passive and endangered instead of active and hybrid, becomes in such circumstances a condition that requires record and rescue by the intervention of the textual forces of cultural nationalism.

The association of orality and oral-memory cultures with an earlier, and now problematic, phase of cultural nationalism might be one of the reasons for postcolonial studies' relative inattention to them. As the UNESCO material referred to earlier suggests, the political imperatives of technological and educational development contrast with the dangers of a romantic attachment to pre-industrial cultural production. Nevertheless, the conjunction of orality and literacy and their contrasting versions of memory cultures in different postcolonial nations do provide suggestive material for postcolonial studies. The work of Eddie Lenihan is a case in point. Lenihan occupies a unique, though, in terms of postcolonial studies, unremarked, place in contemporary Irish culture. He is a scholarly collector of oral narratives, working in western Ireland, where he was born and lives, recording stories of the supernatural, and local history and belief on audio tape and, more recently, on digital film, and transcribing them into written form. However, Lenihan is a folklorist unattached to any academic or government institution, and one committed to demonstrating the living practice of these narratives. He is a teller as well as a recorder, an interpreter through performance as well as through written record and analysis. Lenihan's scholarship, in other words, is an oral scholarship as well as a written one, and one that is active within the popular and scholarly diasporic structures of Irish America, and, to a lesser extent, England, and on radio, television and local newspapers in Ireland. In these ways, it is a practice of memory that seeks to bridge older forms of memorialisation and contemporary circumstances, creating those 'unsuspected bridges' that Wilson Harris defines as essential to postcolonial cultural survival (Harris 1999: 242).

Eddie Lenihan's most recent work, published in written form in the collection *Meeting the Other Crowd* (2003), is interested in the faery, and associated residual practices of belief and custom in the rural west of Ireland. This is, of course, difficult territory for contemporary postcolonial studies. On the one hand, it appears to return to the interests of nineteenth-century patrician folklorists and the nationalist movements with which they were associated. On the other, it can be read in the context of contemporary Ireland's problematic maintenance of ruralist simulacra for cultural export, something exemplified by such diverse products as tourist literature, Irish 'theme' pubs in England and the musical *Riverdance*. It is a version of national culture that national arts organisations, with a developing sense of European contexts, are keen to distance themselves from. The Irish Arts Council, for example, does not fund the work of traditional storytellers and collectors. However, this perception of a tradition compromised by a conservative nationalist past ignores the innovative potential of the work of someone like Lenihan in its development of the resources for a distinctively, but not self-advertisingly, postcolonial memory culture. This involves both the interpretation of traditional materials, and their representation in the diasporic contexts of Irishness.

The stories in *Meeting the Other Crowd*, and Lenihan's performances of them, are both narratives of the faery and intricate social and historical maps. Their articulation of what Lenihan calls a 'parallel' Ireland is one of local landscapes, historical presences and, often, the political and ideological struggles of the 'material' Ireland (Lenihan 2003: 1). Rather than harking back to a pure and distant peasant past, Lenihan's emphasis is upon presence. The stories are contemporary, and articulate the persistence of history within the localities of modernity. Their recurrent interests are in a negotiation between two worlds, the relationship between past and present, the meaning and ownership of land (a key concern of colonial history, of course), and the unpredictable and violent consequences of the breaches of codes of social respect and local knowledge. The cultural embarrassment that Lenihan himself notes in contemporary Ireland about its oral traditions, with its supernatural materials and conservative social connotations, is also a rejection of cultural resource for historical understanding, managing social change and renegotiating contemporary Irish identity in dialogue with its troubled pasts (Interview with author). Eddie Lenihan's particular contribution to this lies in his redefinition of the folklorist or ethnologist as an active teller, as well as a recorder and an archivist.

Performing the stories that he collects allows Lenihan to develop a cultural dynamic very different from that of the more conventional academic folklorist. Without the financial support and grants of that profession, he is also without its demands of discourse and publication and its limitations of audience. Recording a story can mean not only turning it into text, tape or DVD, but also reworking it as a performance for other audiences. That sense of the past as a discourse that penetrates the present, and the museum as a place that opens to and spills out in the world, is given performative expression here. The performances, whilst frequently occupying a stage shaped by tourist expectation or diasporic nostalgia, reject any romanticising of the role. To experience Lenihan's storytelling is to witness a re-articulation of the past, and a performative dialogue between the present and the past – a persistent theme in the stories, of course. Just as, in the tourist economies of the Caribbean, hotel performances can support, rather than erode, indigenous musical forms, so tourist economies and diasporas allow Lenihan a living and fund his collection. He, in turn, redefines rather than memorialises the role of the traditional storyteller in his insistence upon the present as well as the past, and upon the need for the postcolonial nation in Europe to attend to its 'parallel worlds' in order to make sense of that present.

Case Study Three: The Truth and Reconciliation Commission of South Africa

The work of the Truth and Reconciliation Commission (TRC) in South Africa in the period of reconstruction after apartheid provides a vivid case study of the possibilities, dilemmas and dangers involved in the construction of new forms of postcolonial memory and the importance of orality to this process. Formed in 1995 by the passing of the Promotion of National Unity and Reconciliation Act, the TRC was charged with two tasks. The first was to construct through personal testimony a record of the most serious violations of human rights committed between 1960 and 1994. The second was to deliberate on the granting of indemnity from legal prosecution for these crimes, and to identify those entitled to state compensation for their sufferings. Beyond these specific objectives was the less easily definable aspiration to the TRC participating in, and itself defining the means of creating, a new post-apartheid nationhood and a new dynamic between present and past. The latter project required the TRC to engage with the unique circumstances of the South African postcolonial settlement. While the Commission was based upon the model of earlier non-judicial inquiries in post-dictatorship states in South America, the South African TRC operated within more complex and dangerous political dynamics. The reconstitution of the nation embarked upon in the early 1990s was predicated upon the participation of members of the previous apartheid government within the new structures of power, and in the negotiations on the creation of the TRC. There was, therefore, no possibility of a wholly demarcated vision of the past; the latter's presence was palpable within the new administration, and the processes of remembering had to take this into account.

The TRC was divided into a three-part structure that reflected its different objectives: the Human Rights Violations Committee, the Amnesty Committee, and the Reparation and Rehabilitation Committee. These different, but inter-related bodies, were charged with making a new history, and their approaches to that process involved pragmatic decisions that also depended upon a theoretical conception of what a historical record might consist of within the particular context of post-apartheid South Africa. Their methods developed into a deliberated and necessarily improvised historiography that organised a difficult dialogue between competing demands and materials of the past. Thus, whilst the TRC was entrusted to provide an accurate history of human-rights abuses within the fixed parameters of the time of organised state terror after the Sharpeville massacre to the time of the post-apartheid settlement, the possibility of an empirical 'standard history' was precluded by the particular tendentiousness of the process. Any aspiration to objective history was, in fact, offset by a consciousness of a present context imperilled by the pressure of the very past that was being recorded. Telling history here had a purpose that was both a truth in and of itself, and a truth that was designed to defuse the violent potential of that history in the present. The historical method was affected by other factors as well. There was, for example, an absence of documentary records. Many had been destroyed by the state security forces before the transition of power, and many of the victims came from predominantly oral cultures (Bundy 2000: 16). The processes of the commission also challenged accepted practices of historical method. By rejecting a judicial model in which perpetrators were tried for stated crimes, and in which evidence of all participants, victims and perpetrators alike, would be evaluated by adversarial procedures of questioning, a different kind of historical process and record was shaped. The practical procedures of the different arms of the Commission give some sense of this, and suggest the importance of orality and literacy in the process.

In order to be granted amnesty, perpetrators of gross violations of human rights had to submit a written statement of those violations to the Amnesty Commission. Their written statement was judged by reference to the fullness of the statement and to the political motivation of the offences – that the crimes were not committed for obvious personal gain, but under orders from an existing political organisation, be it state-run or revolutionary. There was no requirement to express contrition or accept guilt in the submission. This process was both one of textual interpretation – of the fullness, clarity and motivation of a narrative – and one that resisted the traditional tests of European historiography and law through comparative evaluations of statements, assemblage of material evidence and judgement against defined standards of truth and justice. The collection of evidence from victims of human-rights abuses was more problematic, often because of its social contexts, the hiddenness of those offences, and the potential cultural conflicts between a state commission and the perceptions of the victims. Their evidence was gathered by groups of statement-takers who conducted interviews in local languages. Again, the process of the interview was not an objective collection of evidence. There was no element of questioning, and statements were not made on oath. Rather, it was the eliciting of an oral narrative, an eliciting that formed 'part of the therapeutic and healing work of the Commission' (TRC Report quoted in Deegan 2001: 140). The initial stages of the TRC work, then, involved a mixture of textual and oral collection, interpretation, evaluation and therapeutic process. However, what came to be seen as the most significant, and the most controversial, aspect of the TRC was the development of these texts and interviews into public performances of memory in a series of public hearings.

Beginning in 1996, the TRC held fifty public hearings in different regions of the country. Again, the organisation and conduct of these events were deliberately distinct from those of trials – the process was decentralised away from the capital, Pretoria, there was generally no inquisition and no formal judgement, and only a small number of amnesty applicants or victims who made submissions were called to appear. The Chairman, the former Archbishop of Cape Town, Desmond Tutu, also introduced a variety of 'non-judicial' performative practices into the proceedings. He opened sessions with prayers, for example, encouraged singing at particularly difficult moments in the testimonies, and eschewed the formal behaviour of a European judge by sometimes responding with open emotion to the narratives. This deliberate reconstruction of a non-judicial environment and process of testimony proved extremely controversial, and raises difficult questions about the management of public memory, but it marked off the hearings from the rituals of state law, creating a very different space for historical testament and response. Despite the extreme volatility of these hearings, they were also carefully planned – too carefully, in the opinion of some critics of the process (see Jeffery 1999: 41–3). Participants were selected as representative of the particular histories and cultures of the area in which the hearings were held. The sessions gathered as many perspectives on the history as possible, with cross-sections of gender, race, age and cultural group being represented. Unlike the truth and reconciliation committees in South America, the sessions were public and were also reported and broadcast on radio and television. In this way, the hearings were projected as a means of establishing a national memory of suppressed brutalities in the period from 1960 to 1993, and of achieving a strategy for reconciliation by communicating personal testimonies through mass media.

The work of the TRC was, inevitably, controversial, and in those controversies can be traced particular inflections of the arguments about the theory and practice of postcolonial memory that have been described above. Three issues are particularly significant in these debates. The first is the decision to choose personal testimony over legal process as the primary means both of recording the history of apartheid and of effecting national reconciliation in its aftermath. The second concerns the methods and expectations of interpretation of that testimony by the Commission, and by the wider South African audience that witnessed them through the media. Such harrowing testimonies, of both perpetrators and victims, had no pre-established legal frame to shape and 'use' them, and so the practice of interpretation became uncertain and dangerous. Emotive responses of horror, shame and pity might be necessary reactions, but their role and effectiveness in establishing a new political and social culture remained vague. The third issue concerns the role of the TRC in selecting and presenting the testimonies, and in producing outcomes that met the ambitious terms of reference that it had been set.

Challenges to the TRC's use of personal testimonies without interrogative methods of testing and developing that evidence centred upon the Commission's most radical historiographical innovation: its definition of four different kinds of 'truth', all of which would be accepted in its work. These were: 'factual or forensic' truth; 'personal and narrative' truth; 'social or dialogue' truth; and 'healing and restorative' truth (Truth and Reconciliation Commission of South Africa 1998: 110). The first kind is equivalent to the empirically validated evidence of a European-style court of law. 'Personal and narrative' truth is the uncorroborated narrative of personal perpetration, endurance or witness. Dialogue truth is described by the main architect of these categories, Albie Sachs, as 'social truth, the truth of experience that is established through interaction, discussion and debate [original italics removed]' (113). This implies the acceptance of multiple perspectives on the past, rather than an excision of some narratives or their coalescence into one overriding truth. The fourth category is perhaps the most controversial of them all, defining validity by the effect of its telling, rather than by the factual content of its narrative.

To complicate in these ways the standard of an objective public truth, a concept fundamental to the legal procedures of all nation states, was an extraordinary step. In a sustained critique of this strategy, Anthea Jeffery argues that the consequences of such an abandonment of 'traditional' definitions of verifiable truth was potentially ruinous. 'The rule of law would be undermined', she writes, 'by a judicial process that dispensed with the need for corroboration and substantiation of evidence, and was content to rest upon such things as "instinctive suspicions"' (Jeffery 1999: 18). Despite the avowedly 'non-legal' status of the TRC – it couldn't establish guilt or innocence, acquit or sentence – it nevertheless accepted, evaluated and published narratives that in themselves declared responsibility for gross human rights violations. It also made judgements on cases of amnesty applications. 'For the purpose of making findings of accountability,' Jeffery argues, 'there was only *one* form of truth on which the Commission could rely – the factual or objective truth termed "microscope" truth by Judge Sachs' (70). Yet very little of the evidence considered by the Commission could be validated in this way. History was being defined, in other words, by a deliberated and valued disavowal of established practices of what was or what was not so, and memory culture was taking an unusually central place.

Jeffery's critique of the TRC is one of a range of sceptical appraisals of its strategies and effects. Richard A. Wilson's study *The Politics of Truth and Reconciliation in South Africa* (2001) also argues that the concept of 'human rights' was dangerously subjectified and weakened by the processes of the Commission. '[I]t is misguided to delegitimize human rights at the national level by detaching them from a retributive understanding of justice and attaching them to a religious notion of reconciliation-forgiveness, a regrettable amnesty law and an elite project of nation-building', he concludes (Wilson 2001: 230). The Commission, as a nascent state authority, necessarily appealed to a popular understanding of what Colin Bundy terms 'an official, objective, impartial and authoritative truth'. What it delivered, though, depended upon a 'thoroughly modern historicism' that recognised the past as shifting, contradictory and incomplete – a deconstructive conception of history amenable to the sophistications of theory, but less comprehensible to the victims of apartheid themselves for whom the procedures of criminal prosecution and punishment were more appropriate means of analysis and response (Bundy 2000: 13–14). For Wilson and Bundy, the Commission risked shifting attention from the widespread devastation of apartheid as a colonial social and political practice to a more limited ethical – and dubiously therapeutic – appraisal of selective individual experiences. The political purposes and contexts of the TRC were arguably skewed by its therapeutic discourses of revelation and healing. These allowed certain representative narratives to carry the historical weight of apartheid whilst deflecting attention from the ANC government's own significant concessions on land-ownership and economic stability in the transitional process. As Heribert

Adam and Kanya Adam put it, the concentration on gross human rights violations 'freed the many beneficiaries of apartheid from responsibility and obliterated the reality of structural violence of racial laws for millions of victims who have not been recognised by the TRC process' (Adam and Adam 2000: 34).

These critiques of the TRC centre upon its framing and management of memory cultures. The Commission's commitment to a therapeutic truth over the establishment of social justice, and its redefinition of the meaning and efficacy of personal testimony within a state inquiry, these critics argue, rendered it ineffective as a popular force. Its confused status as a quasi-legal process and a collective historian of apartheid made its practice eccentric and distracted attention from the necessary transformation of state processes of law and economic redistribution. Despite these powerful arguments, however, the South African TRC's decisions and practices do raise significant issues for any consideration of post-colonial history. Its pragmatic engagement with traumatic memory at an urgent and dangerous historical moment, and its management of a public revisitation of a hidden history provide an extraordinary case study of the improvisation of a national historiography that struggled with basic tenets of truth-telling and evidence as it went on. The inconsistencies and problematic elements of its procedures were part of this. Not to have struggled, and, moreover, not to have been seen to struggle, in the making of a new history would also have been damaging. Albie Sachs, who formulated the Commission's four definitions of historical truth, suggests that the 'objective of the whole TRC process was to help humanise South Africa and to move away from abstract characterisations and categories' (Sachs 2000: 96).

The TRC Report also acknowledges a specifically African rationale for its decisions and practices. 'In the (South) African context, where value continues to be attached to oral tradition', it states, 'the process of story telling was particularly important', an acknowledgement that has difficult implications for a legal system founded upon national, metropolitan and textual legal processes (Truth and Reconciliation Commission of South Africa 1998: 112). For Sachs, to initiate the legal procedures and checks that would allow the 'factual and forensic' definitions of truth to be established would be to turn to remote and alien practices of truth-telling, as well as extending the process of 'truth and reconciliation' to lengths that would lead the transitional process to disaster, and requiring equally disastrous penal sanctions or acquittals for lack of substantive evidence. In this interpretation, the apparent flaws in the process were part of the process itself, however distressing they might seem in terms of legal precedent and in the retrospective critiques of legal and political histories of the Commission. Sachs's emphasis, like that of the Chairman of the Commission, Desmond Tutu, is primarily upon the 'experiential truth' that emerged from the process, in however problematic a form. The TRC report's faults were part of its pragmatic engagement with the necessarily contradictory demands that were made upon the commission in its task to shape both history and reconciliation. '[I]t was rough, it had its seams, you could see the stitching', Sachs writes, and in that roughness and incompleteness were complexities and irresolutions vital to its moment (Sachs 2000: 97, 98; see also Tutu 1999). In Sachs's account, the dangers and flaws that legal analysts like Jeffery and Wilson identify are not just excusable, but necessary.

The 'experiential truth' that works, however dangerously, outside the structures of an empirical system of analysis and verification is dependent upon practices of narrative and performance. This is a bleakly formal description of the stories that the TRC elicited, which were harrowing, disturbing testimonies in many different ways. Nevertheless, the Commission depended for its success upon its capacity to provide a forum for the performance of these stories and upon the effects of these stories on a national audience. A striking feature of the TRC report, an official document after all, is the number of references to literary texts and oral narratives, celebrating 'the widest possible record of people's perceptions, stories, myths and experiences' (Truth and Reconciliation Commission of South Africa 1998: 112). This can, of course, add weight to legal critiques of a dangerous subjectivity and impressionism entering an empirical process. In other ways, though, the emphasis upon oral narrative and its particular rhetoric and effects can also suggest a radical revaluation of memory and telling within a diverse cultural context and fraught historical moment. In her account of the hearings, *Country of My Skull* (1998), Antjie Krog dwells upon the testimony of an Eastern Free State shepherd called Lekotse, which describes the devastating effects that a security-service raid on his home had upon himself and his family. Krog presents a literal translation of the account, laid out on the page as though it were a poem (Krog 1998: 210–16). The analysis that follows points up the oral narrative characteristics of its structuring, and analyses the details of the exchanges that Lekotse reports between himself and the policemen. She writes of 'Lekotse's urgent need to understand, to have access, to be informed about the world of the intruders and their thinking'. 'He does not naturally ignore or resist the police', she writes, '[h]is instincts are to give them access to the fulness of his world, and he expects to gain access to their world in return' (219). For Krog, the story becomes a brutal fable of colonial intrusion and thoughtless or deliberated wreckage, both of family and material safety, and of an innately generous social practice.

Krog's illuminating analysis of the testimony that she and the audience of the hearing witnessed also raises difficult questions both of interpretation and politics. In one sense, Lekotse's performance validates the TRC's commitment to the presentation of personal truth. His narrative persists in its own course, and at various points he resists the Chair's attempts to prompt or clarify the story. It also suggests the possibility for African narrative practices to operate on their own terms within new state-controlled institutions. The oppositional, interrogative rhetorical mechanisms of European court procedures would have disallowed the narrative continuities of his account, and would have been antipathetic to the ethical and social values that the narrative embodies. To question the truth and form of the narrative in this way would have been a further assault upon his identity. In other ways, though, Krog's treatment of Lekotse's evidence suggests the very dangers in the TRC process identified by the critiques discussed earlier. To reproduce Lekotse's testimony in the form of a poem and to subtitle it 'The Shepherd's Tale', is to aestheticise its narrative, to emphasise its 'qualities' of expression and eloquence, and so to make it something other than evidence. This rhetorical shift – from testimony to poem – is one encouraged by the 'roughness and incompleteness' of the processes, and by their openness to a cultural pluralism of telling. However, the question is also raised by Krog's treatment of Lekotse of whether the shepherd was best served by an appreciative frame for the rhetorical and memorial power of his testimony or by a process of justice, something that the TRC was unable to inaugurate.

Conclusion

The processes of the TRC, then, focus issues of postcolonial history and memory in a volatile and intractable political moment. Its experiments with the staging and interpretation of historical testimony suggest both the necessity of challenging and rethinking models of evidence and interpretative process in particular cultural and historical situations, and the political dangers of doing so. The TRC can be interpreted as a radical challenge to embedded and inappropriate notions of historical truth, and a distraction from the necessity of profound political and economic change. In such circumstances, the evidence of Lekotse can either be read as proof of the Commission's success in eliciting testimony that works on its own rhetorical terms, or of the tendency of the hearings to invite a liberal celebration of a new multiculturalism when it should be establishing a new justice. The South African Commission, like the 'Transatlantic Slavery' gallery and the oral narratives collected and performed by Eddie Lenihan, in their very different ways, is an example of the diverse practices of postcolonial history and memorialisation, and the theoretical and pragmatic difficulties that they set. Questions of the cultural specificity of historical narrative and evidence, the relationship of memory, history and modernity, the relationship of the form of telling to the history being told, and questions of audience and use, are all differently focused in these performances of postcolonial pasts.

CHAPTER 7

Land

Land – its description, control and exploitation – was both the material and the ideological base of colonialism. Possession of land was a matter of material power and political will – troops, administrators, maps, settlers, communication systems, agriculture and industry. But what shaped, described and communicated these practices were distinctive processes of political and cultural imagination. As Edward Said argues in *Orientalism*, the place of empire had to be made, rather than discovered. 'It is not merely *there*', he writes of the Orient, 'just as the Occident itself is not just *there* either' (Said 2003: 4). Whilst the places of empire are certainly worldly and real, they are also produced by the discourses that define them. '[A]s much as the West itself', Said argues, 'the Orient is an idea that has a history and a tradition of thought, imagery and vocabulary that have given it reality and presence in and for the West' (5). How they are imagined and reproduced is important, not only to the coloniser, but also, through his or her interpretations of that imagining, to the people of that place.

The creation of colonial geographies, 'the process of transforming space into place', as the Australian historical geographer Paul Carter calls it, was also a process of contest and elision (Carter 1987: xxiii). The resources for making a colonial place in 'new worlds' like Australia or the Americas were imported not local. Local geographies, ways of knowing, mapping and shaping the land already existed, of course, but the relentlessness of the importation of colonial ways of geographical seeing at best ignored, and at worst destroyed, those indigenous cultures of landscape. In Australia, for example, local geographies of great complexity were not recognised as geographies at all. A culture predicated upon the essential identity of human societies and their lands remained unseen. The indigenous place was rendered 'space' as local land practices were either by-passed or overridden. On its sites, the colonial place was constructed through the deployment of the perspectives, assumptions and technologies of Europe. In all co- lonised states, to a greater or lesser extent, imported geographical concepts of national borders, private property, desacralisation and the exploitability of natural resources largely superseded already- existing cultural and social practices.

The first priorities of anti-colonial movements were, necessarily, those of defining and recovering political control of coherent local territories. Early anti-colonial struggles tended to be structured and emotionally fuelled by definitions of national identity allied to aspirations to specific national borders. Whilst the physical geo- graphy of this transitional phase in postcolonialism could be relatively simple in islands, such as those of the Caribbean, such territorial definitions were much more traumatic in larger land- masses such as the Indian sub-continent and Africa. There, the frequently arbitrary signage of postcolonial state borders caused – and continues to cause – ethnic conflict, mass migration and international and civil warfare. However, as Frantz Fanon was one of the first to point out, the social and political implications of nationalism were to be extremely problematic for both island and continental postcolonial states.

Identification with what Benedict Anderson famously termed the 'imagined community' of nationhood provided a means of mobilising anti-colonial struggles throughout the world, yet the very force of that imagination came later to expose dangerous faultlines in postcolonial nation states (Anderson 1983). Regions claimed by rival nations or divided by arbitrary national borders have remained dangerous points of dispute – the conflict between India, Pakistan and local nationalists in Kashmir since indepen- dence is just one, particularly severe, example of this. The homo- genising, essentialist tendencies implicit in ideas of national identity have also made the nation state unsteady ground for cultural and ethnic diversity. The violent schisms in nations as various as Rwanda, Guyana and India are testament to this. In the different contexts of settler colonies such as Australia and New Zealand, tensions between the nation-state and its land practices and those of its indigenous populations persist in ongoing legal and social struggles.

These various conflicts over the ownership, control and exploitation of land have remained at the economic and political centre of postcolonial national experience, and they continue to be shaped by changing cultural formations. The intensification of globalisation, for example, with its resultant population movements, developing communication systems and ready transfer of capital has pressured the resources – economic, administrative and imaginative – of the nation state. Older emphases upon ethnic and linguistic purity, as recent postcolonial theories of hybridity have emphasised, have become harder to sustain as cohesive forces of national identity in these circumstances (see Bhabha 1994: 139–70). At the same time, the proliferation of new nationalisms in the wake of the dissolution of Cold War blocs, and the continuation of the legal struggles of some indigenous peoples for land rights have made older conceptions of land and land-use newly politically significant within existing nation states. The frames for the struggles for the possession and control of land and its resources have also diversified. The growth of international tourism, for example, has radically changed the economic and physical geography of some postcolonial states, as land-use changes and different social dynamics are formed.

The case studies that follow concern three different postcolonial contests over the definition, ownership and use of land: the relationship of indigenous Australian and Central American conceptions of land to recent work in cultural studies; the beach as a site both of colonial contact and postmodern tourism; and the landscape of the postcolonial carnival. Developing the book's interest in the postcolonial politics of popular cultural practices, the beach and the carnival are examined as two contrasting sites of leisure and cultural contact and conflict. These sites of pleasure also articulate a continuing history of political struggle and emergent cultural identity. The beach, for example, connects the primal ground of colonial experience – discovery, meeting and describing the 'other' – with an important site of postmodern global travel industries. The negotiations of power conducted in the contemporary places of leisure between indigenous populations and visitors will be examined through a discussion of recent discourses and theories of tourism, particularly those that are interested in tourism's transactions of gender and sexuality. Carnival also connects the colonial past to recent postcolonial encounters and struggles. The history of Caribbean and South American carnival, and its role as a performative negotiation of the forces of colonial power and its subjects will be developed through a discussion of London's Notting Hill Carnival in the 1970s. In a formative period of Black British identity, the carnival and its transformation of local ground in the British capital became an important focus for political action and debate, and a key site for the development of distinctive British–Caribbean connections. The first case study explores the contests and relationships between indigenous and colonial perceptions of land and dwelling. Drawing upon the historical and theoretical work of the Australian Paul Carter and the distinctive postcolonialism of the Guyanan Wilson Harris, it traces some recent discussions about colonial and indigenous geographies, and discusses the possibilities for re-imagining a link between indigeneity, modernity and emergent postcolonial discourses and land practices.

Case Study One: Indigenous Australian and Caribbean Conceptions of Land

Paul Carter's work on the historical geography of Australia is, perhaps, the most sustained scholarly attempt both to define the processes by which land is colonised and to re-imagine land as a potent agency in postcolonial cultures. For Carter, as for Edward Said before him, the act of colonisation involved the rendering of land as manageable and secure in the imagination of the coloniser as well as in his or her political and social life. In *The Road to Botany Bay* (1987), *Living in a New Country* (1992), and *The Lie of the Land* (1996), he explores the 'process of transforming space into place' through rhetorical as well as material means: naming, mapping, drawing, and seeing, as well as settling, planting and building. This 'poetics of colonization' is a way of organising by framing and interpreting it through the aesthetics and value-systems of the coloniser (Carter 1996: 292). The colony is mapped in the cartographer's image, and known through his or her own terms of reference. It is a process that results in a radical restructuring of the landscape, and its recasting from the processes of its 'own' history to those of another.

In Australia, the colonial 're-seeing' resulted in the erasure of an ancient human geography, one that was almost entirely imperceptible to the European arrivants. The inability of colonists to see and understand Aboriginal methods of defining and managing their lands – through 'fire technologies', for example, and by the establishment of implicit boundaries to maintain the viability of natural supplies – led to a landscape long mapped and maintained by indigenous peoples being redefined as 'wilderness' (see Johannes 1989). This ideological enclosure of land, both in the gaze and the map, and its elision of what was already there, had drastic political, as well as cultural, consequences. The transformation of a productive indigenous geography into an unproductive 'European' landscape of desert and unmanaged terrain enabled a straightforward legal dispossession of Aboriginal land and culture. Whilst (cursory and devious) settlements were entered into with the Maori of New Zealand, whose social structures and land management were more obviously explicable within nineteenth-century anthropological categories, the Aboriginal place in Australia could be rendered space by its colonists (see Pawson 1992). This erasure of the gaze then allowed the reconstruction of the place and the nation on a European model.

Indigenous Australian geography was and is radically different to European systems of land description and ownership. Aboriginal belief-systems posit an originary 'mapping' of the land by ancestral beings – a primal making of space into place through its singing into existence from chaos. That ontological act resulted in an inherited obligation for the indigenous peoples. They were required to maintain and 'speak' a land that is itself a fundamental constituent of individuals' and groups' social and spiritual being. 'It would be as correct to speak of the land possessing men as of men possessing land', writes Kenneth Maddock (quoted in Berndt and Berndt 1988: 140). This reciprocal 'ownership' challenges fundamentally First World constructions of property relationships in society. Indigenous Australian world-views, for example, could not countenance a possibility of land being commodified and titles sold (though other kinds of territorial exchange were possible). Likewise, colonial legal systems equated ownership with dwelling, settlement and intensive exploitation of resources, mistaking indigenous nomadism for a way of life beyond any social structure, and implying that Australian Aboriginals, 'alone among the peoples of the earth, have no institutions of tenure in land' (Wilmsen 1989: ix).

Deeply embedded cultural norms of cultivation and development also defined a colonial blindness to Aboriginal land practices. Veronica Strang notes that 'maintaining stable resources was a priority [for indigenous peoples], not just in practical terms, but also because traditional Aboriginal cosmology was predicated on the assumption that, following the example of the ancestral beings, people would live in the same place in the same way for ever' (Strang 1997: 89). But the 'invisible' strategies for maintaining stability of resources in a hunter-gatherer landscape, the lack of obvious human process and the absence of signs of ownership – visible boundaries, fixed settlements – allowed European perceptions of wilderness to define the land. The legal implications of this ideological conflict of seeing and geography were notoriously confirmed in the Blackburn Ruling of 1971, the judgement in the first test case for Aboriginal land rights in the Northern Territories. L. R. Hiatt summarises the ruling as follows:

> In the judge's view, the relationship of the clan to the land failed to meet two vital criteria of a property relationship: the right to alienate, and the right to exclusive use and enjoyment. The fact that the spiritual bond between Aborigines and their territories was so profound as to make alienation unthinkable was thus deemed to render their estates as not owned in any commonly understood legal sense of the word. The Aboriginal ethic of generosity that regarded exclusive use and enjoyment as indecent made comparison even harder. (Hiatt 1996: 29)

The ruling was later overturned and the terms of the debate adjusted to allow limited land rights to indigenous groups. However, the formalisation of fundamental oppositions in conceptions

of land, its use, its ownership and the legal frame for its management remains a stark statement of the conflict about the meanings
of land in the postcolonial settler nation state.

Paul Carter's work is a detailed mapping of the colonial processes
that he terms an urge 'to embrace environmental amnesia' and the
forgetting of 'what wisdom the ground, and its people, might
possess' (Carter 1996: 6). This amnesia, he argues, has resulted in
the ruinous political disenfranchisement and displacement of
indigenous peoples, and all the material and psychological miseries
that have led from that. But Carter also suggests damaging consequences of this forgetting for the culture that displaced those
peoples. In *The Road to Botany Bay*, for example, he argues that 'it
may well be that the relative failure of Whites in Australia to
incorporate aboriginal concepts into their language is one reason
why English here continues to float, as it were, off the ground and
why . . . its poetic power to evoke the living space remains patchy'
(Carter 1987: 136–7). The incorporation of Aboriginal 'poetics' of
land within the rhetorical and cultural appraisal of Australian
history and society is startling in a field that more usually renders
such notions as ideas for sympathetic study rather than as
intellectual tools. To ground an argument in that poesis itself, as
Carter does here and elsewhere in his work, is enough to make any
social scientist edgy. Nevertheless, the most challenging aspect of
Carter's work is its insistence that the insights of indigenous world-
views cannot be neatly translated or contained as objects for
description and analysis within the practices of conventional
study. For Carter, they are performative as well as being source-
materials. Like Erna Brodber, Bessie Head and the anthropologist
Jeanne Favret-Saava, he insists upon a discourse and an intellectual
practice accepting as well analysing cultural difference, however
destabilising that may be for that discourse and practice.

At the centre of Carter's work is the pressure to reconceive the
possibilities for seeing Australia and restoring – without romanti-
cism or nostalgia - indigenous knowledge and culture to the living
cultures of a postcolonial state. In a narrower sense, it is also to
recognise the force of that reconception for the writing of history,
cultural studies, and criticism. In *The Lie of the Land*, for example,
he argues that the writing of Australian cultural history should

acknowledge the complicity of its own strategies of seeing and narrating in the colonial gaze. The acknowledgement of this 'ideological enclosure act', as he calls it, must also be offset by an adjustment in intellectual practice that seeks, without patronage, to include indigenous knowledge, and accepts the consequences of that inclusion. '[A] writing that embraces this shifted perspective [of indigeneity]', he writes,

> must also, presumably, accept its implications. It will not be panoptic, not attempt to see through the "cloudy" passages where linear lines of descent are obscured. It will be "poetic" in the derided sense given this term by serious historians and social scientists – but only because it refuses their off-the-ground generalisation, and insists upon deepening the differences. (Carter 1996: 366)

Such conclusions challenge both the discursive and analytical practices of contemporary postcolonial social geography, most strikingly in Carter's examination of the space/place beyond urban centres, and his serious attention to the 'residual' social practices, as well as social predicaments, of indigenous peoples. The struggle for land rights for Aboriginals becomes not only a contest of contemporary social justice, though it certainly is that, but also a struggle for the maintenance of past and the development of possible future conceptions of land, its meanings, its uses and concepts of its ownership. It embraces a joint strategy of challenging dispossession through legal systems structured by culturally specific definitions of property and settlement whilst maintaining radically other views of the relationship between community and land. The difficulty of this for settler Australians is acknowledged in Carter's own wary sense of the intellectual dangers of writing about indigenous world-views. To do so entails entering 'the realm of representation [that is] the house of Western history', he writes, 'with its books, its windows and doorways', and it risks losing track of the 'new country' on its old terms (Carter 1996: 54). To describe the limits of Western historiography and geography, is, perhaps, to articulate a promise of a new historical geography, but it is not, finally, to perform it, and Carter, like Brodber and Head, is interested as much in the limits of postcolonial discourse as its potential. Nevertheless, Carter remains a geographical historian unusually willing to explore the consequences of the history of colonialism and the possibilities of alternative perceptions of the land. It's a strategy that links him to other postcolonial thinkers, like Wilson Harris, who, as was seen in Chapters 3 and 5, remains steadfastly outside the 'house of Western history' and articulates a more radical reconception of the land in postcolonialism.

Harris's work as a surveyor for hydro-electric projects in the Guyanese interior during the 1950s forms the background for his reconception of the meaning of postcolonial land and of the discourse for representing that land and its peoples. In his various accounts of these river journeys, both fictional and non-fictional (though the opposition has little relevance for Harris), the surveyor's gaze of description and intent of 'modernisation' is transformed by Harris's attention to what he terms a 'landscape of the imagination which can be unravelled to lay bare many complex rooms and dimensions' (Harris 1999: 174). The embedded restrictions of colonial observation that Carter describes and which Harris's surveyors embody are radically disturbed by the land itself. Drawing upon the 'forgotten' world-views of the indigenous peoples of South America and the Caribbean, Harris seeks to construct a new means of addressing landscape beyond the destructive dualisms of the material and the metaphysical, the colonial and postcolonial, 'a world habituated to the pre-emptive strike of conquistadorial ego', as he puts it (Harris 1983: 137). Harris argues for the persistence of the apparently lost languages, histories and world-views of the 'pre-colonial', and for the possibility of a new vision of land and identity. One of Harris's short autobiographical narratives, about two expeditions along the Potaro river in the Guyana interior, gives some sense of the potential and challenge that his distinctive historical geography poses for postcolonial cultural studies.

On their first journey along the river, Harris's team is forced to cut its anchor when the fast-rising river threatens to swamp its boat. A few years later, the team returns to the river and is faced with a similar predicament, but this time the crew is unable to cut the anchor, freeing it only after a difficult struggle. As the danger passes, and the anchor is dragged aboard the boat, they find it was hooked to the anchor that had been abandoned on the previous expedition. 'It is almost impossible to describe the kind of energy that rushed out of that constellation of images', Harris writes,

> I felt as if a canvas around my head was crowded with phantoms and figures. I had forgotten some of my antecedents – the Amerindian/Arawak ones – but now their faces were on the canvas. One could see them in the long march into the twentieth century out of the pre-Columbian mists of time . . . There was a sudden eruption of consciousness, and what is fantastic is that it all came out of a constellation of two ordinary objects, two anchors. (Quoted in Ashcroft et al. 1995: 187)

The tale is, characteristically, at once rooted in a traumatic worldly event and presents a fabulous reordering of perception through that event. A scientific expedition aimed at developing the river as a modern hydro-electric resource becomes a journey of historical and cultural revelation as the resources of physical safety have to be abandoned. The crew must depend upon the loss of moorings rather than upon the securities of (physical and intellectual) anchorage in order to survive. The peril of the second journey is revealed as that of their own history, not that of the geography of the river. To survive, the crew have to overcome their own paralysis, and dredge the hidden connections of the mysteriously joined anchors that Harris associates with 'the lost expeditions, the people who had gone down in these South American rivers'. The postcolonial landscape, in the process of being mapped and its material resources exploited, is revealed in the story as a complex and unstable place, a threat not only through natural currents, but historical currents, too. The surveyor – the functionary of colonial and postcolonial development (and, in Harris's cross-cultural bridging, of Kafkaesque modernity) – is rendered visionary as well as empiricist. In the strange trauma that is a frequent feature of Harris's narratives, the European-trained observer is forced to re-see the land and its inscribed histories and cultures.

More even than Carter's sketches of a new poetics of the land, Harris's work challenges the discourses available to postcolonial geographies. The task set by Carter of re-seeing, as well as repossessing, the land of the colony, is pursued by Harris through a wholesale reconstruction of perception and language, through often extreme experiences and realisations about the nature of the historical ruptures caused by imperialism. His work, again like Carter's, also sets problems for a cultural studies that is grounded in the principles and practices of Western social science. Its terms are – quite deliberately – untranslatable into those of analytical practice. As in the autobiographical fragment discussed earlier, Harris's version of postcolonialism is sited precisely on the points of rupture and revelation in apparently monolithic, globalising practices of material exploitation and linguistic and cultural domination. His discourse is similarly outside analytical norms, and draws upon a repetitive metaphysics of performance, bridging and Native American myth. Yet the very density and difficulty of that discourse is important, too. Harris resists any simplistic return to or celebration of pre-Columbian world-views or an ecological perspective that is unattached to the particular historical crises of the various stages of colonial encounters. His work simultaneously resists entrapment within what he sees as damaging fixtures of perception, whether those of Western scientific positivism or those which would seek to deny the realities of a Europeanised presence in the Caribbean. The task of a truly postcolonial culture, Harris suggests, is to find a language and means of perception to see and read the 'living text' of old landscapes (Quoted in Gilkes 1991: 33).

The apparently metaphysical mode of Wilson Harris's work, as has been noted before, is troubling for an emergent discipline that is both schooled in the methods of social science and in the materialist politics of economic dispossession. Nevertheless, it provides a valuable counter-discourse and challenge to a postcolonial studies that must necessarily be wary of its own terms of engagement with the cultures and world-views of its subjects. The very difficulty and strangeness of Harris's writing force a confrontation with potentially normative discourses of analysis that are themselves implicated in the acts of dispossession that they decry. The next case study, with its emphasis on international tourism and the discourses of pleasure and consumption, is in many ways distant from Harris's visionary cartography. In other ways, though, it develops his and Carter's themes, particularly their insistence upon the continuities of historical and cultural meaning embedded in land, and their sense of postcolonial landscapes as performance spaces for struggles of power and meaning.

Case Study Two:
The Beach as Postcolonial Landscape of Pleasure

Beaches are important places for a discussion of postcolonial land. They staged both the earliest moments of colonial encounters and host some of the most powerful cultural and economic transactions of the contemporary postcolonial condition. From its early stages, colonialism recognised the shore as both a material and metaphorical site of power and exchange. Daniel Defoe's novel *Robinson Crusoe* (1719), an early investigation of the ideologies and strategies of colonialism, classically defines its island's shoreline as a primal site of power and interpretation, a colonial 'contact zone', as Mary Louise Pratt calls it. Pratt defines such a site as a 'space in which peoples geographically and historically separated come into contact with each other and establish ongoing relations, usually involving coercion, radical inequality, and intractable conflict' (Pratt 1992: 6). This staging of power, resistance and interaction underpins the history of colonialism and its aftermath. Greg Dening, in his study of eighteenth-century Pacific trade and exploration, sees the beach as a place of cultural experiment and uncertain negotiation. It is 'a marginal space', he writes, where 'neither otherness nor familiarity holds sway, where there is much invention and blending of old and new'. In his discussion of these contact zones in Tahiti, he describes the development of a common 'grammar' of colonial encounters. Their 'meaning came out of the paradoxes of violence and quiet, sea and land, stranger and nature, politics and cosmology', he writes. 'No one met on the beach at Tahiti without bending to that grammar' (Dening 1992: 179). The texts and performances that the grammar generated belonged to neither indigenous people, nor colonist, but were generated by the process of contact. It is a delicate balance, of course, and one readily swayed in the colonialist's favour on progression inland and the establishment of settlements. Nevertheless, as Dening's book suggests, the liminality of the beach staged an uncertain, and often dangerous, theatre of communication and misunderstanding. It is one that has held its metaphorical power in recent texts from Jane Campion's *The Piano* (1993) to Alex Garland's novel of tourist paranoia, *The Beach* (1996), and in the social and economic life of many postcolonial states.

Economies from the Caribbean, to West Africa, to the South Pacific now depend upon the presence of the First World tourist's hedonistic body upon the beaches that were previously stages for entry and consolidation of colonial control. This reshaping of the beach reflects changes in the perception and use of land in the post- or neocolonial context of the international leisure resort, even as it preserves something of that liminal uncertainty and grammar of exchange that Dening describes in the eighteenth century. It thus offers a counter-narrative to that of the urban environment that has preoccupied postcolonial cultural theory. Whilst the city has increasingly become the political and cultural centre of postcolonial nations, in the wake of rural depopulation, it is also the space that maintains most forcefully the ideological assumptions and physical markers of space and power implicit in the nineteenth-century colonial design. Jane M. Jacobs argues that the 'spatial template of the grid', which continues to define the city, 'placed a rational spatiality of urban order over the unknown ("irrational") spatiality of Aborigines/Nature' (Jacobs 1996: 21). Whether the city is Bombay or Lagos or Kingston, that 'rational' spatiality maintains old social orderings, and, of course, generates the most influential postcolonial intellectual perspectives (Salman Rushdie's evocation of the hybridities of Bombay are perhaps the most famous of these urban representations). What is interesting about the postcolonial beach is its evasions of this urban colonial modernity. Having become economically powerful only at a relatively late stage of postcolonial development, after the general collapse of traditional export economies and the subsequent development of tourist industries, the beach retains the dynamics of a formative contact zone, even as it is integrated into postmodern global economies of leisure.

The representative place of postmodernity, Marc Augé argues, is the non-place. Airport terminals, motorways, service areas, shopping malls are its defining landscapes, places that are beyond anthropology and history. They are stages only for what he terms 'solitary contractuality'. Old markers of place and community, achieved through 'complicities in language, local references, the unformulated rules of living know-how', are bleached away, or are rendered only as consumable signs of past usages – self-conscious replicas of a disappearing culture (Augé 1995: 94, 101). The non-place's authority is at once absolute and invisible, an ultimate projection of what Fredric Jameson sees as the 'waning of affect' that marks the 'cultural logic' of global capitalism (Jameson 1984: 200). The tourist beach can be seen as another such non-place. Stripped of geographical and political specificity and fixed within its elements of white sand, blue sea and clear skies, the tropical beach can be endlessly reconfigured as a desirable tourist destination that is almost independent of social context. Remove the signifiers 'Goa', 'Cuba', 'Gambia' or 'Barbados' from photographs in tourist brochures, and the resorts become indistinguishable places arranged for tourist pleasure, and reached as an end point of a journey through the circuits of terminals, transit areas and transport systems that process the consumption of the experience. Tourist authorities cultivate a predictability of facilities and services, a provision normally set at a distance from the environments of postcolonial urban modernity. The hedonistic, leisured non-place of the beach resort thus becomes a postcolonial place apparently stripped of its postcolonialism. History is removed, local geography restyled, and the troubled modernity of postcolonial nationhood elided in a strange conjunction of the exoticist signifiers of old colonial primitivism and First World air-conditioning, buffets and room-service. The tourist beach, to reverse Paul Carter's summary of the process of colonial enculturation, becomes a postcolonial place apparently transformed back into a (leisured, postmodern) space.

Yet the non-place of the beach does have a politics, and is shaped by a history. From the very solidity of the demarcations of the beach from the postcolonial landscapes and cultures that surround it emerge strange processes of encounter and inter-relation that suggest a new anthropology of the postcolonial at its apparently most developed.

An intriguing guide to the dynamics of the postcolonial non-place is provided by Terry McMillan's popular novel *How Stella*

Got Her Groove Back (1996). McMillan's novel is an account of a wealthy, professional African-American woman's holiday in 'Castle Beach', an exclusive beach resort hotel in Negril, Jamaica, and her romance with a younger Jamaican man whom she meets there. The argument of the novel is that Stella's groove is restored by her 'escape' from the limitations of an affluent, but ultimately sterile, California, and her encounter with the 'other' place of the Caribbean and its romantic embodiment, Winston. However, her engagement with the 'otherness' that she discovers there conforms to the anticipated versions of place, culture, class and aesthetics that the exclusive resort itself defines. Whilst Stella's first-person narrative is a beguiling (and beguiled) account of her discovery of the tropical place, that place consists of a calculated deployment of signs of cultural authenticity in an environment removed from the economic and social predicaments of its island. Stella commits herself wholeheartedly and unquestioningly to what John Urry has termed 'the tourist gaze', an engagement with an 'other' place which, he argues, is 'structured by culturally specific notions of what is extraordinary and therefore worth viewing. This means that the services provided . . . must take a form which does not contradict or undermine the quality of the gaze, and ideally should enhance it' (Urry 2002: 59). Castle Beach, like all such resorts, is a simulacrum, a carefully managed assemblage of signs that allows privileged visitors to interpret that environment as an authentically tropical place on established terms of exoticism.

Stella's response to Castle Beach indicates the process of this construction and its economic and political implications. Her gaze upon 'Jamaica' is consistently filtered through a repertoire of images and rhetoric drawn from film, television and tourist literature. Her first description of the resort, for example, is that it is 'like a modern tropical version of *Casablanca*', and she finds herself 'sitting on a live postcard' when she ventures into the hills (McMillan 1996: 41, 80). In other ways, though, Stella's engagement with Castle Beach is that of a demanding consumer. She dwells upon and relishes its surfaces' compatibility with First World standards of order as well as with exotic stereotypes. Her constant affirmation of clean beaches, elegant surroundings and designer brands is extended to the Jamaicans that she meets.

Stella's knowledge and use of perfumes, deodorants and douches is extensive, and her physical aesthetics are prescriptive. The first encounter with her Jamaican lover is defined by his use of Calvin Klein's Escape, a cologne that she knows and of which she approves. Winston himself, although a hotel worker, is also the middle-class son of a surgeon, a social position confirmed both by the geography of their encounters and his body culture. In the Jamaican section of the book, he is never seen outside of tourist hotel complexes, and he knows the perils of body odour and how to deal with them. Indeed, it is his use of globalised brand toiletries such as Calvin Klein that renders him a recoverable commodity for Stella when, trapped in the non-place of Miami airport on the way home, she obtains a dab of Escape to restore her lover to her.

The 'double vision' of otherness and fulfilled expectations is founded upon Stella's own – largely unacknowledged – economic and cultural power, and the elision of the postcolonial place that is Jamaica. She leaves the hotel only once, to take an unsatisfactory horse trek into the hills led by a Jamaican who 'looks and smells as if he has been afraid of water for a long time and does not know what deodorant is' (75). This dirty body is set in opposition to the desirable geography and physiques of Castle Beach and their orderly, clean exoticism. It is an opposition that the narrative occasionally registers, but never analyses. Stella pays $60 for a pass to allow Winston to return and see her after he has left the resort, for example, but the implication of this transaction in the wider economics and social conflicts of the postcolonial place remains unexplored. While she is in Castle Beach, Stella accepts without comment the quality of its cultivated geography and its material luxury. The actions and interpretations of Stella in the resort embody the processes of cultural and economic power that sustain the tourist industry in such places. Her rigorous discriminations between the acceptable and unacceptable body, between sweat and scent, and between the beautiful beach and the unseen 'other' social life of the island reflect the social processes of the resort itself. Its strategy is to define itself as an exotic place, but not as a postcolonial place, distancing itself from the historical and material distresses of the island. Hotel and guest become allied in a system of physical and ideological surveillance that enforces an attractive, consumable version of 'the Caribbean' within the securities of the resort's perimeter fences. However, whilst the resort aspires to the leisure transactions of a pleasurable non-place, and its guest to an unproblematised consumption of a repertoire of exotic signs, the performance of this tourism does not remain outside the politics of postcolonialism.

Tim Edensor argues that tourism in former colonies is imbued with a complex nostalgia. The tourist anticipates an unmediated encounter with authenticity and otherness, whilst at the same time relishing a version of the material comforts and protection that colonialism created and maintained (Edensor 1998). The exclusive resort, whilst appearing to be part of a postmodernist leisure economy, also replicates the physical demarcations of the economic divisions of past colonial occupation. Its success is predicated upon an elision of pernicious history and of the current consequences of that history in favour of an aestheticised styling of the local, whether of landscape or of body. Construction of land and culture in the service of postmodern consumption can – must – feed upon an unacknowledged history in the land. Such tourism plays with an access to an idealised exoticism, and the glamour of the lifestyles of imperial control, whilst fencing out the later economic and social troubles of postcolonial nationhood. In McMillan's novel, the tourist Stella exerts economic power and consumes the version of the Caribbean place that she desires. In the process, she abolishes both the violent history of colonialism and the contemporary strains of American-Caribbean economic relations. In some ways, this process is easily replicated in the central sexual romance. The main Jamaican character, Winston, is a callow, almost voiceless presence as the Jamaican man is rendered a willing, decultured component in a tourist experience that holds to its 'exclusive' tag with a vengeance. Winston is Stella's sexual escape; she is, in a sense, his economic escape. But the sexual transactions open up a more intimate and troubled experience of postcolonialism that presses at complex questions of the body, identity, experience and power. Desire, even in exclusive resorts, is difficult to control.

In McMillan's novel, Winston is a problematically passive figure. His sensitivity, responsibility and boyish charm can be read as a challenge to racial stereotypes of Jamaican machismo.

However, his pliancy and voicelessness render him uncomfortably close to colonial fantasies of a conjunction of native simplicity, physical beauty and sexual prowess, despite the novel's ostensibly feminist premise. Winston, the pliant object of Stella's desire, causes her no cultural problems; like his cologne, he is readily accessible, knowable and ultimately transportable to America. But the presence of desire – however it is shaped by the surveillance systems of luxury tourism – complicates the aspirations of the leisured non-place to be a zone of unproblematic 'solitary contractuality'. Dean MacCannell identifies the desire for 'authentic experiences' as a primary factor in 'touristic consciousness' and, even in the increasingly controlled environments of exclusive tourism, this poses problems (MacCannell 1999: 101). Such desire is dangerously poised. It works between an encounter with an authenticity already known and complete in the image-banks of colonial memory – Stella's perception of the resort as *Casabalanca* – and a more vulnerable anticipation and revision of such presumptions through intimacy and contact, however compromised or limited they may be. In these circumstances, tourist beaches are dynamic, permeable locations, and the very extent of the exertions made to control them is indicative of the cultural instabilities that they can both host and inspire. Desire, as Robert Young argues, is an ambivalently powerful component of colonial practice that provokes both the possibility of transgression and the necessity for its repression (Young 1995).

Dean MacCannell presents a broadly optimistic version of such tourist transactions, even within a post- or neo-colonial environment. Whilst recognising ways in which they are skewed in economic and cultural terms, he argues for the basically heuristic, exploratory motives of its participants. The desire of the tourist, unlike the purpose of the colonist, is for experience rather than power. Whilst the former might be implicated in the latter, the dynamics and outcomes of the process, MacCannell suggests, are not wholly predictable or pernicious. Tourist resorts are meant to be staged versions of cultures, their signs of otherness expunged of the economic and social realities of Third World distress, and organised for consumption by First World guests on the terms of the latter's choosing. But the absolutism or disinfection to which non-places aspire cannot be achieved in this context, however well fenced and surveilled the beach might be. The very act of staging a controlled version of otherness, such as that described in *How Stella Got Her Groove Back*, introduces practices of resistance and mimicry that allow unpredictable and unmanageable inter-cultural transactions to take place. Somebody always gets through the fence. For MacCannell, this transgression is part of the process of travel; tourists' urges to seek the 'authentic', however clumsily these are framed and executed, will themselves ensure the conditions for social and cultural acts that cannot be contained within the apparent securities of the non-place.

Using the sociologist Erving Goffman's terms, MacCannell describes the Western tourist experience as one that is impelled to move beyond the staged 'front' region to the 'back' region. The place constructed by the hotel and resort always leads to a cultural space that, although it may be invisible and of restricted access, actually provides the dynamic that the tourist wishes to experience (MacCannell 1999: 95ff). The desire to know the 'other' is, MacCannell argues, on the whole, an honest one, and is, in some ways, achievable. Of course, the aspiration and its execution are themselves freighted with economic power and cultural assumptions – Goffman's metaphors of front and back performance are uncomfortably close to colonialism's old metaphors of penetration and discovery. Nevertheless, the desire to know arguably inaugurates a contact that has to be one of negotiation rather than simple appropriation. As Tim Edensor argues in his study of the Taj Mahal as a tourist site, the activity cannot be totally controlled. Whilst it is an act of seeing and experiencing that is, in some ways, staged in historical contexts of colonialism and within the more recent economic and ideological determinants of a globalised leisure industry, there are other dynamics at play which are indigenous and localised. 'If we consider . . . tourist spaces to be performative spaces, or ' "stages" ', he writes, 'it is clear that certain types of performance are constrained by carefully managed stages, whereas less overtly controlled stages potentially permit wider scope for improvisation' (Edensor 1998: 8). The totalising aspiration of tourist management is resisted by different kinds of local engagements, and these are organised both by the interests of the visitors and of the hosts.

Tim Edensor's model of a negotiated postmodern tourism re-places that of First World control and deculturation with a dynamic of dominant and emergent discourses and cultures that are in unequal, but also unpredictable, relationships. If the tourist beach is, in one sense, an idealised landscape of neocolonial reconfigura-tions and re-articulations of older exoticisms, it is also a stage for postcolonial responses to those initiatives. The rendering of the shore as privatised, deodorised and effectively divorced from the postcolonial cultural dynamics of the 'place beyond' is indicative of the wider processes of a globalised leisure economy. However, those acts of enclosure cannot in themselves satisfy or control all the participants in the exchange. The passive, middle-class Win-ston is a problematic means of entry into Goffman's 'back region' of Jamaican culture. Nevertheless, Stella's desire to make such an entry through a sexual relationship does test the rules of contact and interpretation implicit in the growth of global leisure. Eden-sor's sense of competing stages within a wider economy of neo-colonial tourism is at its most pressing in the intimacies that the novel invokes. It is noticeable how hard *How Stella Got Her Groove Back* works to evade the political questions raised by its cross-cultural sex. McMillan tends to displace these anxieties onto Stella's concern with the disparity of age in the relationship, rather than the difference of their economic and cultural positions, and there are, of course, no cultural complications caused by racial difference. The personal worries about appearance and social propriety are more easily resolved than the cultural and economic imbalances between America and the Caribbean that shape the encounter. Power is displaced, as the novel itself suggests in a rare moment of political candour. ' "I like the fact that you don't know your own power" ', Stella tells Winston during his first visit to Los Angeles. ' "What power?" "That's my point" ', she replies (309). Despite this, though, the question of power persists on the clean sands of Castle Beach.

Stella's sexual relationship with Winston is poised between an intimate encounter of individuals from different cultures and an exploitative dynamic that mirrors the economic and cultural power structures in the neo-colonial Caribbean. Inter-cultural sex, parti-cularly in the context of global tourism industries, has provoked some contentious debates in the recent sociology of leisure and travel. Simon Carter and Stephen Clift's work, for example, emphasises the ways in which contemporary sex tourism links the most intimate of personal encounters with a complex of colonial and postcolonial historical, economic and social forces. They argue that the transactions of sex tourism in South-east Asia need to be seen in a context of 'a violent international conflict involving the transportation of hundreds of thousands of men; the local and international division of gendered labour; social and technological changes in world tourism markets; international trade and investment; and a series of intersecting ideologies and discourses around sexuality, gender and race' (Carter and Clift 2000: 12). And if this is an exploitative example of the globalisation of tourism, it also carries with it a long history of colonial formations of sexuality, desire and otherness developed through the more recent processes of postmodern travel and leisure (see Hyam 1991; McClintock 1995; Said 2003: 188–90). However, whilst the links between Western male sex tourism and neo-colonial militarism and economic power are unarguable, more difficult political questions have arisen when the 'sex tourist' is a woman. In the sociological debates surrounding Stella's groove on the beach, faultlines in postcolonial and feminist approaches to such encounters become more marked.

The most provocative account of the sociology of female 'sex tourism' is perhaps that of Deborah Pruitt and Suzanne LaFont. In their study of Jamaican beach resorts, they seek to separate the dynamic of women tourists' sexual relationships with local men from that of male sex tourists. Pruitt and LaFont argue that the former offers the possibility of mutual development whereas the latter replicates existing social and economic conditions. Women tourists' liaisons with local men, they suggest, tend to be 'constructed through a discourse of romance and long-term relationship, an emotional involvement usually not present in sex tourism' (Pruitt and LaFont 1995: 423). Because of the radical reversal of the gendered power relationships established by colonialism, these encounters create a space within the norms of sexual behaviour that provides new possibilities of identity and expression for both participants. 'In a unique conjunction of need, hope, and desire', they write, 'the romance relationships between tourist women and local men serve to transform traditional gender roles across cultural boundaries, creating power relations distinctive from those existing in either native society' (436). For Pruitt and LaFont, the tourist beaches of Jamaica and the Caribbean become true contact zones, creative liminal spaces in which cultural roles of gender can be renegotiated, both in the relationship that is formed, and in its participants' private acknowledgement of their past restrictions. Stella's groove thus becomes not just a sense of romantic well-being, but also a space of social and gendered change.

Pruitt and LaFont's account of romance tourism has been challenged in other studies of the relationship between sex and contemporary Third World tourism. The argument of the former is predicated upon a clear distinction between Western women's and Western men's behaviour and political significance in the postcolonial place. Travel, as in Dean MacCannell's most positive sense of the process, frees women from gender constraints and – crucially – from their own agency as Westerners who embody dominant power formations that are genderless. However, as Jacqueline Sánchez Taylor has argued, such assumptions are dangerously close to the political evasions that Terry McMillan's novel struggles to achieve in its attempts to render Stella's relationship as one of equal individual vulnerability, rather than one that involves unequal economic and social power. 'The tendency to de-sexualize female sex tourism by labelling it as "romance"', Sánchez Taylor suggests, 'hides the complexities involved in the social interaction between affluent, Western women and poor Black men' (Sánchez Taylor 2000: 45). Whilst there might be a challenge to the patriarchal structure of the women's home society through the sexual or romantic negotiations and expressions on the tourist beach, Sánchez Taylor argues, that challenge is conducted through, and compromised by, the exertion of financial and cultural agencies held in common with that patriarchy. These remain untouched by the development of romance. Women's sex tourism consequently only challenges the male version within their own limited perception of the activity. The postcolonial context of economic and cultural power is not only untouched, but reaffirmed.

Interpretation of the participants' accounts of these most intimate of postcolonial cultural transactions is a particularly problematic issue. As in the exchange between Stella and Winston quoted earlier, both parties tend to deny the operation of power within the relationship. In their essay on women's sex tourism in the Dominican Republic, Edward Herold, Rafael Garcia and Tony DeMoya suggest that 'most [Western women] truly believe that they are engaging in consensual romantic relationships [whilst] the beach boys believe that they are, for the most part, in control of the relationship' (Herold et al. 2001: 995). Local codes and discourses of masculinity are here set against an imported frame of feminised (and feminist) romance on the tourist beach. The beach boy's status is difficult to define in this, both for himself and for the Western woman. As Herold et al. imply, the roles of the postcolonial female prostitute and her Western client are clear enough in their reference to structures of sexual and political power, but the roles of those involved in 'romance tourism' are not. Both can develop very different explanations of the transactions while they remain in the liminal space of the beach. The woman can evoke a discourse of romance. The beach boy, however, needs to perform an ambivalent role. His financial dependence upon sexual tourists equates him with the stereotypically 'female' cultural role of the prostitute. However, his ability to define a sexually dominant role within the sexual relationship with the visitor liberates him from that subservience – at least in his own eyes, and, perhaps, in those of his local community. This ambiguity poses challenges for the ethnographers who seek to disentangle the transactions of power within such relationships. For example, a Cuban beach boy called Juan tells Sánchez Taylor, 'I would rather be "caliente" than intelligent . . . What use is being intelligent if no one wants to fuck you?' Sánchez Taylor reads this comment as confirmation that his 'subjective identity was directly related to the oppressive historical and cultural ideology used by colonial white males to construct Black male identity' (49). In other words, Juan is enforcing upon himself the body/mind division characteristic of colonial structures of power. However, in the deceptive theatre of the tourist beach (a performance space that inevitably involves its sociologists as well as its sex tourists) it might also suggest an intelligent insight into a particular economic predicament, and a complex performative means of managing it. What Juan also reveals is an understanding of the cultural transactions in which he is involved.

The beach, then, despite the increasing incorporation of its geography into the processes of postmodern artifice and Augé's non-places, remains a contact zone. If tourism is an activity that is at once coercive and conservative, and heuristic and emancipatory, as MacCannell suggests, the postcolonial beach is a liminal space that encourages cultural negotiations that are unequal but also indeterminate. The apparently neutral space in which such trans-actions are conducted is, in fact, fraught with the histories of colonialism and the more recent perils and freedoms of postcolo-nialism. How the participants define the groove and establish political identities through negotiations that involve gender, eco-nomics, romance and cultural difference remain raw and difficult processes, as the sociology, social geography and fiction discussed in this case study suggest. However, the discourses and transact-ions of such tourism have become central to the experience of postcolonial cultures – and hence to postcolonial cultural studies.

Case Study Three: The Moving Landscapes of Carnival

Carnival, like the beach, provides a way of studying a site for the performances of colonial and postcolonial pleasure and power-struggles. However, those performances take place in the streets of urban centres rather than on the liminal stages of the beach. Originating in pre-modern European festivals, exported to colonies of Catholic powers, such as Trinidad and Haiti, and then re-exported to Protestant First World nations in the postcolonial era, carnival presents a complex urban theatre both for challenging and reinforcing physical and ideological limits. The playing of 'mas' in 'Europe's biggest street festival', the Notting Hill Carnival, for example, still bears the traces and arguments of the long, contested history of the Trinidad carnival that was its model. Its peculiar mixture of consumption, display and challenge to the practices of urban policing made it both a means of performing changing circumstances of emigration and settlement – particularly in the 1970s – and maintaining a cultural continuity between that process and earlier forms of self-expression in colonial contexts.

The currency of carnival and the carnivalesque in recent cultural studies owes much to the rediscovery and dissemination of the work of the Russian literary theorist Mikhail Bakhtin. Bakhtin's classic account of medieval European carnival, *Rabelais and His World* (1984), defines the carnival as a circumscribed, temporary desecration of place and a deliberated and playful deconstruction of the signs and practices of secular and religious power. The human body and the body-politic are made grotesque, unstable and vulnerable for the festival period in city streets transformed into what Bakhtin terms 'a pageant without footlights and without a division into performers and spectators' (quoted in Vice 1997: 151). This seductive account of social transformation and possibility has to be treated with caution when thinking about postcolonial carnival traditions, however. The movement of carnival from Europe to the Caribbean and South America was a translation of a pre-modern social practice into sites of unstable, developing modernity. In place of relatively homogeneous hierarchies of estate and social function through which carnival was enacted in Europe, colonies were organised in rigidly demarcated frames of race and culture, structured by slavery, new labour practices and by developing ideological preoccupations with racial difference. The meaning and practice of carnival were adapted to these new circumstances, and became a means of control as much as a means of challenge, reinforcing the conservative management of popular expression through licensed play which was always implicit in Bakhtin's model of the carnivalesque.

John Cowley's and Joseph Roach's work has traced the ways in which Caribbean carnival was used to reinforce, rather than challenge, patterns of demarcation and hierarchy (Cowley; 1996, Roach 1996). The planters' exclusive masquerades in Trinidad and the elite, racially segregated 'krewes' of New Orleans carnival, with their prioritised position in the street parades and exclusive, private balls, restated existing patterns of cultural and social value rather than abolishing them, however temporarily. Colonial carnival traditions maintained difference even as they allowed mimicry and mockery of that difference in the occupation and transformation of public ground. Power was not suspended in Bakhtinian fashion in colonial carnival, and whatever blurrings of social identity that were achieved under cover of mask or of night were contested by colonial authority. Nevertheless, carnival did provide an alternative structure and discourse for the performative con-testation of that power. Its public geography and its traditions of mockery and mimicry provided political and cultural resources for acts of resistance in carnival cities such as New Orleans and Port of Spain.

The postcolonial history of carnival maintained the tension between legitimated disorder and the potential for a performative expression of emergent social organisation and political expression. It is a history that interestingly diverged between the experience of 'original' colonial carnival in places like Port of Spain, and that which emerged as a force of emigrant expression in London. After independence, carnival became a settled, economically profitable occasion for Trinidad, and part of its national, civic identity. John Stewart has traced this transformation of Trinidadian carnival into what he terms 'a venture in cultural patriotism' since the 1960s (Stewart 1986: 306). 'The Trinidad carnival has never occurred in an atmosphere of political neutrality', he argues, 'but whereas in the past the festival construed an alternate context with reflexive and rebellious potentials, in recent times it has become more openly an extension of a moderating (modernizing) process central to the overall objectives of current political leadership' (302). This post-colonial moderation idealises and promotes the concept of the carnivalesque, even as it incorporates its practices within state and (increasingly) commercial control. Such incorporation results in the regulation of costume and behaviour, the restrictive pricing of entry to the masquerade bands, and an emphasis upon an adjudicated spectacle that introduces the very separation of per-former and spectator that carnival fundamentally denies. The development of an elaborate and costly carnival aesthetic geared towards a performance before judges and television cameras, and best exemplified by the extraordinary designs of Peter Minshall, has restated divisions and distances of social identity (see Nunley 1993; Hill 1997: xx–xxi). The carnival's appeal is primarily directed to the visitor and the international viewer rather than to the local participant. As Niels Sampath comments, '[t]he images [of Trinidad carnival] are now essentially detached from their previous intrinsic relation to everyday life' (Sampath 1997: 153). And whilst Sampath argues that this creates 'a more equitable identity' in terms of global and expatriate participation, it also ensures that control of the ground of carnival is managed by political elites and commercial interests.

The period that marked the increased regulation of Trinidadian carnival also initiated the exportation and adaptation of carnival practices to First World centres, most notably to London. Notting Hill Carnival's history, since its inception in the 1960s, provides a counter-narrative to the exportation of pre-modern European festival practices to Caribbean and South American colonies. In his history of the London carnival, Abner Cohen insists on the continuing social importance of its traditions in the postcolonial period. 'Although it is essentially a cultural, artistic spectacle, saturated by music, dancing and drama', he argues, 'it is always political, intimately and dynamically related to the political order and to the struggle for power within it' (Cohen 1993: 4). The initial project was that of reviving an old London fair in the then-deprived area of Notting Hill. It was initiated by a social worker who was born of Russian and Native American parents, but, in a cultural bridging or transformation that Wilson Harris would recognise, it became linked, by the early 1970s, to the traditions of the significant number of Trinidadian emigrants in the area (Cohen 1993: 10–11). As Notting Hill endured the economic and material pressures of social migration and housing problems, as well as the physical division of the place by motorway construction in the 1960s, the carnival became intensively 'West Indianised'. This development was shaped by three forces: the increasing permanence of settlement of emigrant West Indians, who, nevertheless, wished to maintain a specific Caribbean identity within London; the development of community organisation and politically radical groups in some influential sections of that community; and the particular local political meanings of Notting Hill for Black British politics following the racial conflicts there in 1958.

As Cohen suggests, the history of the Notting Hill Carnival from the 1970s to the present is, in many ways, a material performance of the metropolitan politics of postcolonial Britain. The introduction of steel-pan bands as the musical markers of the Trinidadian redefinition of postcolonial carnival in the early 1970s was quickly offset by that of reggae-based sound systems in the mid-1970s. This was both a recognition of the significant presence of Jamaican emigrants in London, and a sign of the broadening cultural meanings of both the Carnival and the Caribbean in England. Whilst Jamaica, a Protestant society, had no indigenous carnival tradition, reggae had become the dominant music and wider cultural expression of a broadly West Indian culture in Britain. The nationalism that shaped post-independence carnival in Trinidad was thus performatively rerouted in the particular circumstances of postcolonial London to reflect a 'Caribbean-ness' that was, ironically, disappearing in the Caribbean itself, after the failure of the political project of island Federation in the period after independence. As the Notting Hill Carnival became the performative focus for a wide range of debates and conflicts about policing, social conditions and racism in Black Britain, so did the local markers of a newly exported Trinidadian cultural tradition become itself transformed into a complex of emergent Black British politics. The extensive networks of black organisations necessary for the preparation of a growing carnival led it to be what Cohen calls 'a symbol of, as well as a mechanism for achieving corporate identity, unity and exclusiveness' among West Indians in Britain and the first generations of British West Indians (79). This transformation was both charted and influenced by *Race Today*, the most articulate organ of British black politics in the 1970s.

Race Today always presented the Notting Hill Carnival as central to its cultural and political project. In a collection of polemical essays published in the aftermath of the civil disturbances that marked the 1976 Carnival, the journal sought to assert itself as the festival's historian and as the keeper of its values. Darcus Howe, the editor of *Race Today*, became Chair of one of the organisations competing for control of the carnival's organisation, and the collective performed 'mas' (that is, performed as a masquerade band) in the festival – 'social realism it is', writes Howe about its militant 'Forces of Victory' theme of 1978 (Howe 1978: 102). Eliding the origins that Cohen traces, the Carnival is projected both as a 'working-class festival' and a celebration that found its source in Trinidadian exile, the founders being three emigrant panmen.

Notting Hill was chosen as the location because it was 'the closest to being liberated territory', a reference to the bitter racial conflicts in the area in 1958 (Race Today Collective 1977: 2). This mythologising of the Carnival's origins is entirely within the spirit of carnival practices, of course, and the collection develops a distinctive amalgam of radical Marxist polemic and a vivid carnivalising of that materialist rhetoric. In his account of the 1976 Carnival riots, for example, Howe himself creates a narrative in which a Caribbean unity is organically shaped in a Babylonic exile of '[b]ottle and stone and no place to shelter' (15). The Trinidadian core of the carnival spirit, expressed in the saying 'all o'we is one' (i.e. we are a communal identity) is both radicalised to meet the oppressive forces of the British state, and buttressed by the input of other Caribbean exiles in the midst of creating a distinctively Black British-Caribbean political performance. In a striking anecdote of this new merging, a prophet of Dread arises from the apparently very un-Rastafarian context of Trinidadian celebration to make common cause:

> Near Cambridge Gardens, about 30 yards away from where 300 police are forming up behind dustbin lids, a rastaman is haranguing the crowd. He stands in front of about 500 youths and he waves his red, green and gold stick at the police lines. 'Burn the wicked,' he shouts . . . 'I walk through fire,' he screams and begins walking towards the police ranks waving his stick. (17)

Rasta apocalypticism emerges from the secular release of Catholic Trinidadian carnival as newly emergent forms of political organisation and expression are shaped in the 'liberated territory' of Notting Hill.

The strategy of Howe and the *Race Today* Collective was to make the Notting Hill Carnival both the expression and the process of a new politics in a postcolonial Britain. Carnival became metaphor and practice for an emergent black consciousness. '[T]he strength and weakness of a Carnival festival is the measure of the stage of development of the West Indian community in Britain', Race Today states categorically (Race Today Collective 1977: 3). Essays and articles in the journal in the mid- and late 1970s carefully develop

this carnival politics in different directions. The resistance to
council and police attempts to move the Carnival from the streets
to a park or stadium is seen as exemplifying a more profound
opposition to restrictions of public movement and cultural expression, and that expression itself becomes both emblem and enaction
of a political process. To create a carnival is to create a politics. The
Collective notes the 'disciplined organization that shapes a mas
band', and reads the power struggles within the overall carnival
management as part of a process to 'mobilise the autonomous units'
to create a unified cultural force (17). The transformation of
European carnival traditions to the circumstances of the colonial
and postcolonial Caribbean, and their further transformation on
their return to Europe, are Black Atlantic processes of the assertion
of political will. The carnival landscapes of London in the 1970s
were not those of 'leisure', but those of the 'changing same' of
resistance and cultural remaking. '[W]e have captured the streets of
Notting Hill', *Race Today* declares, after the 1978 carnival, 'and
transformed it [sic] into an arena of cultural rebellion. We stage a
festival which is a direct antithesis to that which has been laid on
for us by the dominant culture' (Race Today Collective 1978: 123).

The history of Notting Hill Carnival in the twenty-five years or
so since these *Race Today* pieces can be seen as a retreat from the
clear political positions articulated there. The Carnival's easy
absorption into a civic discourse of multiculturalism ('Europe's
biggest street-festival'), the growth in its attendance accompanied
by the pressures upon the policing of its performance structures,
and the corporate sponsorship of its bands, all suggest a retreat
from or a defeat by the kind of problematics defined by Howe and
Race Today in the 1970s. In what sense is it 'liberated territory'
when crash barriers separate audience from 'mas', in defiance of
carnival dynamic, for much of the route, and when Richard
Branson can wave to those crowds from his Virgin float? The
processes of cultural inclusion, political defusion and commercial
incorporation, familiar from its Trinidadian model, are recognisable
in all engagements between dominant and subaltern cultures. In
other ways, though, the carnival, even in its current engorged and
commercial form, remains an effective expression of the issues of
postcolonial Britain. After all, carnival was always Janus-faced. Its

capacity to harness and express popular discontent and energy was always in tension with the pragmatic strategy of containing such culture in bounded forms and within ritual reversals. And, in presenting the alliances of corporate cultures and black Britain, the negotiations between metropolitan civic politics and the 'minorities' it seeks to incorporate, and the concentration of postcolonial fantasies of the Caribbean carnivalesque, the Carnival still serves its purpose as a performance space for contemporary arguments and alliances of race, history and the aftermath of empire.

Conclusion

The landscapes that have formed the bases of this final chapter have ranged from Aboriginal land economies, through the changing streets of carnival cultures to the apparently controlled simulacra of the exotic postmodern non-places. Their various performances and contests suggest both the persistence of colonial histories within postcolonial environments and the capacity for transformation and expression that such new environments allow. The questions of perception, agency and interpretation posed by indigenous Australian and South American conceptions of the relationships between people and landscapes, for example, are important to postcolonial studies' interests in the continuities and discontinuities of the pre-colonial, colonial and postcolonial. Notting Hill Carnival is a contemporary manifestation of both a complex pattern of diasporic forces and of the strategies of inclusion and control deployed in a self-consciously 'multicultural' postcolonial state. The transactions that occur on the tourist beach suggest the development of the controlled and simulated spaces that Marc Augé describes as 'non-places' in postcolonial places. However, as *How Stella Got Her Groove Back* and the sociological arguments surrounding tourism suggest, those non-places host both pleasurable and politically fraught negotiations. The beach, like the streets of carnival, like postcolonial studies itself, remains a stage for often ambivalent encounters and exchanges.

Bibliography

Abram, Simone, Waldren, Jacqueline D., and Macleod, Donald V. L. (eds) (1997) *Tourists and Tourism: Identifying with People and Places*, Oxford and New York: Berg

Adam, Heribert and Adam, Kenya (2000) 'The Politics of Memory in Divided Societies,' in Wilmot James and Linda van de Vijver (eds), *After the TRC*, 32–47

Ahmad, Aijaz (1992) *In Theory: Classes, Nations, Literatures*, London and New York: Verso

Ahmed, Sara (2000) *Strange Encounters: Embodied Others in Post-Coloniality*, London and New York: Routledge

Ahmed, Sara and Stacey, Jackie (eds) (2001) *Thinking Through the Skin*, London and New York: Routledge

Alcoff, Linda (1991/2) 'The Problem of Speaking for Others,' *Cultural Critique*, 20, 5–32

Ambrose, Timothy and Paine, Crispin (1993) *Museum Basics*, London and New York: ICOM and Routledge

Anderson, Benedict (1983) *Imagined Communities: Reflections on the Origin and Spread of Nationalism*, London and New York: Verso

Anderson, Kay and Gale, Fay (eds) (1992) *Inventing Places: Studies in Cultural Geography*, Melbourne: Longman Cheshire

Antze, Paul and Lambek, Michael (eds) (1996) *Tense Past: Cultural Essays in Trauma and Memory*, New York and London: Routledge

Apache Indian (1993) *No Reservations*, Island [CD]

Appadurai, Arjun (1991) 'Global Ethnoscapes: Notes and Queries for a Transnational Anthropology', in Richard G. Fox (ed.), *Recapturing Anthropology*, 191–210

Appiah, Kwame Anthony (1992) *In My Father's House: Africa in the Philosophy of Culture*, London: Methuen

— (1991) 'Is the Post- in Postmodernism the Post- in Postcolonial?', *Critical Inquiry* 17.2, 336–57

Armes, Roy (1987) *Third World Film Making and the West*, Berkeley: University of California Press

Ashcroft, Bill, Griffiths, Gareth, and Tiffin, Helen (eds) (1995) *The Post-Colonial Studies Reader*, London and New York: Routledge

Augé, Marc (1995) *Non-Places: Introduction to an Anthropology of Super-modernity*, tr. John Howe, London and New York: Verso

Bailey, Trevor (1992) 'Talking Cricket', *Daily Telegraph*, 22 June, 31

Baker, Houston A. (1984) *Blues, Ideology and Afro-American Literature*, Chicago: University of Chicago Press

Baker, Richard (1999) 'Land is Life: A Cultural Geography of Australian Contact History', in Elaine Stratford (ed.), *Australian Cultural Geographies*, 25–47

Bakhtin, Mikhail (1968) *Rabelais and his World*, tr. Hélène Iswolsky, Bloomington: Indiana University Press

Bale, John and Maguire, Joseph (1994) *The Global Sports Arena: Athletic Talent Migration in an Interdependent World*, London: Frank Cass

Baraka, Amiri (1991) *The LeRoi Jones/Amiri Baraka Reader*, ed. William J. Harris, New York: Thunder's Mouth Press

Barker, Chris (2000) *Cultural Studies: Theory and Practice*, London: Sage

Baxandall, Michael (1991) 'Exhibiting Intention: Some Preconditions of the Visual Display of Culturally Purposeful Objects', in Ivan Karp and Steven D. Lavine (eds), *Exhibiting Cultures*, 33–41

Beckles, Hilary McD. (1998) *The Development of West Indies Cricket*, London and Stirling: Pluto Press

Beckles, Hilary McD. and Stoddart, Brian (eds) (1995) *Liberation Cricket: West Indies Cricket Culture*, Manchester and New York: Manchester University Press

Bennett, Tony (1995) *The Birth of the Museum: History, Theory, Politics*, London and New York: Routledge

Berndt, Ronald M. and Berndt, Catherine H. (1988) *The World of the First Australians: Aboriginal Traditional Life: Past and Present*, 4th edn, revised, Canberra: Aboriginal Studies Press

Beverley, John (1999) *Subalternity and Representation: Arguments in Cultural Theory*, Durham and London: Duke University Press

Bhabha, Homi K. (1994) *The Location of Culture*, London and New York: Routledge

—— (ed.) (1990) *Nation and Narration*, London and New York: Routledge

Bourdieu, Pierre (1990) *In Other Words: Essays Towards a Reflexive Sociology*, tr. M. Adamson, Cambridge: Polity Press

Bray, Tamara L. (ed.) (2001a) *The Future of the Past: Archaeologists, Native Americans, and Repatriation*, New York and London: Garland
— (2001b) 'American Archaeologists and Native Americans: A Relationship Under Construction', in Tamara L. Bray (ed.), *The Future of the Past*, 1–8
Brodber, Erna (1988) *Myal*, London and Port of Spain: New Beacon Press
— (1987) 'Marcus Garvey and the Politicisation of Some Afro-Jamaicans', *Jamaica Journal*, 20.3, 66–72
— (1982) *Perceptions of Caribbean Woman: Towards a Documentation of Stereotypes*, Cave Hill, Barbados: Institute of Social and Economic Research, UWI
— (1975) *Yards in the City of Kingston*, Kingston, Jamaica: Institute of Social and Economic Research
Brown, Adam (ed.) (1998) *Fanatics! Power, Identity and Fandom in Football*, London and New York: Routledge
Browning, Barbara (1995) *Samba: Resistance in Motion*, Bloomington and Indianapolis: Indiana University Press
Buena Vista Social Club (1999) dir. Wim Wenders (USA)
Bundy, Colin (2000) 'The Beast of the Past: History and the TRC', in Wilmot James and Linda van de Vijver (eds), *After the TRC*, 9–20
Carter, Alexandra (ed.) (1998) *The Routledge Dance Studies Reader*, London and New York: Routledge
Carter, Paul (1996) *The Lie of the Land*, London and Boston: Faber
— (1992) *Living in a New Country: History, Travelling and Language*, London and Boston: Faber
— (1987) *The Road to Botany Bay: An Essay in Spatial History*, London and Boston: Faber
Carter, Simon and Clift, Stephen (2000) 'Tourism, International Travel and Sex: Themes and Research', in Stephen Clift and Simon Carter (eds), *Tourism and Sex*, 1–19
Cashman, Richard and McKernan, Michael (eds) (1982) *Sport: Money, Morality and the Media*, Kensington: New South Wales University Press
Castillo, Richard J. (1997) *Culture and Mental Illness: A Client-Centered Approach*, Pacific Grove, CA: Brooks/Cole Publishing
Castle, Gregory (ed.) (2001) *Postcolonial Discourses: A Reader*, Oxford: Blackwell
Chakrabarty, Dipesh (1992) 'Postcoloniality and the Artifice of History: Who Speaks for "Indian" Pasts?' *Representations*, 37, Winter, 1–26
Chevannes, Barry (ed.) (1998) *Rastafari and Other African-Caribbean Worldviews*, Houndmills: Macmillan

Chopra, Anupama (2002) *Dilwale Dulhania Le Jayenge*, London: British Film Institute

Chrisman, Laura and Parry, Benita (eds) (2000) *Postcolonial Theory and Criticism*, Cambridge: D. S. Brewer

Clifford, James (1997) *Routes: Travel and Translation in the Late Twentieth Century*, Cambridge, MA, and London: Harvard University Press

— (1988) *The Predicament of Culture: Twentieth-Century Ethnography, Literature, and Art*, Cambridge, MA, and London: Harvard University Press

Clift, Stephen and Carter, Simon (eds) (2000) *Tourism and Sex: Culture, Commerce and Coercion*, London and New York: Pinter

Cohen, Abner (1993) *Masquerade Politics: Explorations in the Structure of Urban Cultural Movements*, Oxford and Providence, RI: Berg

Constantine, Learie (1954) *Colour Bar*, London: Stanley Paul

— (1946) *Cricket in the Sun*, London: Stanley Paul

— (1933) *Cricket and I*, London: Philip Allan

Coombes, Felicity and Gemmell, Suzanne (eds) (1999) *Piano Lessons: Approaches to* The Piano, Sydney and London: John Libbey

Cooper, Carolyn (1995) *Noises in the Blood: Orality, Gender and the 'Vulgar' Body of Jamaican Popular Culture*, Durham: Duke University Press

Couling, Katherine and Grummitt, Karsten-Peter (1998) *Cinemagoing Australasia*, Leicester: Dodona Research

Cowley, John (1996) *Carnival, Canboulay and Calypso: Traditions in the Making*, Cambridge: Cambridge University Press

— (1990) 'London is the Place: Caribbean Music in the Context of Empire 1900–60', in Paul Oliver (ed.), *Black Music in Britain*, 58–76

— (1985) 'Cultural "Fusions": Aspects of British West Indian Music in the USA and Britain 1918–51', *Popular Music*, 5, 81–96

Coxall, Helen (1997) 'Speaking Other Voices', in Eilean Hooper-Greenhill (ed.), *Cultural Diversity*, 99–115

Crapanzano, Vincent and Garrison, Vivian (eds) (1977) *Case Studies in Spirit Possession*, New York and London: John Wiley and Sons

Daily Express (n.d.) *The Greatest Show on Earth/Trinidad Carnival/Minshall: The Man and his Mas'*, Daily Express: Port of Spain, Trinidad

Das Gupta, Chidananda (1991) *The Painted Face: Studies in India's Popular Cinema*, New Delhi: Roli Books

Dayan, Joan (1995) *Haiti, History, and the Gods*, Berkeley: University of California Press

De Boeck, Filip (1998) 'Beyond the Grave: History, Memory and Death in Postcolonial Congo/Zaïre', in Richard Werbner (ed.), *Memory and the Postcolony*, 21–57

Deegan, Heather (2001) *The Politics of the New South Africa: Apartheid and After*, Harlow: Longman

Delgado, Celeste Fraser and Muñoz, José Esteban (eds) (1997a) *Everynight Life: Culture and Dance in Latin/o America*, Durham and London: Duke University Press

— (1997b) 'Rebellions of Everynight Life', in Celeste Fraser Delgado and José Esteban Muñoz (eds), *Everynight Life*, 9–32

Dening, Greg (1992) *Mr Bligh's Bad Language: Passion, Power and Theatre on the Bounty*, Cambridge: Cambridge University Press

Desmond, Jane C. (1997) 'Embodying Difference: Issues in Dance and Cultural Studies', in Celeste Fraser Delgado and José Esteban Muñoz (eds), *Everynight Life*

Diagnostic and Statistical Manual of Mental Disorders (1994) 4th edn, Washington, DC: American Psychiatric Association

Dickey, Sara (1993) *Cinema and the Urban Poor in South India*, Cambridge: Cambridge University Press

Dilwale Dulhania Le Jayenge (1995) dir. Aditya Chopra (India)

Dirlik, Arif (1998) *The Postcolonial Aura: Third World Criticism in the Age of Global Capitalism*, Boulder: Westview Press

— (1994) 'The Postcolonial Aura: Third World Criticism in the Age of Global Capitalism', *Critical Inquiry*, 20.2, Winter, 328–56

Duff, Alan (1993) *Maori: The Crisis and the Challenge*, Auckland: HarperCollins

Dwyer, Rachel (2000) *All You Want is Money, All You Need is Love: Sexuality and Romance in Modern India*, London and New York: Cassell

Dyson, Lynda (1999) 'The Return of the Repressed? Whiteness, Femininity and Colonialism in *The Piano*', in Felicity Coombes and Suzanne Gemmell (eds), *Piano Lessons*, 111–21

Eagleton, Terry (1998) 'Postcolonialism and "Postcolonialism"', *interventions*, 1.1, 24–6

Eco, Umberto, Ivanov, V. V., and Rector, Monica (1984) *Carnival!*, ed. Thomas A. Sebeok, Berlin: Mouton Publishers

Edensor, Tim (1998) *Tourists at the Taj: Performance and Meaning at a Symbolic Site*, London and New York: Routledge

Eichberg, Henning (1998) *Body Cultures: Essays on Sport, Space and Identity*, ed. John Bale and Chris Philo, London and New York: Routledge

Eilersen, Gillian Stead (1995) *Bessie Head: Thunder Behind Her Ears: Her Life and Writing*, Portsmouth, NH, London, Cape Town and Johannesburg: Heinemann, James Currey and David Philip

Engel, Matthew (ed.) (1994) *Wisden Cricketers' Almanack*, Guildford: J. Wisden

Erlmann, Veit (1993) 'The Politics and Aesthetics of Transnational Musics', *The World of Music*, 35.2, 3–15

Fairley, Jan (2001) 'The "Local" and the "Global" in Popular Music', in Simon Frith, Will Straw and John Street (eds), *The Cambridge Companion to Pop and Rock*, 272–89

Fanon, Frantz (1986) [1952] *Black Skin, White Masks*, tr. Charles Lam Markmann, London: Pluto Press

— (1967) *The Wretched of the Earth*, tr. Constance Farrington, Harmondsworth: Penguin

Favret-Saada, Jeanne (1980) *Deadly Words: Witchcraft in the Bocage*, tr. C. Cullen, Cambridge and Paris: Cambridge University Press and Editions de la Maison des Sciences de L'Homme

Fentress, James and Wickham, Chris (1992) *Social Memory*, Oxford, UK, and Cambridge, MA: Blackwell

Finnegan, Ruth (1992) *Oral Traditions and the Verbal Arts: A Guide to Research Practices*, London and New York: Routledge

— (1988) *Literacy and Orality: Studies in the Technology of Communication*, Oxford: Basil Blackwell

Foley, Catherine E. (1997) 'Traditional Step-Dance in North Kerry: Local Body Dialects', in Thérèse Smith and Mícheál Ó Súilleabháin (eds), *Blas*, 53–63

Foster, Susan Leigh (ed.) (1996) *Corporealities: Dancing Knowledge, Culture and Power*, London and New York: Routledge

Foucault, Michel (1971) *Madness and Civilization: A History of Insanity in the Age of Reason*, tr. Richard Howard, London: Routledge

Fox, Richard G. (ed.) (1991) *Recapturing Anthropology: Working in the Present*, Santa Fe: School of American Research Press

Free, Marcus (1998) ' "Angels" with Drunken Faces?: Travelling Republic of Ireland Supporters and the Construction of Irish Migrant Identity in England', in Adam Brown (ed.), *Fanatics!*, 219–32

Freud, Sigmund (1953) *Totem and Taboo and Other Works*, tr. James Strachey, London: Hogarth Press and the Institute of Psycho-Analysis

Frith, Simon (1996) *Performing Rites: On the Value of Popular Music*, Oxford: Oxford University Press

Frith, Simon, Straw, Will, and Street, John (eds) (2001) *The Cambridge Companion to Pop and Rock*, Cambridge: Cambridge University Press

Frow, John (1997) *Cultural Studies and Cultural Value*, Oxford: Clarendon Press

Fuller, Nancy J. (1992) 'The Museum as a Vehicle for Community Empowerment: The Ak-Chin Indian Community Ecomuseum Project', in Ivan Karp, Christine Mullen Kreamer and Steven D. Lavine (eds), *Museums and Communities*, 327–65

Gabriel, Teshome H. (1989) 'Towards a Critical Theory of Third World Films', in Jim Pines and Paul Willemen (eds), *Questions of Third Cinema*, 30–52

Gallop, Jane (1988) *Thinking Through the Body*, New York: Columbia

Ganguly, Suranjan (2000) 'A Cinema on Red Alert: Mrinal Sen's *Interview* and *In Search of Famine*', *Journal of Commonwealth Literature*, 35.1, 55–70

Gates, Henry Louis, Jr (1991) 'Critical Fanonism', *Critical Inquiry*, 17.3, Spring, 457–70

Geertz, Clifford (2000) *Available Light: Anthropological Reflections on Philosophical Topics*, Princeton and Oxford: Princeton University Press

— (1972) 'Deep Play: Notes on the Balinese Cockfight', in Clifford Geertz (1993) [1973] *The Interpretation of Cultures: Selected Essays*, London: Fontana, 412–53

Gilbert, Sandra M. and Gubar, Susan (1979) *The Madwoman in the Attic: The Woman Writer and the Nineteenth-Century Literary Imagination*, New Haven and London: Yale University Press

Gilkes, Michael (1991) 'The Landscape of Dreams', in Hena Maes-Jelinek (ed.), *Wilson Harris: The Uncompromising Imagination*, 31–8

Gilroy, Paul (2000) *Between Camps: Race, Identity and Nationalism at the End of the Colour Line*, London: Allen Lane/The Penguin Press

— (1997) 'Exer(or)cising Power: Black Bodies in the Black Public Sphere', in Helen Thomas (ed.), *Dance in the City*, 21–34

— (1993a) *The Black Atlantic: Modernity and Double Consciousness*, London and New York: Verso

— (1993b) *Small Acts: Thoughts on the Politics of Black Cultures*, London and New York: Serpent's Tail

— (1987) *'There Ain't No Black in the Union Jack': The Cultural Politics of Race and Nation*, London: Routledge

The Gladiators (1977) *Trenchtown Mix Up*, Island [CD]

Goldberg, David Theo and Quayson, Ato (eds) (2002) *Relocating Post-colonialism*, Oxford: Blackwell

Good, Byron J. (1994) *Medicine, Rationality, and Experience: An Anthropological Perspective*, Cambridge: Cambridge University Press

Gordon, Lewis R., Sharpley-Whiting, T. Denean, and White, Renée (eds) (1996) *Fanon: A Critical Reader*, Oxford: Blackwell

Guha, Ramachandra (2002) *A Corner of a Foreign Field: The Indian History of a British Sport*, London: Picador

Hall, Reginald (1994) 'Irish Music and Dance in London, 1890–1970: A Socio-Cultural History', Doctoral Dissertation, University of Sussex

Hallam, Elizabeth and Street, Brian V. (eds) (2000a) *Cultural Encounters: Representing 'Otherness'*, London and New York: Routledge

Hallam, Elizabeth and Street, Brian V. (2000b) 'Cultural Encounters – Representing "Otherness" ', in Elizabeth Hallam and Brian V. Street (eds), *Cultural Encounters*, 1–10

Hannigan, Dave (1998) *The Garrison Game: The State of Irish Football*, Edinburgh and London: Mainstream

Hargreaves, Jennifer (2000) *Heroines of Sport: The Politics of Difference and Identity*, London and New York: Routledge

— (1994) *Sporting Females: Critical Issues in the History and Sociology of Women's Sports*, London and New York: Routledge

Harris, Wilson (1999) *Selected Essays of Wilson Harris: The Unfinished Genesis of the Imagination*, ed. A. Bundy, London: Routledge

— (1983) *The Womb of Space: The Cross-Cultural Imagination*, Westport, CN, and London: Greenwood Press

Harvey, David (1990) *The Condition of Postmodernity*, Cambridge, MA, and Oxford: Blackwell

Head, Bessie (1977) *The Collector of Treasures and Other Botswana Village Tales*, London: Heinemann

— (1974) *A Question of Power*, London: Heinemann

Hebdige, Dick (1987) *Cut 'n' Mix: Culture, Identity and Caribbean Music*, London: Comedia

Herold, Edward, Garcia, Rafael, and DeMoya, Tony (2001) 'Female Tourists and Beach Boys: Romance or Sex Tourism?', *Annals of Tourism Research*, 28.4, 978–97

Hiatt, L. R. (1996) *Arguments about Aborigines: Australia and the Evolution of Social Anthropology*, Cambridge: Cambridge University Press

Hill, Donald R. (1993) *Calypso Calaloo: Early Carnival Music in Trinidad*, Gainesville: University Press of Florida

Hill, Errol (1997) [1972] *The Trinidad Carnival: Mandate for a National Theatre*, London: New Beacon Books

Hjort, Mette and MacKenzie, Scott (2000) *Cinema and Nation*, London and New York: Routledge

Holmes, Michael (1994) 'Symbols of National Identity and Sport: The Case of the Irish Football Team', *Irish Political Studies*, 9, 81–98

hooks, bell (2001) *Salvation: Black People and Love*, London: Women's Press

— (2000) *All About Love*, London: Women's Press

Hooper-Greenhill, Eileen (ed.) (1997) *Cultural Diversity: Developing Museum Audiences in Britain*, London and Washington, DC: Leicester University Press

Howat, Gerald (1975) *Learie Constantine*, London: George Allen and Unwin

Howe, Darcus (1978) 'Playing Mas'', *Race Today*, 10.5, July–August, 102–3

Huggan, Graham (2002) 'Postcolonial Studies and the Anxiety of Interdisciplinarity', *Postcolonial Studies*, 5.3, 245–75

Hutnyk, John (1997) 'Adorno at Womad: South Asian Crossovers and the Limits of Hybridity-Talk', in Pnina Werbner and Tariq Modood (eds), *Debating Cultural Hybridity*, 106–36

Huyssen, Andreas (2003) *Present Pasts: Urban Palimpsests and the Politics of Memory*, Stanford: Stanford University Press

Hyam, Ronald (1991) *Empire and Sexuality: The British Experience*, Manchester: Manchester University Press

Irwin-Zarecka, Iwona (1994) *Frames of Remembrance: The Dynamics of Collective Memory*, New Brunswick and London: Transaction Publishers

Jacobs, Jane M. (1996) *Edge of Empire: Postcolonialism and the City*, London and New York: Routledge

James, C.L.R. (2001) [1938] *The Black Jacobins: Toussaint L'Ouverture and the San Domingo Revolution*, London: Penguin

— (1993) *American Civilization*, ed. Anna Grimshaw, Oxford and Cambridge, MA: Blackwell

— (1992) *The C. L. R. James Reader*, ed. Anna Grimshaw, Oxford and Cambridge, MA: Blackwell

— (1989) *Cricket*, ed. Anna Grimshaw, London: Allison and Busby/W. H. Allen

— (1985) [1953] *Mariners, Renegades and Castaways: The Story of Herman Melville and the World We Live In*, London: Allison and Busby

— (1984) *At the Rendezvous of Victory: Selected Writings*, London: Allison and Busby

— (1980a) *Notes on Dialectics: Hegel, Marx, Lenin*, London: Allison and Busby

— (1980b) *Spheres of Existence: Selected Writings*, London: Allison and Busby

— (1977a) *The Future in the Present: Selected Writings*, London: Allison and Busby

— (1977b) *Nkrumah and the Ghana Revolution*, London: Allison and Busby

— (1971) [1936] *Minty Alley*, London: New Beacon

— (1969) [1963] *Beyond a Boundary*, London: Stanley Paul

James, Wilmot and van de Vijver, Linda (eds) (2000) *After the TRC: Reflections on Truth and Reconciliation in SA*, Athens and Cape Town: Ohio University Press/David Philip

Jameson, Fredric (1984) 'Postmodernism, or the Cultural Logic of Late Captialism', in Fredric Jameson (2000) *The Jameson Reader*, ed. Michael Hardt and Kathi Weeks, Oxford: Blackwell, 188–232

Jeffery, Anthea (1999) *The Truth About the Truth Commission*, Johannesburg: South Africa Institute of Race Relations

Johannes, Robert E. (ed.) (1989) *Traditional Ecological Knowledge: A Collection of Essays*, Gland, Switzerland, and Cambridge, UK: IUCN, World Conservation Union

Jones, Simon (1988) *Black Culture, White Youth: The Reggae Tradition from JA to UK*, Basingstoke: Macmillan

Karp, Ivan and Lavine, Steven D. (eds) (1991) *Exhibiting Cultures: The Poetics and Politics of Museum Display*, Washington, DC, and London: Smithsonian Institution Press

Karp, Ivan, Mullen Kreamer, Christine, and Lavine, Steven D. (eds) (1992) *Museums and Communities*, Washington, DC, and London: Smithsonian Institution Press

Kaschula, Russell H. (ed.) (2001a) *African Oral Literature: Functions in Contemporary Contexts*, Claremont, South Africa: New Africa Books

— (2001b) 'Oral Literature in Contemporary Contexts', in Russell H. Kaschula (ed.), *African Oral Literature: Functions in Contemporary Contexts*, xi–xxvi

Kavanagh, Gaynor (2000) *Dream Spaces: Memory and the Museum*, London and New York: Leicester University Press

Keane, Roy (2002) *Keane: The Autobiography*, with Eamon Dunphy, London: Michael Joseph

Kenny, Michael G. (1996) 'Trauma, Time, Illness, and Culture: An Anthropological Approach to Traumatic Memory', in Paul Antze and Michael Lambek (eds), *Tense Past*, 151–71

Kirshenblatt-Gimblett, Barbara (1991) 'Objects of Ethnography', in Ivan Karp and Steven D. Lavine (eds), *Exhibiting Cultures*, 386–443

Koritz, Amy (1996) 'Re/Moving Boundaries: From Dance History to Cultural Studies', in Gay Morris (ed.), *Moving Words: Re-Writing Dance*, 88–103

Krog, Antjie (1998) *Country of My Skull*, London: Jonathan Cape

Kurin, Richard (1991) 'Cultural Conservation through Representation: Festival of India Folklife Exhibitions at the Smithsonian Institute', in Ivan Karp and Steven D. Lavine (eds), *Exhibiting Cultures*, 315–43

Ladd, Edmund J. (2001) 'A Zuni Perspective on Repatriation', in Tamara L. Bray (ed.), *The Future of the Past*, 107–15

Lady Saw (1998) *99 Ways*, VP Records [CD]

— (1996) *Give Me the Reason*, VP Records [CD]

Lambek, Michael (1996) 'The Post Imperfect: Remembering as Moral Practice', in Paul Antze and Michael Lambek (eds), *Tense Past*, 235–54

Larsen, Neil (2000) 'Imperialism, Colonialism, Postcolonialism', in Henry Schwarz and Sangeeta Ray (eds), *A Companion to Postcolonial Studies*, 23–52

Lazarus, Neil (1993) ' "Unsystematic Fingers at the Conditions of the Times": "Afropop" and the Paradoxes of Imperialism', in Jonathan White (ed.), *Recasting the World*, 137–60

Lenihan, Eddie (2003) *Meeting the Other Crowd: The Fairy Stories of Hidden Ireland*, Dublin: Gill and Macmillan

Lhamon, W. T., Jr (1990) *Deliberate Speed: The Origins of a Cultural Style in the American 1950's*, Washington, DC, and London: Smithsonian Institution Press

Lindfors, Bernth (ed.) (1999) *Africans on Stage: Studies in Ethnological Show Business*, Bloomington and Indianapolis/Cape Town: Indiana University Press/David Philip

Lipsitz, George (1994) *Dangerous Crossroads: Popular Music, Postmodernism and the Poetics of Place*, London and New York: Verso

— (1990) *Time Passages: Collective Memory and American Popular Culture*, Minneapolis: University of Minnesota Press

Littlewood, Roland (1998) *The Butterfly and the Serpent: Essays in Psychiatry, Race and Religion*, London and New York: Free Association Books

Littlewood, Roland and Dein, Simon (eds) (2000) *Cultural Psychiatry and Medical Anthropology: An Introduction and Reader*, London and New Brunswick, NJ: Athlone Press

London is the Place for Me: Trinidadian Calypso in London, 1950–1956 (2002) Honest Jon's Records [CD]

MacCannell, Dean (1999) [1976] *The Tourist: A New Theory of the Leisure Class*, Berkeley and Los Angeles: University of California Press

McClintock, Anne (1995) *Imperial Leather: Race, Gender and Sexuality in the Colonial Contest*, London and New York: Routledge

McCulloch, Jock (1995) *Colonial Psychiatry and 'the African Mind'*, Cambridge: Cambridge University Press

— (1983) *Black Soul White Artifact: Fanon's Clinical Psychology and Social Theory*, Cambridge: Cambridge University Press

Macey, David (2000) *Frantz Fanon: A Life*, London: Granta

McMillan, Terry (1996) *How Stella Got Her Groove Back*, London and New York: Viking

McRobbie, Angela (1984) 'Dance and Social Fantasy', in Angela McRobbie and Mica Nava (eds), *Gender and Generation*, 130–61

McRobbie, Angela and Nava, Mica (eds) (1984) *Gender and Generation*, Basingstoke: Macmillan

Maes-Jelinek, Hena (ed.) (1991) *Wilson Harris: The Uncompromising Imagination*, Sydney: Dangaroo Press

Malone, Jacqui (1996) *Steppin' on the Blues: The Visible Rhythms of African American Dance*, Urbana and Chicago: University of Illinois Press

Mandle, W. F. (1987) *The Gaelic Athletic Association and Irish Nationalist Politics, 1884–1924*, London and Dublin: Christopher Helm, and Gill and Macmillan

Mangan, J. A. (ed.) (1996) *Tribal Identities: Nationalism, Europe, Sport*, London: Frank Cass

— (ed.) (1992) *The Cultural Bond: Sport, Empire, Society*, London: Frank Cass

— (ed.) (1988) *Pleasure, Profit, Proselytism: British Culture and Sport at Home and Abroad, 1700–1914*, London: Frank Cass

Marley, Bob (1979) *Survival*, Island [CD]

Mattelart, Armand (2000) *Networking the World, 1794–2000*, tr. Liz Carey-Libbrecht and James A. Cohen, Minneapolis and London: University of Minnesota Press

Mayer, Geoff (1995) 'Going Home: *Once Were Warriors*', *Metro*, 100, 3–6

Minh-ha, Trinh T. (1989) 'Outside In Inside Out', in Jim Pines and Paul Willemen (eds), *Questions of Third Cinema*, 133–49

Mitchell, Tony (1996) *Popular Music and Local Identity: Rock, Pop and Rap in Europe and Oceania*, London and New York: Leicester University Press

Monsoon Wedding (2001) dir. Mira Nair (USA/Italy/Germany/France)

Moorhouse, H. F. (1996) 'One State, Several Countries: Soccer and Nationality in a "United" Kingdom', in J. A. Mangan (ed.), *Tribal Identities*, 55–74

Morley, David and Chen, Kuan-Hsing (eds) (1996) *Stuart Hall: Critical Dialogues in Cultural Studies*, London and New York: Routledge

Morris, Gay (ed.) (1996) *Moving Words: Re-Writing Dance*, London and New York: Routledge

Naficy, Hamid (2001) *An Accented Cinema: Exilic and Diasporic Filmmaking*, Princeton and Oxford: Princeton University Press

Nanda, Meera (2002) *Breaking the Spell of Dharma and Other Essays*, New Delhi: Three Essays Press

Nandy, Ashis (ed.) (1998a) *The Secret Politics of Our Desires: Innocence, Culpability and Indian Popular Cinema*, New Delhi: Oxford University Press

— (1998b) 'Indian Popular Cinema as a Slum's Eye View of Politics', in Ashis Nandy (ed.), *The Secret Politics of Our Desires*, 1–18

Neill, Anna (1999) 'A Land Without a Past: Dreamtime and Nation in *The Piano*', in Felicity Coombes and Suzanne Gemmell (eds), *Piano Lessons*, 136–47

Nelson, Cary and Grossberg, Lawrence (eds) (1988) *Marxism and the Interpretation of Culture*, Basingstoke: Macmillan Education

Ness, Sally Ann (1996) 'Dancing in the Field: Notes from Memory', in Susan Leigh Foster (ed.), *Corporealities: Dancing Knowledge, Culture and Power*, 129–54

Niles, John D. (1999) *Homo Narrans: The Poetics and Anthropology of Oral Literature*, Philadelphia: University of Pennsylvania Press

Newman, Judie (1995) *The Ballistic Bard: Postcolonial Fictions*, London: Arnold

Nunley, John (1993) 'Peter Minshall: The Good, the Bad, and the Old in Trinidad Carnival', in Dorothea S. Whitten and Norman E. Whitten (eds), *Imagery and Creativity*, 288–307

Ó Giolláin, Diarmuid (2000) *Locating Irish Folklore: Tradition, Modernity, Identity*, Cork: Cork University Press

Okely, Judith (1996) *Own or Other Culture*, London and New York: Routledge

Oliver, Paul (ed.) (1990) *Black Music in Britain: Essays on the Afro-Asian Contribution to Popular Music*, Milton Keynes and Philadelphia: Open University Press

Once Were Warriors (1994) dir. Lee Tamahori (New Zealand)

Ong, Walter J. (1988) [1982] *Orality and Literacy: The Technologizing of the Word*, London and New York: Routledge

O'Regan, Tom (1996) *Australian National Cinema*, London and New York: Routledge

Orr, Bridget (1999) 'Birth of a Nation? From *Utu* to *The Piano*', in Felicity Coombes and Suzanne Gemmell (eds), *Piano Lessons*, 148–60

Ottley, Rudolph (1995) *Calypsonians from Then to Now, Part I*, Arima

Paddy in the Smoke (1997) [1968] Topic [CD]

Parry, Benita (2002) 'Directions and Dead Ends in Postcolonial Studies', in

David Theo Goldberg and Ato Quayson (eds), *Relocating Postcolonialism*, 66–81

— (1987) 'Problems in Current Theories of Colonial Discourse', *The Oxford Literary Review*, 9.1 and 2, 27–55

Pawson, Eric (1992) 'Two New Zealands: Maori and European', in Kay Anderson and Fay Gale (eds), *Inventing Places: Studies in Cultural Geography*, 15–33

Perren, Alisa (2001–2) 'Sex, Lies and Marketing: Miramax and the Development of the Quality Indie Blockbuster', *Film Quarterly*, 55.2, 30–9

Phillips, Mike and Phillips, Trevor (1998) *Windrush: The Irresistible Rise of Multi-Racial Britain*, London: HarperCollins

The Piano (1993) dir. Jane Campion (Australia)

Pines, Jim and Willemen, Paul (eds) (1989) *Questions of Third Cinema*, London: British Film Institute

Polan, Dana (2001) *Jane Campion*, London: British Film Institute

Porter, Roy (2002) *Madness: A Brief History*, Oxford: Oxford University Press

— (1987) *A Social History of Madness: Stories of the Insane*, London: Weidenfeld and Nicholson

Pratt, Mary Louise (1992) *Imperial Eyes: Travel Writing and Transculturalisation*, London and New York: Routledge

Pruitt, Deborah and LaFont, Suzanne (1995) 'For Love and Money: Romance Tourism in Jamaica', *Annals of Tourism Research*, 22.2, 422–40

Race Today Collective (1978) 'Carnival Review', *Race Today*, 10.6, 123

— (1977) *The Road Make to Walk on Carnival Day: The Battle for the West Indian Carnival in Britain*, London: Race Today

Rajadhyaksha, Ashish and Willemen, Paul (1999) *Encyclopaedia of Indian Cinema*, London and New Delhi: British Film Institute and Oxford University Press

Rector, Monica (1984) 'The Code and Message of Carnival: "Escolas-de-Samba"', in Umberto Eco, V. V. Ivanov and Monica Rector, *Carnival!*, 37–165

Reed, Ishmael (1988) [1972] *Mumbo Jumbo*, London: Allison and Busby

Rhys, Jean (1966) *Wide Sargasso Sea*, London: Andre Deutsch

Roach, Joseph (1996) *Cities of the Dead: Circum-Atlantic Performance*, New York: Columbia University Press

Rose, Jacqueline (1994) 'On the "Universality" of Madness: Bessie Head's *A Question of Power*', *Critical Inquiry*, 20, Spring, 401–18

Rose, Tricia (1994) *Black Noise: Rap Music and Black Culture in Contemporary America*, Hanover and London: Wesleyan University Press

Ross, Andrew (1989) *No Respect: Intellectuals and Popular Culture*, London and New York: Routledge

Rowan, Paul (1994) *The Team That Jack Built*, Edinburgh: Mainstream

Sachs, Albie (2000) 'His Name Was Henry', in Wilmot James and Linda van de Vijver (eds), *After the TRC*, 94–100

Said, Edward W. (2003) [1978] *Orientalism*, London: Penguin

— (1994) *Representations of the Intellectual: The 1993 Reith Lectures*, London: Vintage

— (1993) *Culture and Imperialism*, London: Chatto and Windus

— (1983) *The World, the Text, and the Critic*, Cambridge, MA: Harvard University Press

— (1981) *Covering Islam: How the Media and the Experts Determine How We See the Rest of the World*, London and Henley: Routledge and Kegan Paul

— (1980) *The Question of Palestine*, London and Henley: Routledge and Kegan Paul

Said, Edward, Buttigieg, Joseph A., and Bové, Paul A. (2001) 'An Interview with Edward W. Said', in Patrick Williams (ed.), *Edward Said*, Vol. I, 152–72

Salaam Bombay! (1988) dir. Mira Nair (India, France, UK)

Sampath, Niels (1997) *'Mas'* Identity: Tourism and Global and Local Aspects of Trinidad Carnival', in Simone Abram, Jacqueline D. Waldren and Donald V. L. Macleod (eds), *Tourists and Tourism*, 149–71

Sánchez Taylor, Jacqueline (2000) 'Tourism and "Embodied" Commodities: Sex Tourism in the Caribbean', in Stephen Clift and Simon Carter (eds), *Tourism and Sex*, 41–53

Sarvan, Charles (1990) 'Bessie Head: Two Letters', *Wasafiri*, 12, Autumn, 11–15

Savigliano, Marta E. (1995) *Tango and the Political Economy of Passion*, Boulder: Westview Press

Scally, John (1998) *Simply Red and Green: Manchester United and Ireland: A Story Of a Love Affair*, Edinburgh and London: Mainstream

Schiller, Dan (1999) *Digital Capitalism: Networking the Global Market System*, Cambridge, MA, and London: MIT

Schreiner, Claus (1993) *Música Brasileira: A History of Popular Music and the People of Brazil*, tr. Mark Weinstein, New York and London: Marion Boyars

Schwarz, Henry (2000) 'Mission Impossible: Introducing Postcolonial

Studies in the US Academy', in Henry Schwarz and Sangeeta Ray (eds), *A Companion to Postcolonial Studies*, 1–20

Schwarz, Henry and Ray, Sangeeta (eds) (2000) *A Companion to Postcolonial Studies*, Malden, MA, and Oxford: Blackwell

Sen, Mrinal (2002) *Montage: Life. Politics. Cinema*, Calcutta: Seagull Books

Sen, Mrinal and Bandyopadhyay, Samik (1983) *In Search of Famine (Ākāler Sandhāney)*, Calcutta: Seagull Books

Sharma, Ashwani (1996) 'Sounds Oriental: The (Im)possibility of Theorizing Asian Music Cultures', in Sanjay Sharma, John Hutnyk and Ashwani Sharma (eds), *Dis-Orienting Rhythms*, 15–31

Sharma, Sanjay (1996) 'Noisy Asians or "Asian Noise"?', in Sanjay Sharma, John Hutnyk and Ashwani Sharma (eds), *Dis-Orienting Rhythms*, 32–57

Sharma, Sanjay, Hutnyk, John, and Sharma, Ashwani (eds) (1996) *Dis-Orienting Rhythms: The Politics of New Asian Dance Music*, London and New Jersey: Zed Books

Shelton, Anthony Alan (2000) 'Museum Ethnography: An Imperial Science', in Elizabeth Hallam and Brian V. Street (eds), *Cultural Encounters*, 155–93

Simpson, Moira G. (1996) *Making Representations: Museums in the Post-Colonial Era*, London and New York: Routledge

Small, Stephen (1997) 'Contextualising the Black Presence in British Museums: Representations, Resources and Response', in Eilean Hooper-Greenhill (ed.), *Cultural Diversity: Developing Museum Audiences in Britain*, 50–66

Smith, Thérèse and Ó Súilleabháin, Míchael (eds) (1997) *Blas: The Local Accent in Irish Traditional Music*, Limerick: Irish World Music Centre, University of Limerick

Spivak, Gayatri Chakravorty (1993) *Outside in the Teaching Machine*, New York and London: Routledge

— (1988) 'Can the Subaltern Speak?' in Cary Nelson and Lawrence Grossberg (eds), *Marxism and the Interpretation of Culture*, 271–313

Stewart, John (1986) 'Patronage and Control in the Trinidad Carnival', in Victor W. Turner and Edward M. Brumer (eds), *The Anthropology of Experience*, 289–315

Stoddart, Brian (1988a) 'Cricket and Colonialism in the English-Speaking Caribbean to 1914: Towards a Cultural Analysis', in J. A. Mangan (ed.), *Pleasure, Profit, Proselytism*, 231–57

Stoddart, Brian (1988b) 'Sport, Cultural Imperialism, and Colonial Response in the British Empire', *Comparative Studies in Society and History*, 30.4, 649–73

Stoddart, Brian and Sandiford, Keith A. P. (eds) (1998) *The Imperial Game: Cricket, Culture and Society*, Manchester and New York: Manchester University Press

Stolzoff, Norman C. (2000) *Wake the Town and Tell the People: Dancehall Culture in Jamaica*, Durham and London: Duke University Press

Strang, Veronica (1997) *Uncommon Ground: Cultural Landscapes and Environmental Values*, Oxford and New York: Oxford

Stratford, Elaine (ed.) (1999) *Australian Cultural Geographies*, Melbourne: Oxford University Press

Sugden, John and Bairner, Alan (1994) 'Ireland and the World Cup: "Two Teams in Ireland, O There's Only Two Teams in Ireland"', in John Sugden and Alan Tomlinson (eds), *Hosts and Champions*, 119–40

Sugden, John and Tomlinson, Alan (eds) (1994) *Hosts and Champions: Soccer Cultures, National Identities and the USA World Cup*, Aldershot: Arena

Surin, Kenneth (1995) 'C. L. R. James's Materialist Aesthetic of Cricket', in Hilary McD. Beckles and Brian Stoddart (eds), *Liberation Cricket*, 313–41

Taussig, Michael T. (1980) *The Devil and Commodity Fetishism in South America*, Chapel Hill: University of North Carolina Press

Thomas, Helen (ed.) (1997) *Dance in the City*, Basingstoke and London: Macmillan

Thomas, Nicholas (1994) *Colonialism's Culture: Anthropology, Travel and Government*, Cambridge: Polity

Thomas, Rosie (1985) 'Indian Cinema: Pleasures and Popularity. An Introduction', *Screen*, 26. 3–4, 116–31

Tibbles, Anthony (1996) 'Against Human Dignity: The Development of the Transatlantic Slavery Gallery at Merseyside Maritime Museum, Liverpool', *Proceedings, IXth International Congress of Maritime Museums*, 95–102

Tiffin, Helen (1982) 'Cricket, Literature and the Politics of De-Colonisation: The Case of C. L. R. James', in Richard Cashman and Michael McKernan (eds), *Sport: Money, Morality and the Media*, 177–93

Transatlantic Slavery: Against Human Dignity (n.d.) Exhibition Catalogue, Liverpool: National Museums and Galleries on Merseyside

Truth and Reconciliation Commission of South Africa (1998) *Truth and Reconciliation Commission of South Africa Report*, Vol. 1, Cape Town: Truth and Reconciliation Commission

Turner, Victor W. and Brumer, Edward M. (eds) (1986) *The Anthropology of Experience*, Urbana and Chicago: University of Illinois Press

Tutu, Desmond (1999) *No Future Without Forgiveness*, London: Rider

UNESCO (2002) 'Literacy as Freedom' UNESCO Institute for Statistics, unesco.org

— (2003) *The New Courier*, 3.1, unesco.org

Urry, John (2002) *The Tourist Gaze*, 2nd edn, London: Sage

Vansina, Jan (1985) *Oral Tradition as History*, Madison: University of Wisconsin Press

Vergès, Françoise (1996) 'To Cure and to Free: The Fanonian Project of "Decolonized Psychiatry" ', in Lewis R. Gordon, T. Denean Sharpley-Whiting, and Renée White, *Fanon*, 85–99

Vianna, Hermano (1999) *The Mystery of Samba: Popular Music and National Identity in Brazil*, ed. and tr. John Charles Chasteen, Chapel Hill and London: University of North Carolina Press

Vice, Sue (1997) *Introducing Bakhtin*, Manchester: Manchester University Press

Walker, Sam (1997) 'Black Cultural Museums in Britain: What Questions Do They Answer?', in Eilean Hooper-Greenhill (ed.), *Cultural Diversity*, 32–49

Werbner, Pnina (1997) 'The Dialectics of Cultural Hybridity', in Pnina Werbner and Tariq Modood (eds) *Debating Cultural Hybridity*, 1–26

Werbner, Pnina and Modood, Tariq (eds) (1997) *Debating Cultural Hybridity: Multi-Cultural Identities and the Politics of Anti-Racism*, London and New Jersey: Zed Books

Werbner, Richard (ed.) (1998) *Memory and the Postcolony: African Anthropology and the Critique of Power*, London and New York: Zed Books

Whannel, Gary (1995) 'Sport, National Identities and the Tale of Big Jack', *Critical Survey*, 7.2, 158–64

White, Jonathan (ed.) (1993) *Recasting the World: Writing after Colonialism*, Baltimore: Johns Hopkins University Press

Whitten, Dorothea S. and Whitten, Norman E. (1993) *Imagery and Creativity: Ethnoaesthetics and Art Worlds in the Americas*, Tucson and London: University of Arizona Press

Williams, Patrick (ed.) (2001) *Edward Said*, Vol. I, London: Sage

Wilmsen, Edwin N. (ed.) (1989) *We Are Here: Politics of Aboriginal Land Tenure*, Berkeley: University of California Press

Wilson, Richard A. (2001) *The Politics of Truth and Reconciliation in South Africa: Legitimizing the Post-Apartheid State*, Cambridge: Cambridge University Press

Wood, Marcus (2000) *Blind Memory: Visual Representations of Slavery in*

England and America, 1780–1865, Manchester and New York: Manchester University Press

Young, Robert J. C. (2003) *Postcolonialism: A Very Short Introduction*, Oxford: Oxford University Press

— (2001) *Postcolonialism: An Historical Introduction*, Oxford: Blackwell

— (1995) *Colonial Desire: Hybridity in Theory, Culture and Race*, London and New York: Routledge

Zé, Tom (1992) *The Return of Tom Zé: The Hips of Tradition*, Luaka Bop [CD]

Zuberi, Nabeel (2001) *Sounds English: Transnational Popular Music*, Urbana and Chicago: University of Illinois Press

Index